A Sarah Cox

Graciela Iturbide

Images of the Spirit

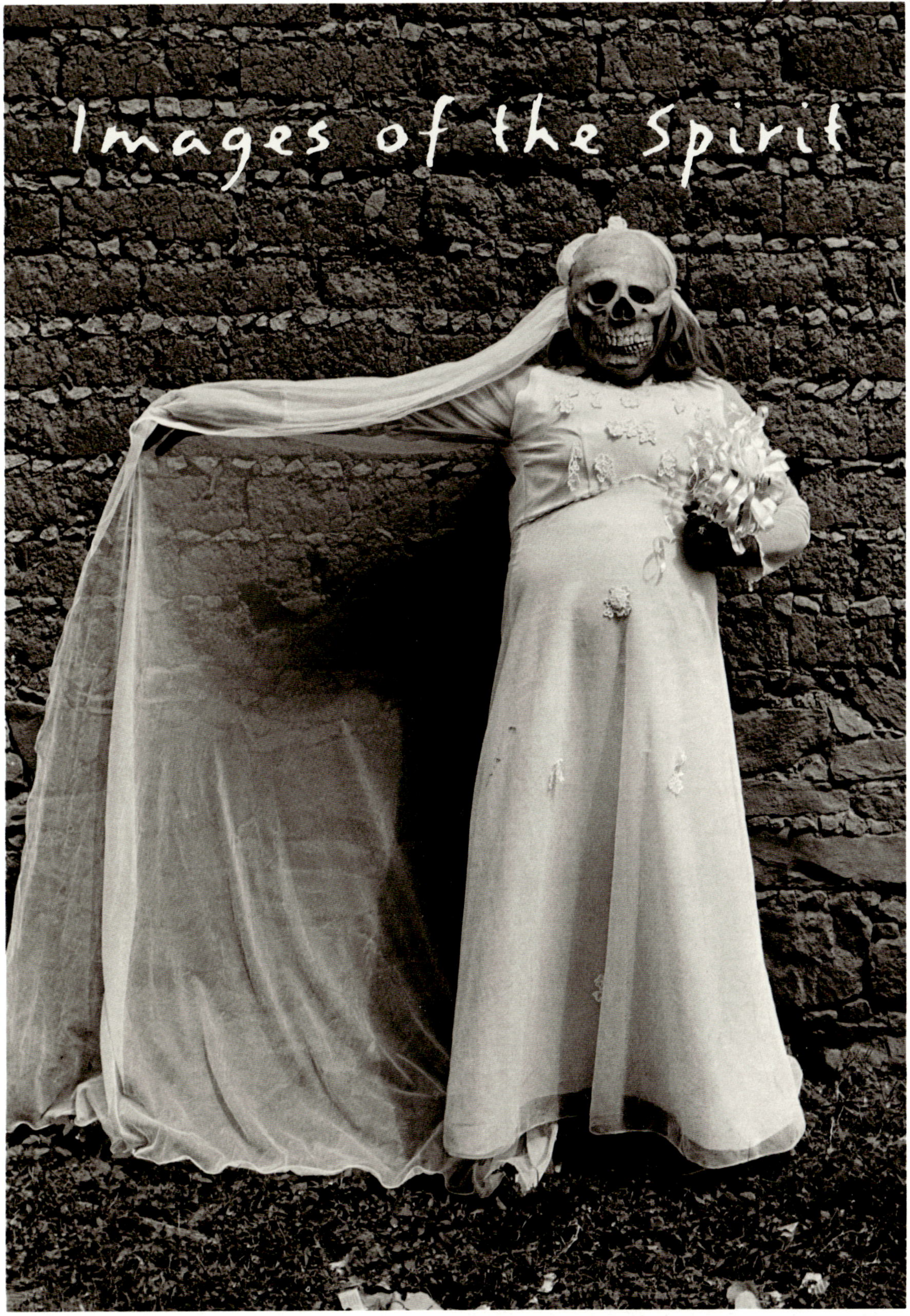

1999. S. José.

IMAGES OF THE SPIRIT

PHOTOGRAPHS BY

Graciela Iturbide

Preface by ROBERTO TEJADA

Epilogue by ALFREDO LÓPEZ AUSTIN

APERTURE / Philadelphia Museum of Art

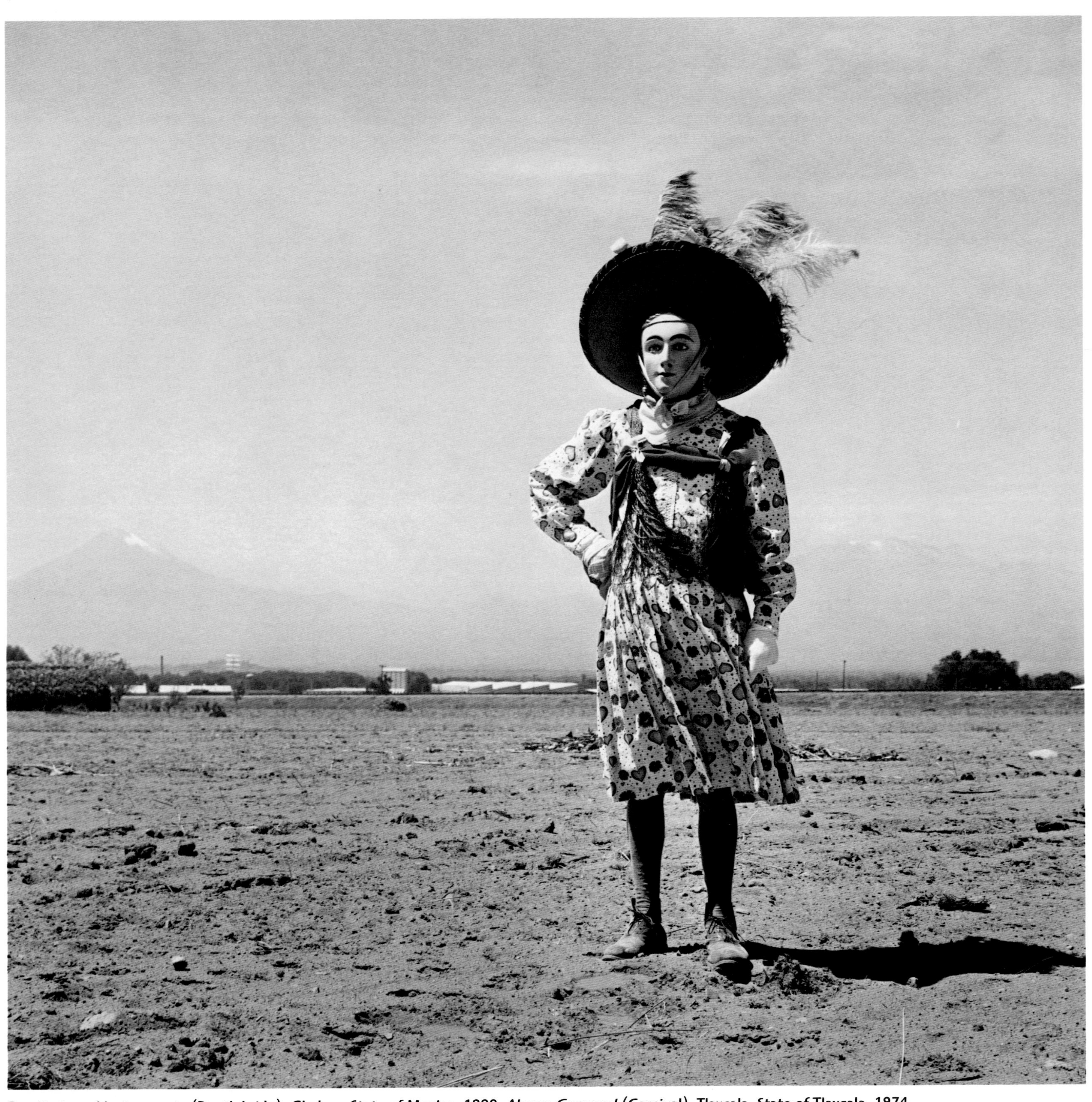

Frontispiece: *Novia muerte* (Death bride), Chalma, State of Mexico, 1990. *Above*: *Carnaval* (Carnival), Tlaxcala, State of Tlaxcala, 1974

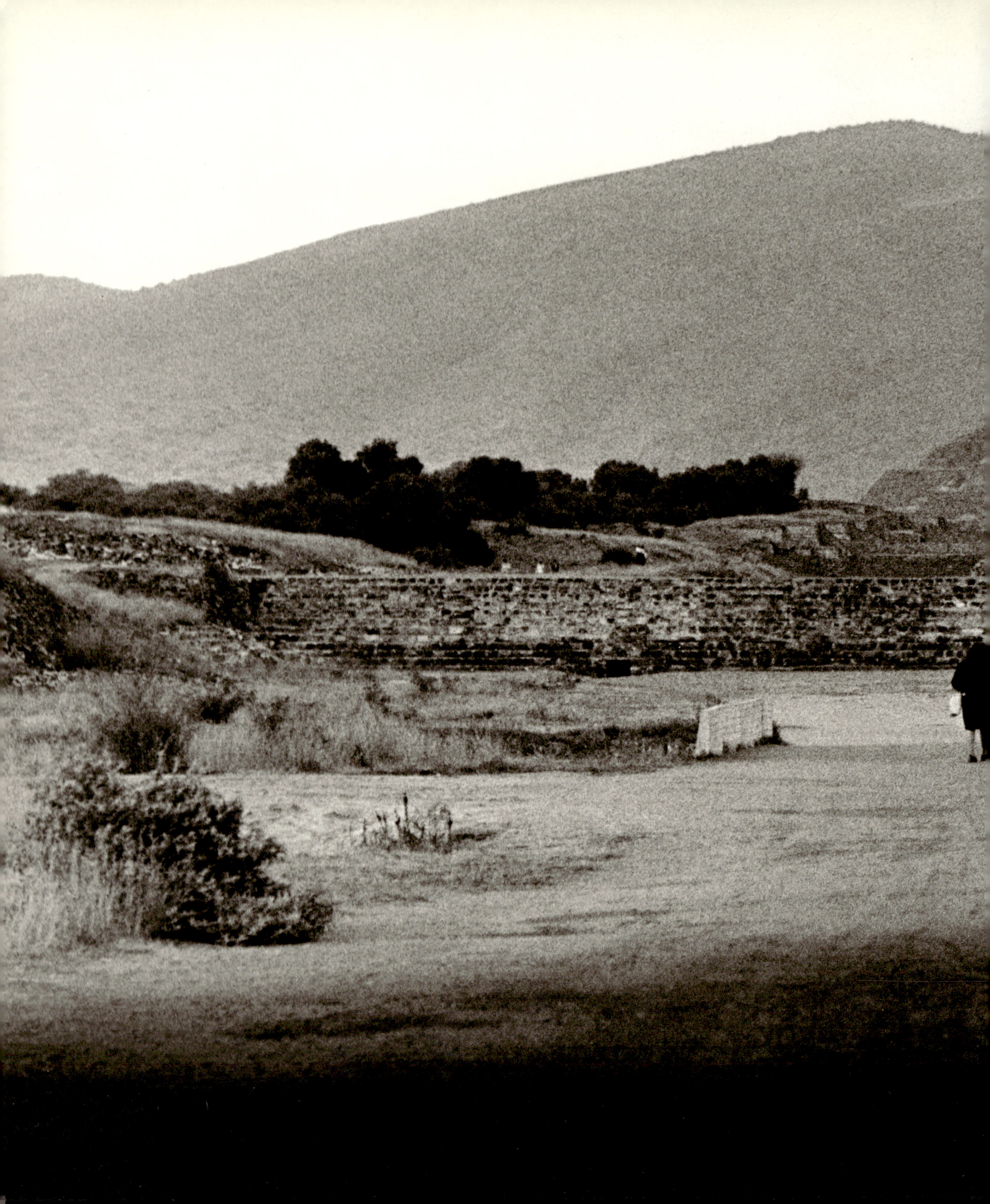

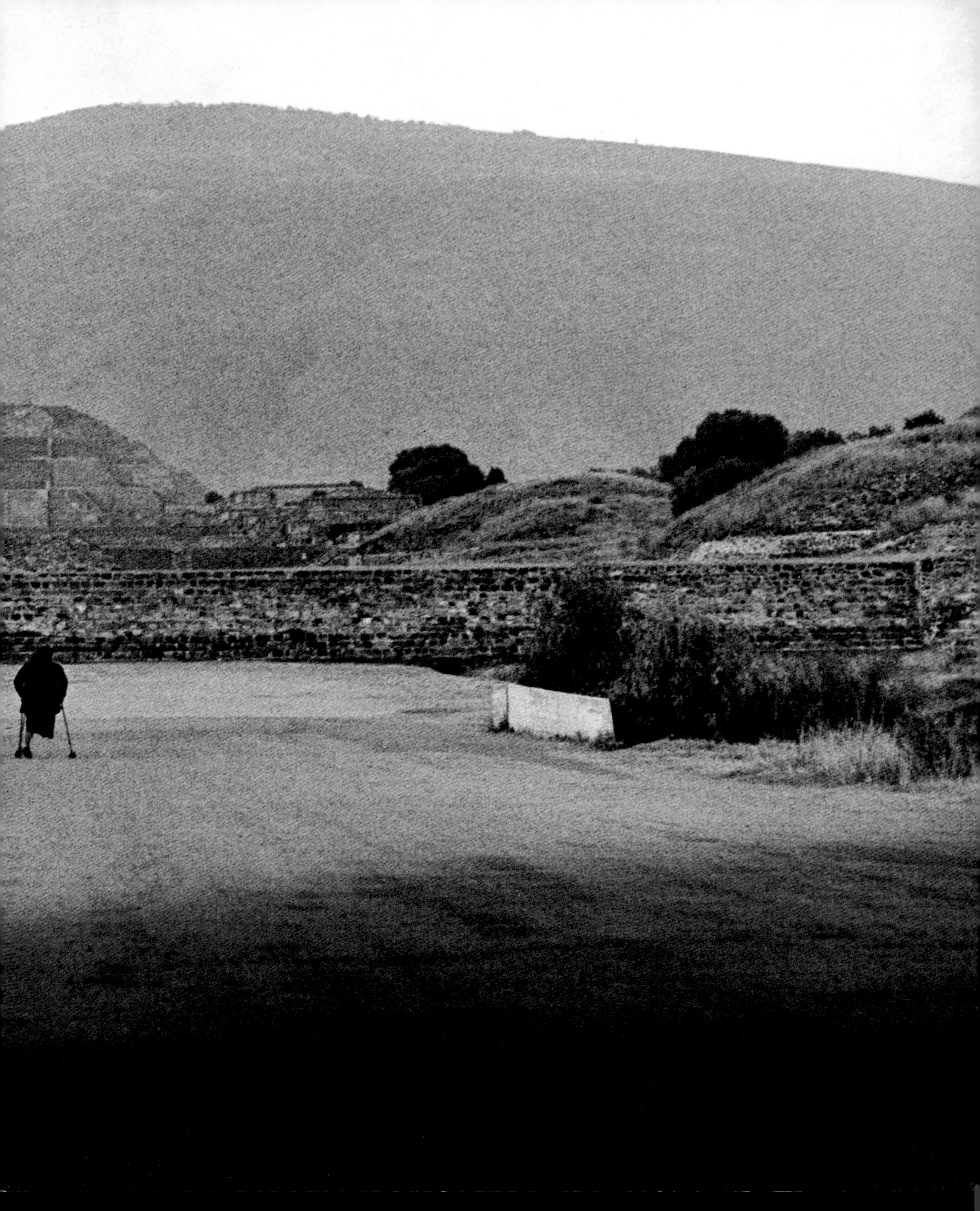

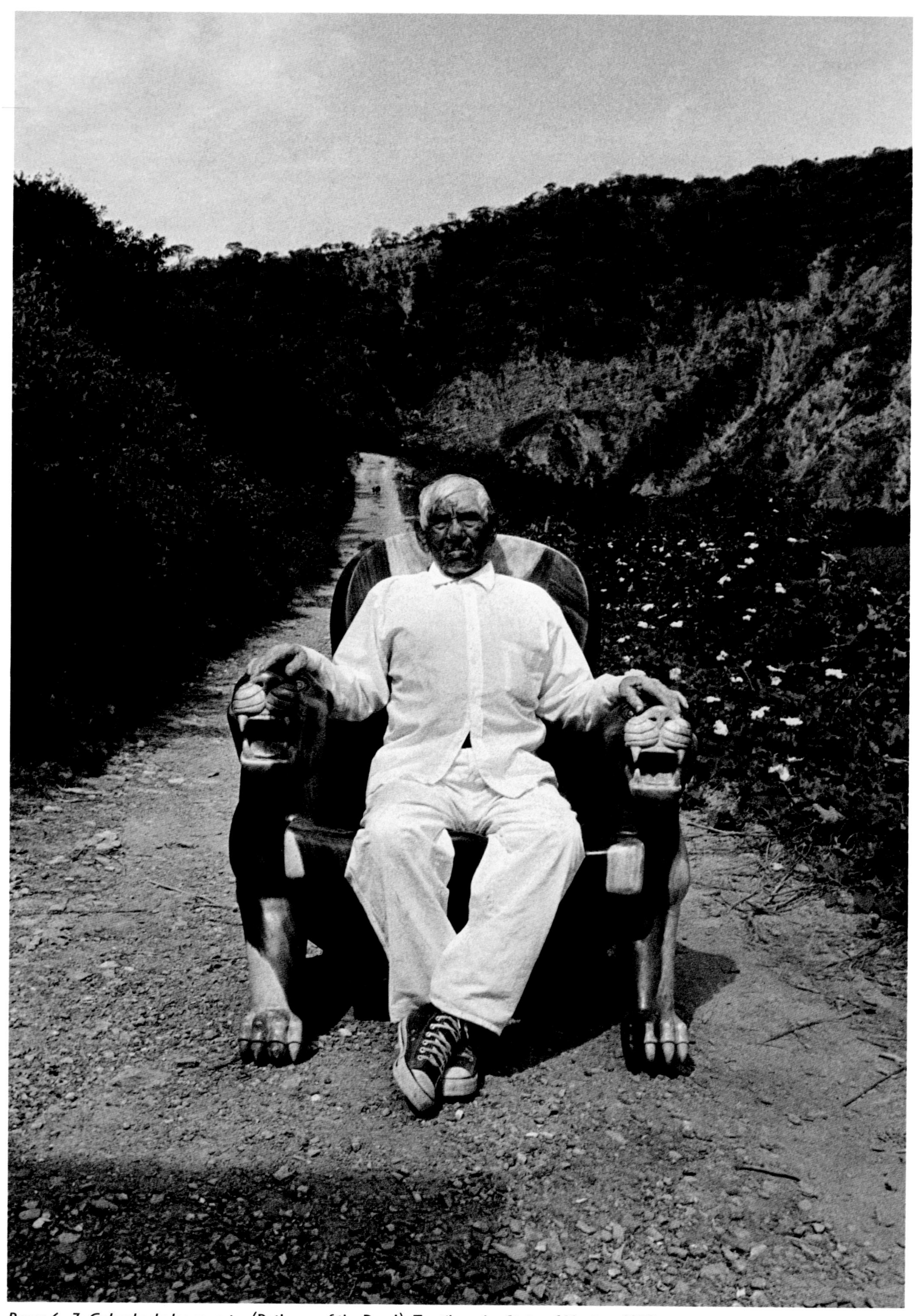

Pages 6–7: *Calzada de los muertos* (Pathway of the Dead), Teotihuacán, State of Mexico, 1979
Above: *Guardián de los caminos* (Keeper of the roads), Guerrero, State of Mexico, 1995

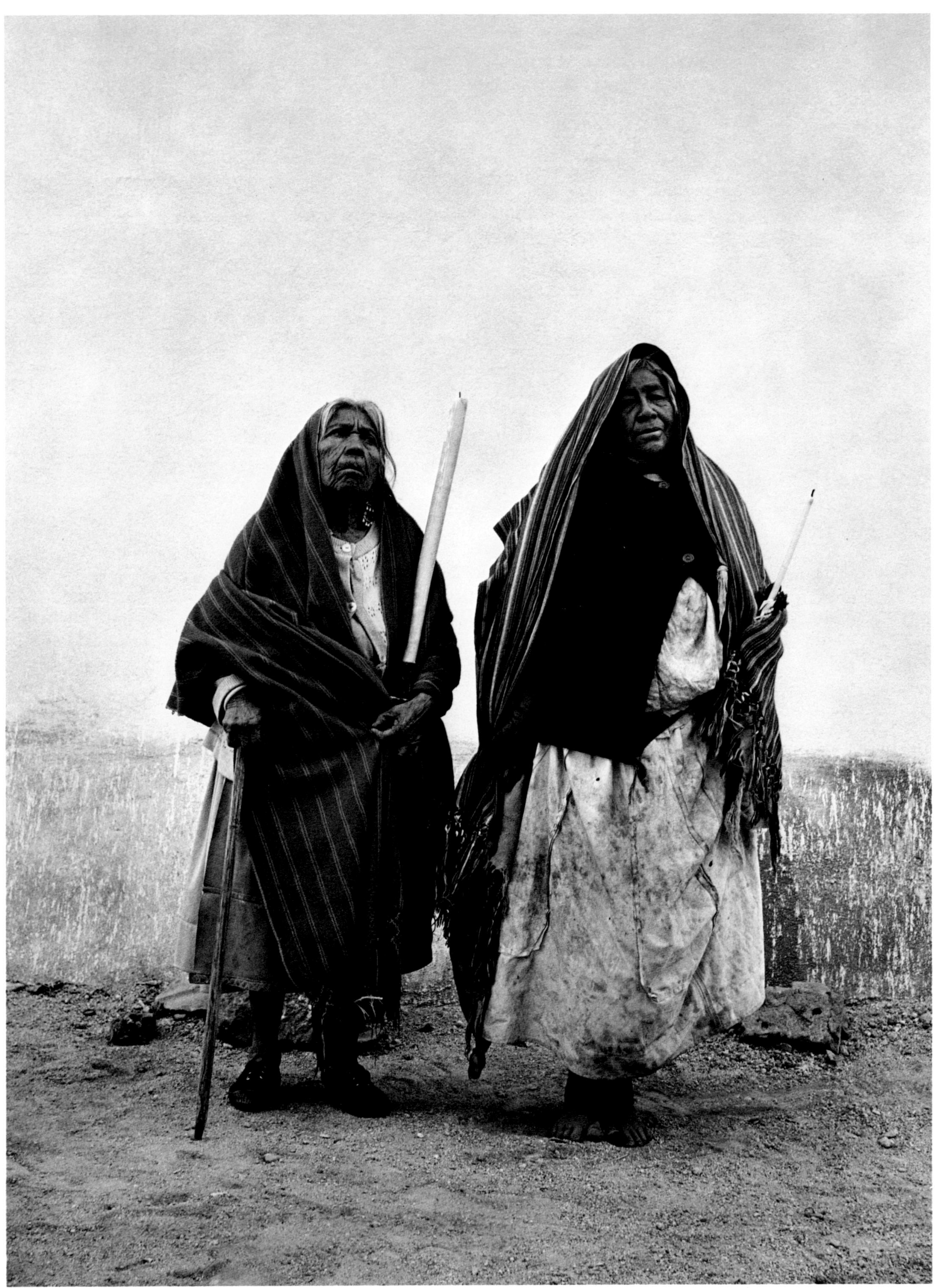

Año nuevo (New Year), Ocumichu, Michoacán, 1981

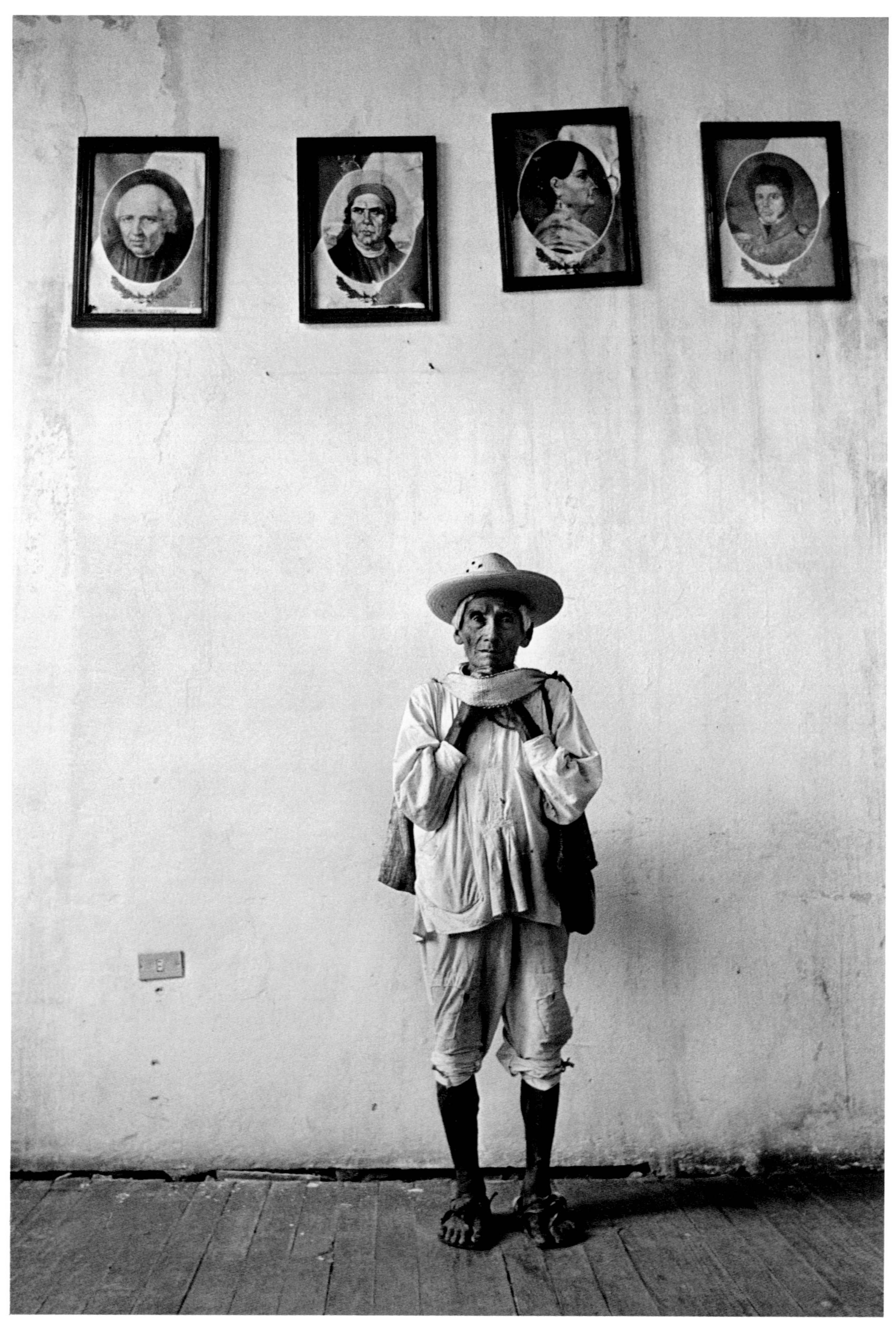

 Héroes de la patria (National heroes), Cuetzalan, Puebla, 1993

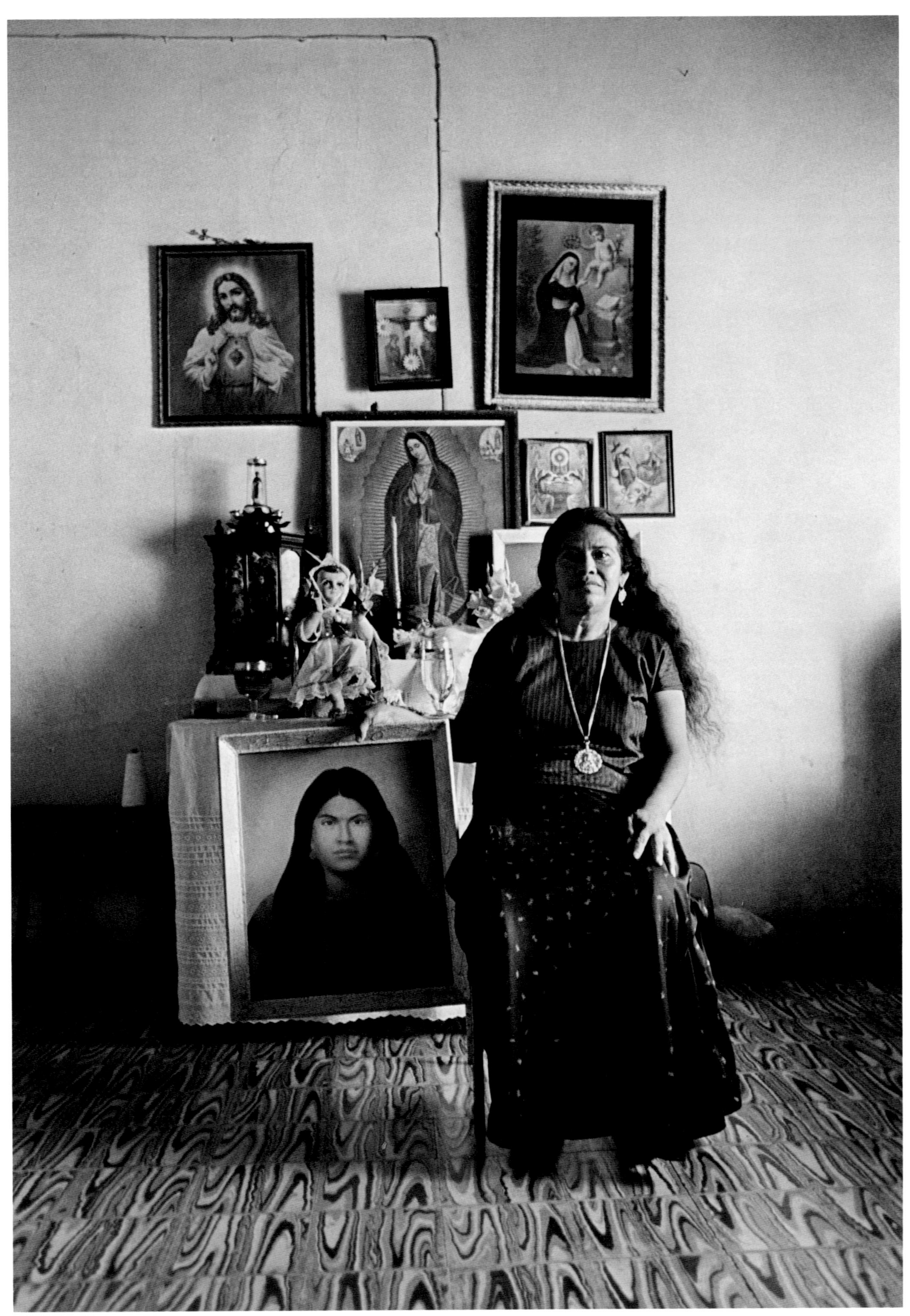

Na' Marcelina, Juchitán, Oaxaca, 1984

Sidelong Mirrors & Invisible Masks

THE PHOTOGRAPHY OF GRACIELA ITURBIDE

by Roberto Tejada

Sun-cracked or rain-washed, the desolate open stretches, the abrupt volcanic risings and the exuberant enclosures of Mexico's landscapes have long been in collision with the erratic forms and symptoms of a reckless, makeshift modernity. In Mexico, the countryside looms with the massive stone profiles of its pre-Hispanic past, with the extreme austerity or lavish excess of its colonial Catholic pageantry, and with the bold flare of its vernacular expression; but also with the concrete-brick and fiberglass of its tentative present—all reminders of the intense historical changes wrought here by a continuous clashing of cultures.

But the land resonates with the intricate patterns of human events and the resolve for durable meaning, regardless of the transitory promises made by the future order of things. Where cultural wealth is often at odds with blatant material indigence—or caught between the closing spheres of the rural and the urban—the singular force by which these communities form comes swelling into full view with their unmistakable signs and commanding visual intensity. Mexico is alive in the flesh and bones from which it draws its contradictions and diversity, a manifold collective body whose intentions burn in every gesture.

For the past twenty-five years, Graciela Iturbide has remarkably engaged the workaday life and seasonal celebrations of various communities throughout Mexico, exploring ways to extend the scope of the "objective" photograph, with a tale of her own to tell about the immeasurable totality of a country and its innumerable corners of experience; about everyday life and festival; about collaborative effort and communal perseverance; about the ages of life, the decisive role of women, and the passion play of popular Catholicism; about the strange in the familiar and the limits of the knowable when actual phenomena emerge in the generous or unspeakable guises of dream.

These images are political. One of the major concerns in the work of Graciela Iturbide has been to explore and articulate the ways in which a vocable such as "Mexico" is meaningful only when understood as an intricate combination of histories and practices. Mexico's contemporary culture is inextricably bound to a complex weft of ideas regarding its indigenous presence: its *mestizaje*—or mixed racial genesis—has served alternately as founding myth and as official rhetoric, in both politics and art.

Graciela Iturbide's images are powerful because they underline time and again the rift between belonging and citizenship, rendered often against a backdrop of Mexican icons or heroes—be it the frail displacement of a rural campesino in Puebla, or the triumph of locals in East Los Angeles. These images speak of outsider culture within larger constricting divisions, images seen now as having anticipated the present-day crisis with regard to the exhausted rhetoric that once sustained Mexico's long-presumed cultural cohesion—a monolithic identity now under revision thanks largely to legitimate standpoints that are defined and defended by borderland identity, by Mexico's increasingly organized and outspoken indigenous communities, and by seasonal migration and its inevitable acculturations.

In sharp contrast with certain formalist resolves to detain the process of becoming, Graciela Iturbide welcomes the occurrence of theatricality and the play of appearances—the iconic epiphanies that come to life within the traffic of the everyday—giving full foreground to the inherent nature of Mexican feast days and carnivals, and provisional release through representation. At times, the work clearly evokes Mexico's particular brand of early studio photography, as in the portraits-within-portraits, or the images of figures behind veils or frames, or set against curtains and painted murals, or against the time-weathered textures of a paint-dripped or graffitied wall, or against natural backdrops that serve as genuine stage-settings. As if mediated through a sidelong mirror or invisible mask, these performative moments are either prompted by the photographer, willingly offered by the subject, or—more likely—created mutually between the two.

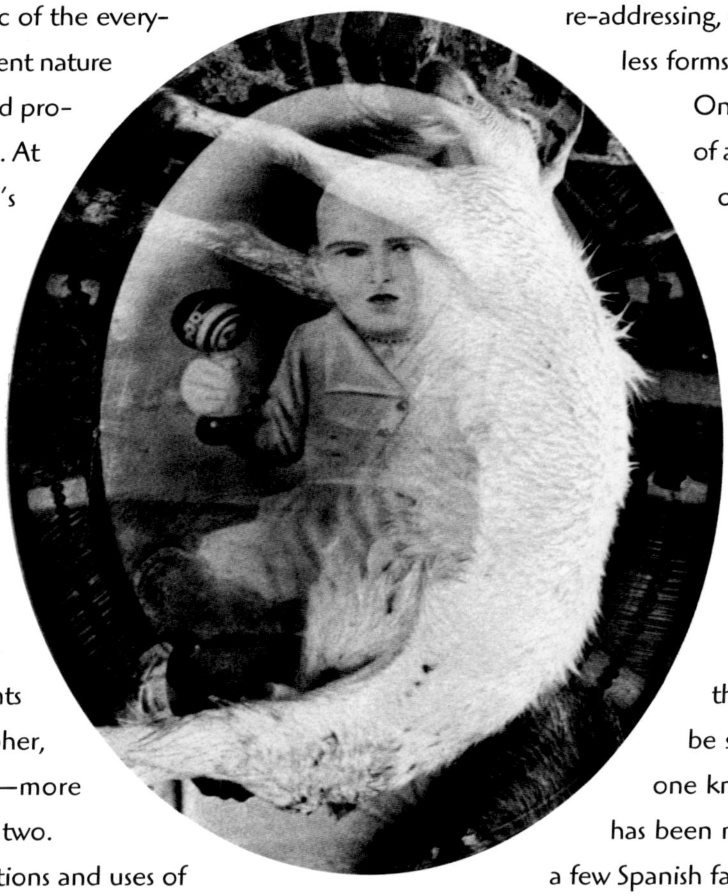

These images question the intoxications and uses of looking. They move comfortably between emotional precision and ambiguity. They invite the possibility of accident. They provide a document about the desire that drives photography, rendering the play of seduction enacted between photographer and subject. But, more importantly, these images celebrate how such a subject can be delivered from immanence through the flux of mutuality. Porous images about the present, they give voice to a history and its foundational violence.

The occupation of Mexico during the sixteenth century forever altered the cultural and religious landscape of the diverse civilizations that existed prior to the arrival of the Spaniards. The five hundred years following that initial destruction and historic upheaval have been witness to a less visibly violent, though complex and multiform process, described optimistically as an ongoing, syncretic cultural mixing—*mestizaje*. Despite the near-total dominance exerted here by the colonial culture of New Spain (churches built using the rubble of razed temples), Mexico was hardly immune to the influx of indigenous expression. In fact, it is nearly impossible to discuss any aspect of Mexican culture today without re-addressing, to greater or lesser degrees, its countless forms of syncretism.

One result of the conquest was the rise of an emerging class of Spanish hacienda-owners who brought various kinds of major and minor livestock to the New World, replacing much of the agriculture that sustained Amer-indian civilizations. The *matanza* (or bloodshed), a commercial slaughter of goats, has long taken place almost exclusively in the regions of Huajuapan de León (Oaxaca) and nearby Tehuacán (Puebla). At the end of the rainy season, Mixtec shepherds lead their flocks down from the highlands to be sold at the Huajuapan stockyard. No one knows exactly how long the institution has been managed by the same descendants of a few Spanish families. There, the animals are slaughtered in a body, and then butchered. Ritual and rite are certainly suggested by the structured prayer and dancing traditionally performed before each *pica*, or killing—a powerful juxtaposition with the painstaking aspect of work, and the collective and family routine that underscores this seasonal-animal economy.

Juchitán, a Zapotec town on the Isthmus of Tehuantepec, is a place where women have long been a visible public presence, actively taking part in the political and economic life of the community. As elsewhere in Mexico, traditional attire speaks of standing—or it can become the victorious aura of a woman at a political rally. Bisexuality and male cross-dressing are at home here, in this social web whereby conventional roles for women have been

Retrato de familia **(Family portrait), La Mixteca, Oaxaca, 1992**

noticeably inverted. *Curanderas*, or healers, fulfill a fusion of emotion, hope, and intimate foreboding within the collective sense of well-being; and household altars are set equally with Catholic saints, copal, and flowers, as well as sacred wooden hands and the cherished items of family observance. A mix between extraneous and native rites of passage may well have given rise to a practice known as *el rapto*, or "the abduction" (of the virgin bride-to-be), a staged transgression of matrimonial prohibitions reinforcing interfamily bonds, and perhaps channeling a latent violence toward women here who nonetheless exert their particular and rare form of autonomy.

Cultural amalgamations are hardly a thing of the past, nor a concluded totality. They are a series of changes still in the making. The carnivalesque feast day of San Miguel Arcángel in Chalma was originally a pre-Hispanic pilgrimage; children can be seen there dressed as angels or ghoulish brides, while adults give free reign to subverting the social norms, dressed as hybrids of skeletons, political figures, and television personalities, in a ceremony of sheer derisiveness.

Perhaps the image by Graciela Iturbide that best embodies the blend of traditional ways of living and the accelerated modernity that can now be seen throughout much of rural and indigenous Mexico is that of a Seri Indian, seemingly veiled by her waist-long hair, as she scurries away on the stone ridge of a mountain overlooking an expanse of the Sonora desert. Like other images rendered by the photographer, the scale of the human, in transit, is poignantly pitted against the limitless appearance of the landscape—worn as a daily thing, and really no one's property in particular. As if suddenly catching her balance on a boulder to her left side, the woman is shown clutching, in her right hand, a portable radio-cassette player.

I'm thinking about these images of Mexico, about the possibilities of representation, about bringing collective or personal deficit into fullness and complexity, about the meanings of an independent life in art, and about the transformative efforts involved in forging sense out of one's most immediate, determining facts. For to address this photographer's achievement accurately is to keep in mind that Graciela Iturbide virtually had to reinvent herself by thoroughly disowning the given—the conventional patterns made available to a woman of her class by the dominant systems of bourgeois values that, to this day, still shape much of Mexico's rarefied salon-society.

I'm thinking about Graciela Iturbide and the responsibilities of the imagination as framed by the artist and woman; about the tragedy of individual loss; about the pregnancy of death in a bridal gown; about images of motherhood expressed as gift and verdict; about the transfiguration of death into something tangible—into intimacy, into witness. To understand her indelible vision of Mexico and its diverse human drama is to sense that a death-in-life inhabits these images—the premature death of Graciela's second child, a reality out of which a daughter of memory is repeatedly evoked, and by which the self and other are confused, or waived momentarily of their rigid dichotomies. It is a death through which Graciela came into her own, into a kind of voluntary exile within the provisional residence of photography, into the festival aspect and everyday multiplicity of Mexico and its peoples.

These are images that are passionately engaged with the rifts in the human. In this poetics of violence and purity—of death, daily life, and duality—Graciela Iturbide explores those spaces between the observer and the observed; between the system and the gesture; between cultural inheritance and the damages of history; between the liquid undertones of collective memory and its wagers on the future. The evidence she has gathered is a virtual territory unto itself. Look. You can see it stretching from the black gore of sacrificed flesh to the open hand of a lone cactus emerging upright, steadfast, from the hard, cracked earth.

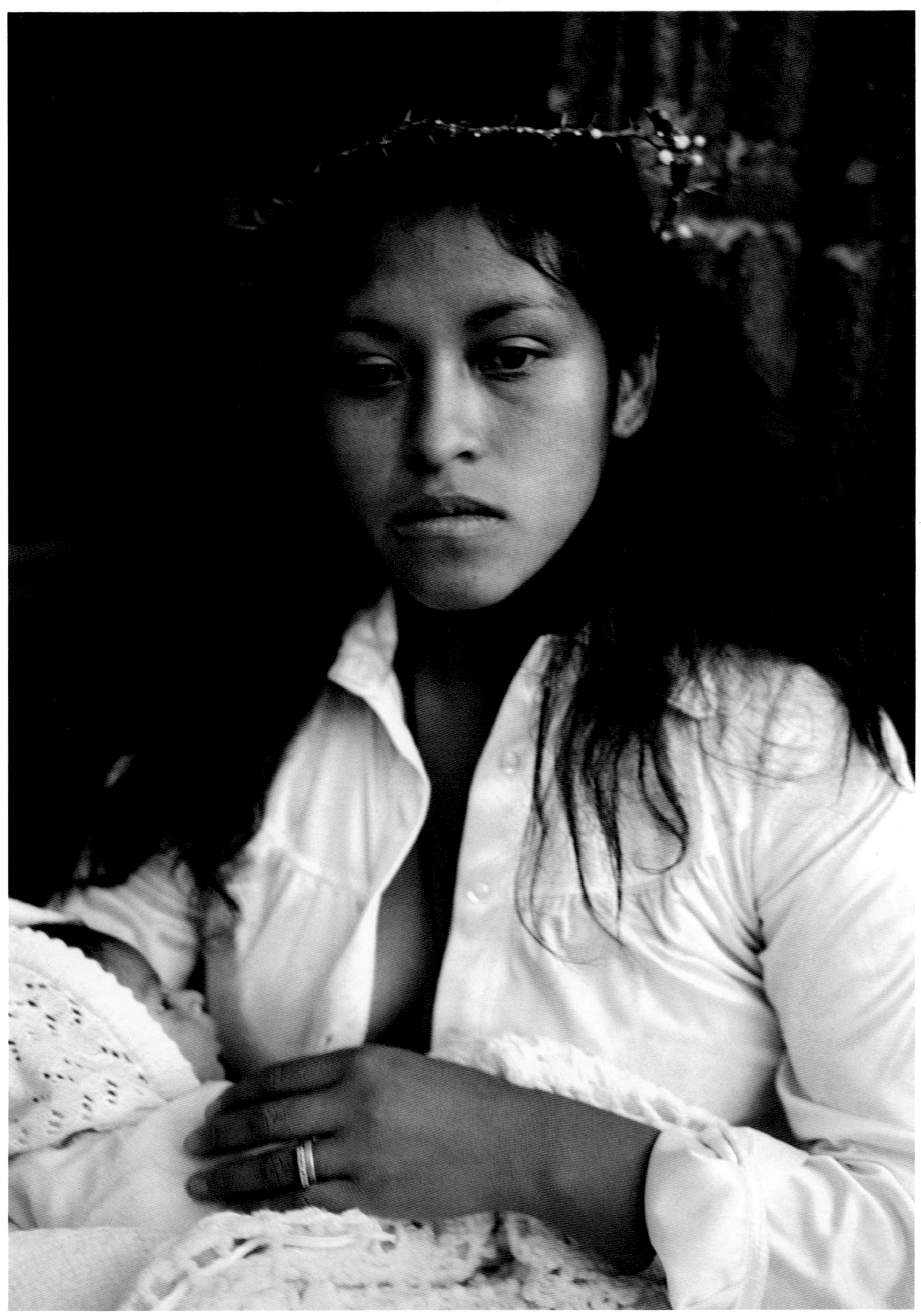

Madonna, Mexico City, 1980

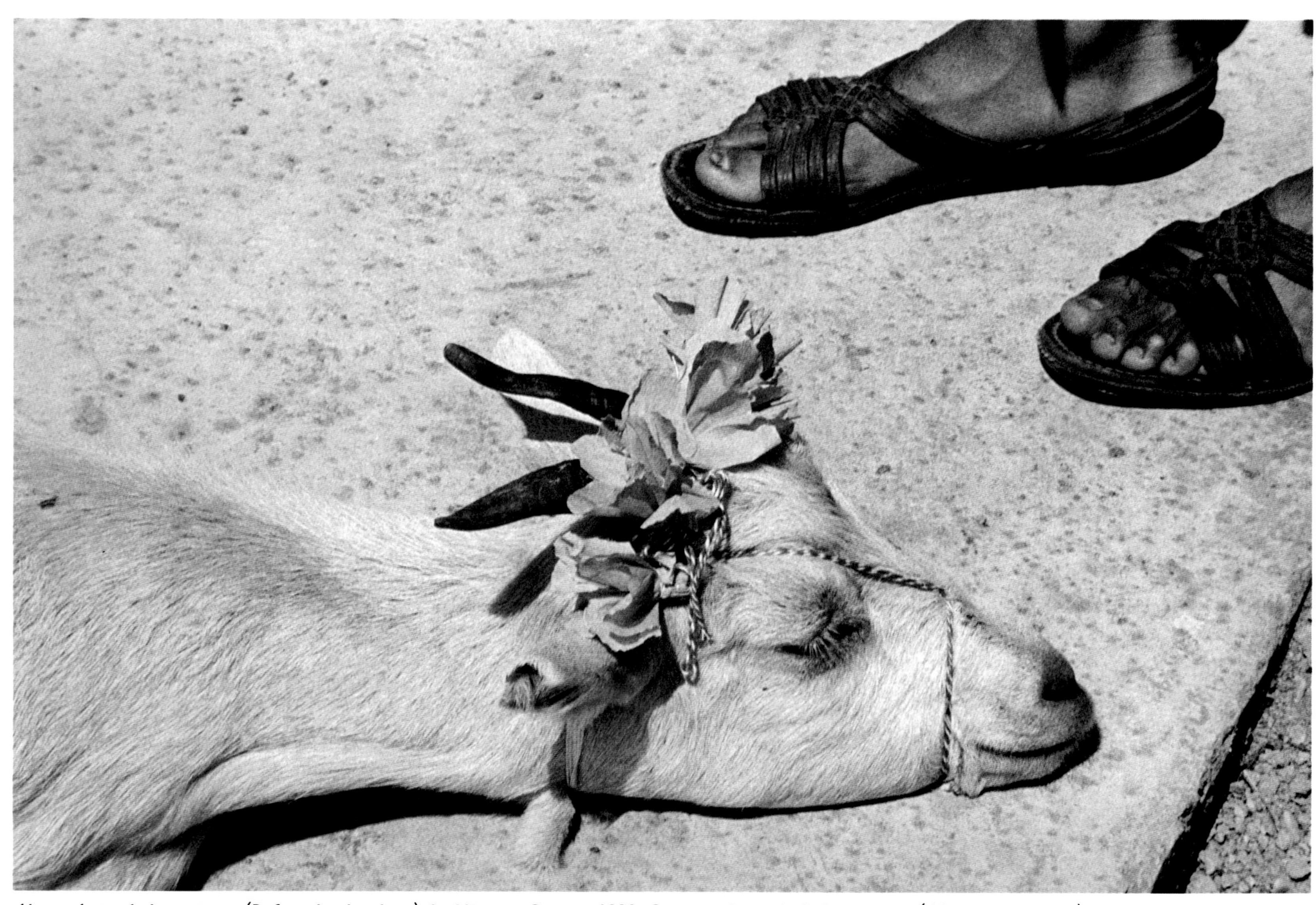

Above: *Antes de la matanza* (Before the slaughter), La Mixteca, Oaxaca, 1992. *Opposite*: *Después de la matanza* (After the slaughter), La Mixteca, Oaxaca, 1992

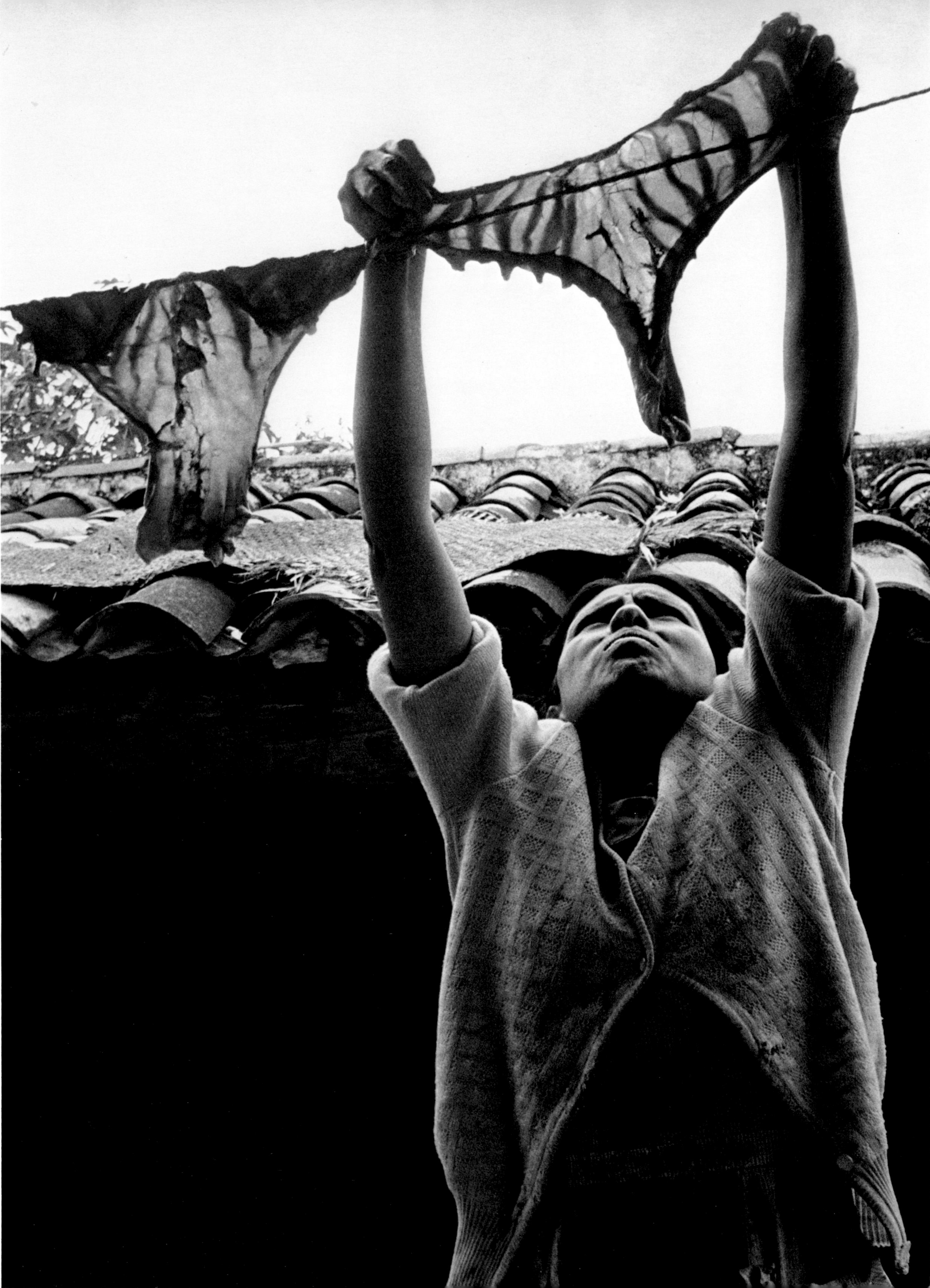

El sacrificio (The sacrifice), La Mixteca, Oaxaca, 1992

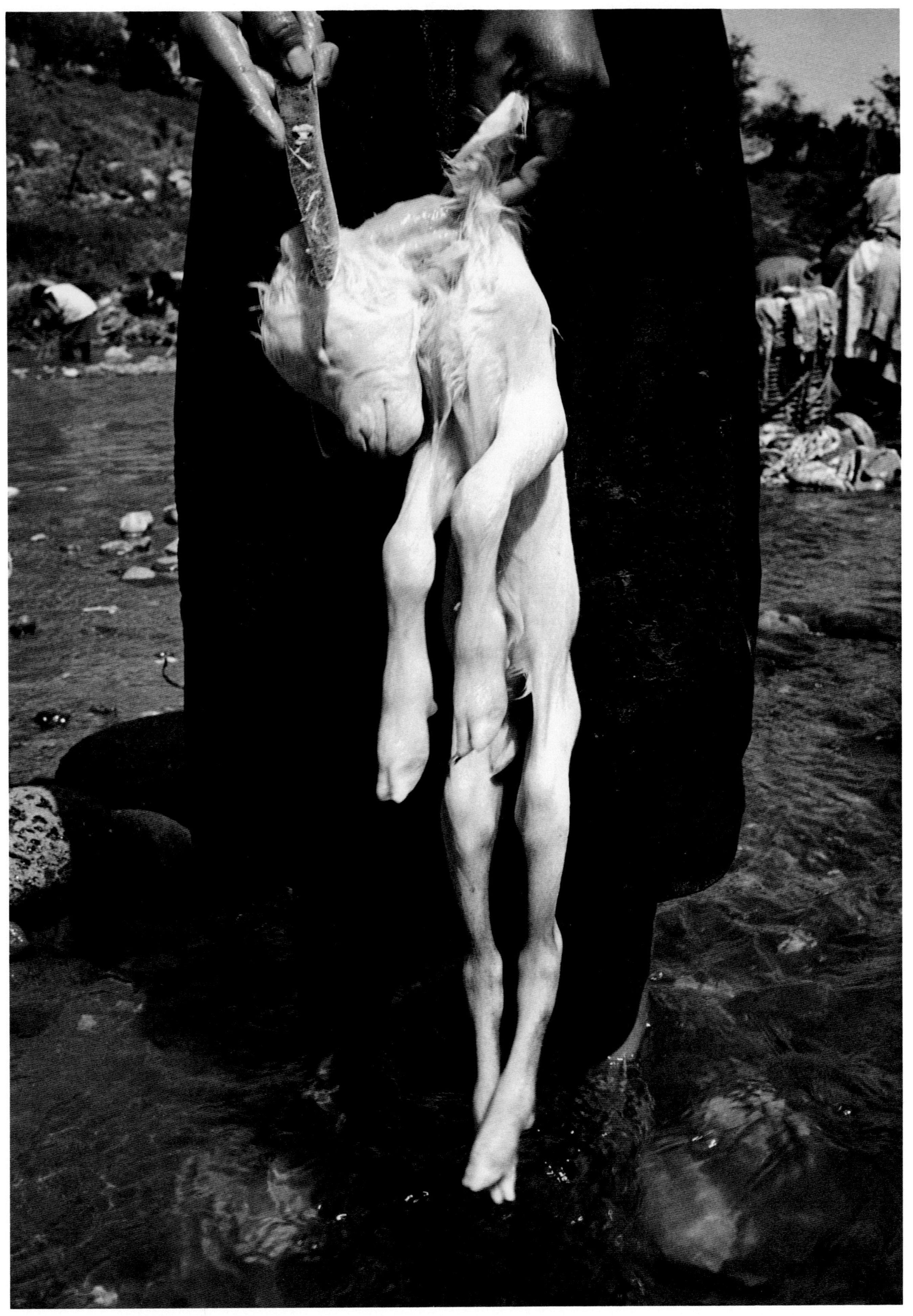

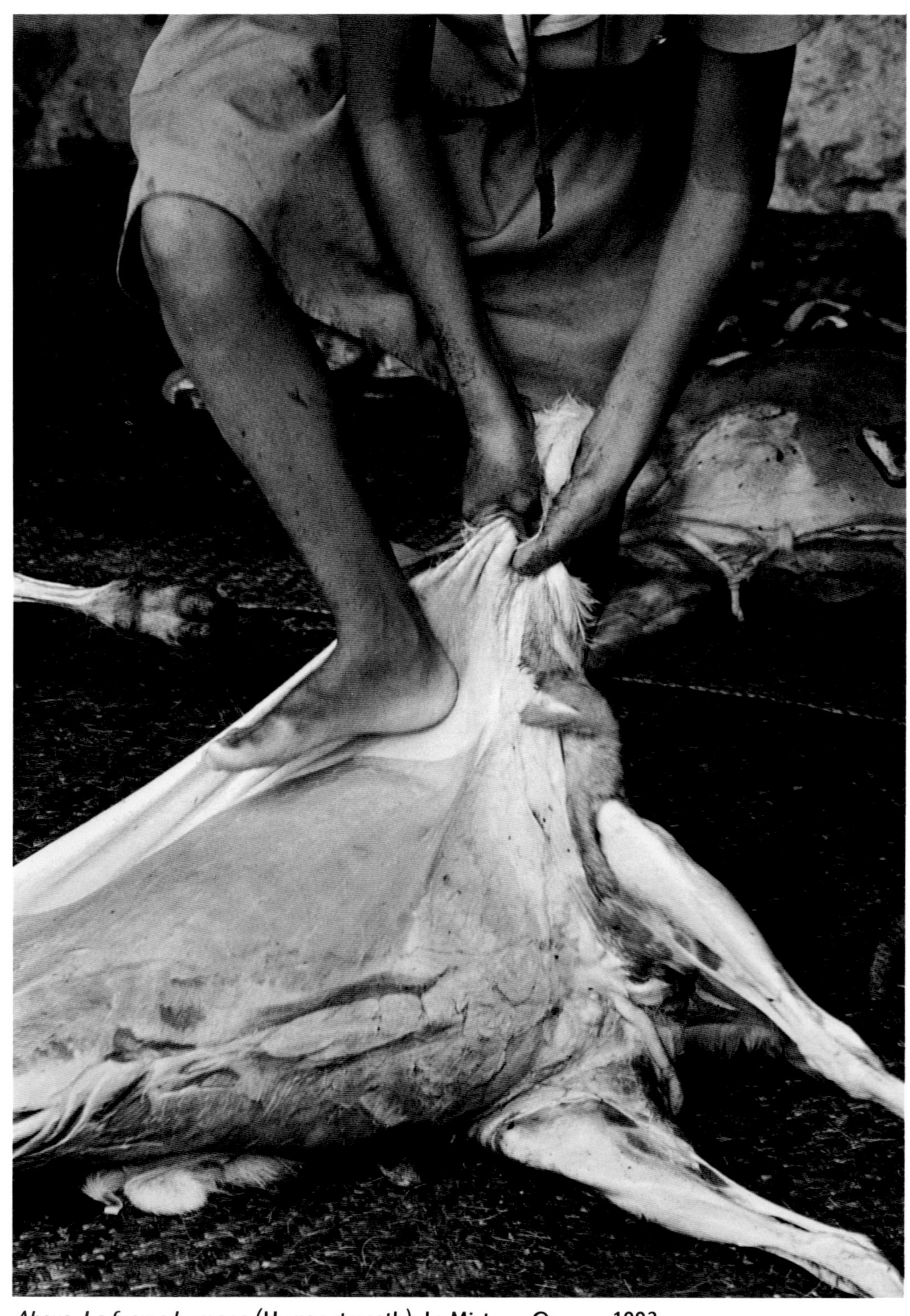

Above: *La fuerza humana* (Human strength), La Mixteca, Oaxaca, 1992
Opposite: *Cabritas* (Goats), La Mixteca, Oaxaca, 1992

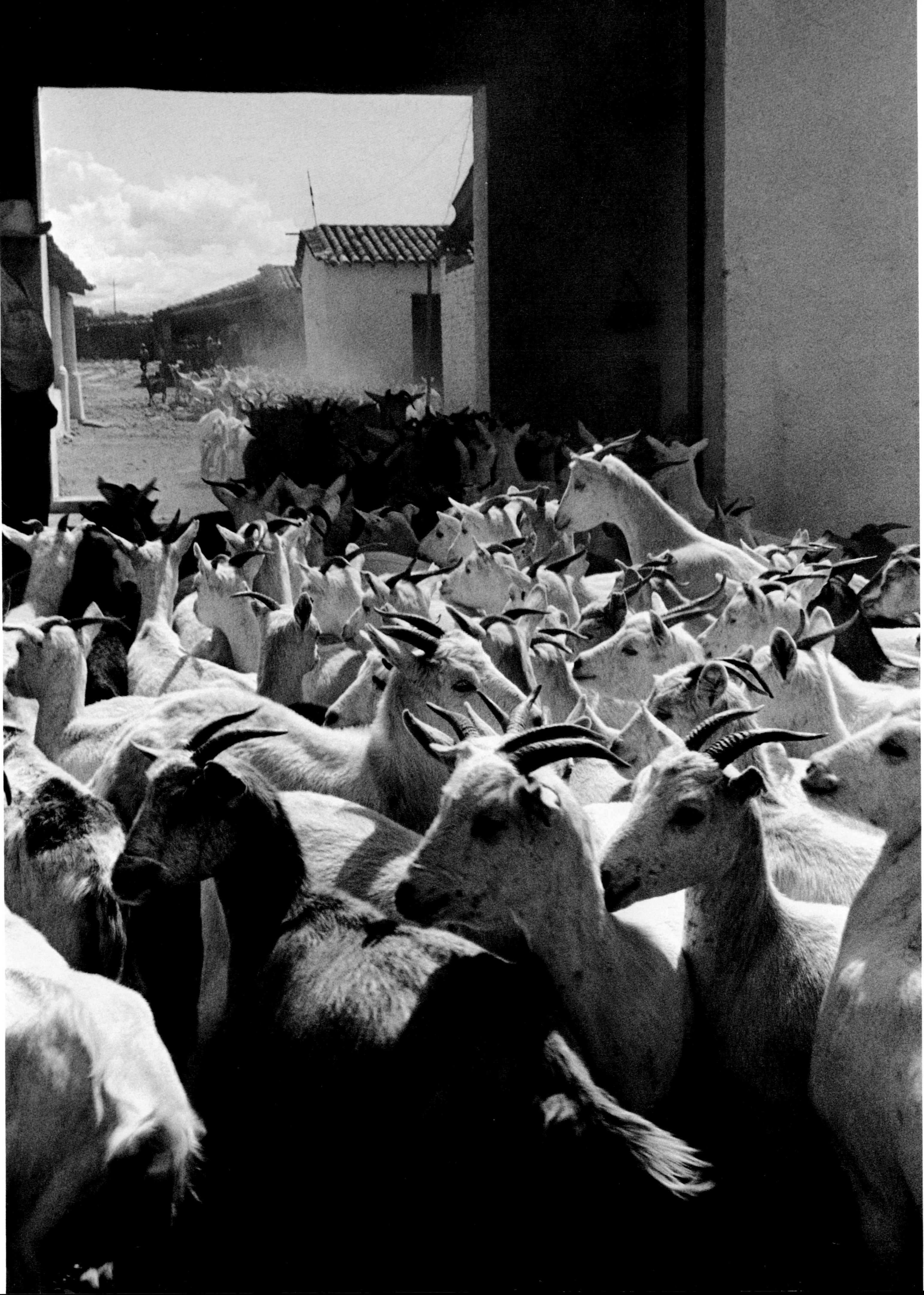

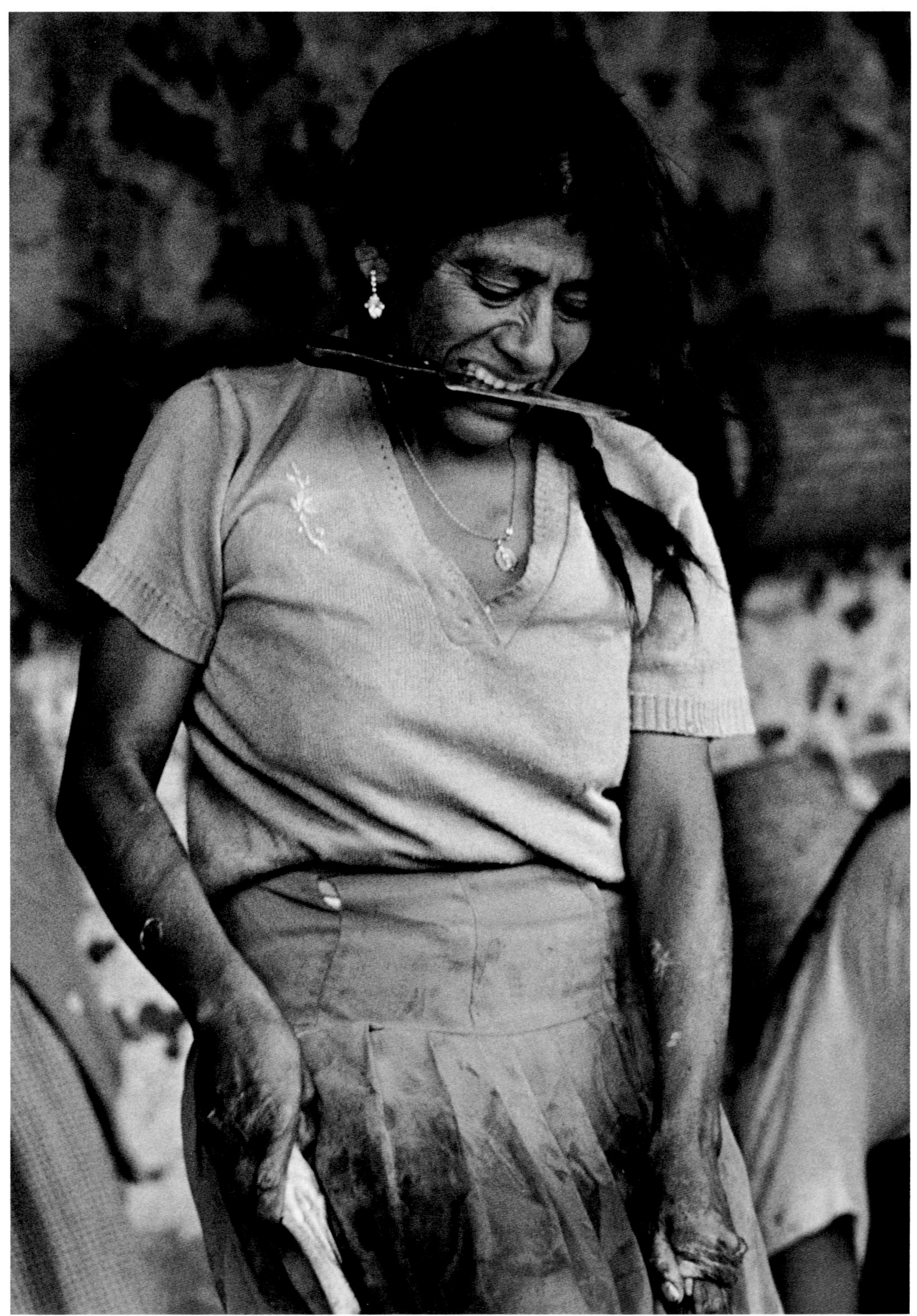

 Above: *Carmen*, La Mixteca, Oaxaca, 1992. *Opposite*: *Cordero de dios* (Lamb of God), La Mixteca, Oaxaca, 1992

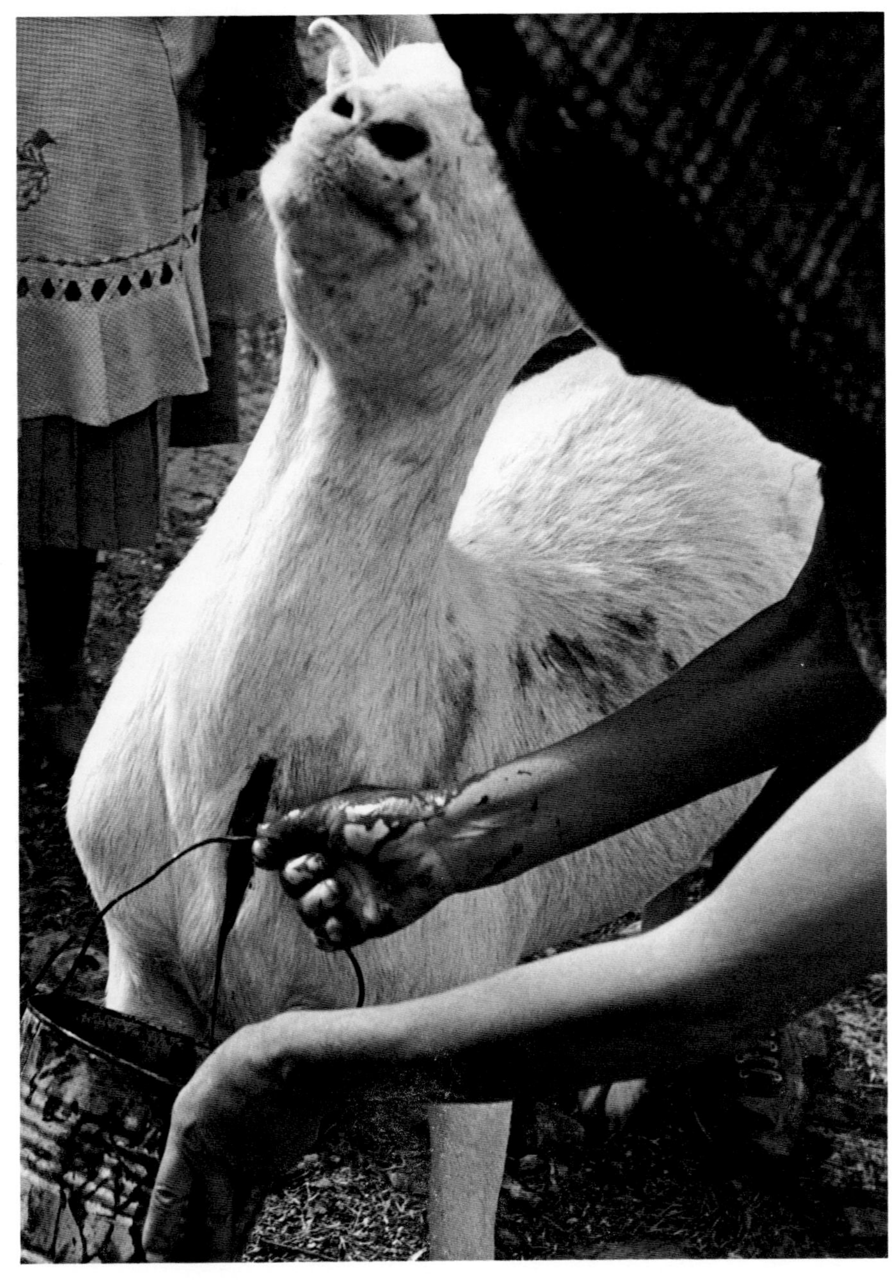

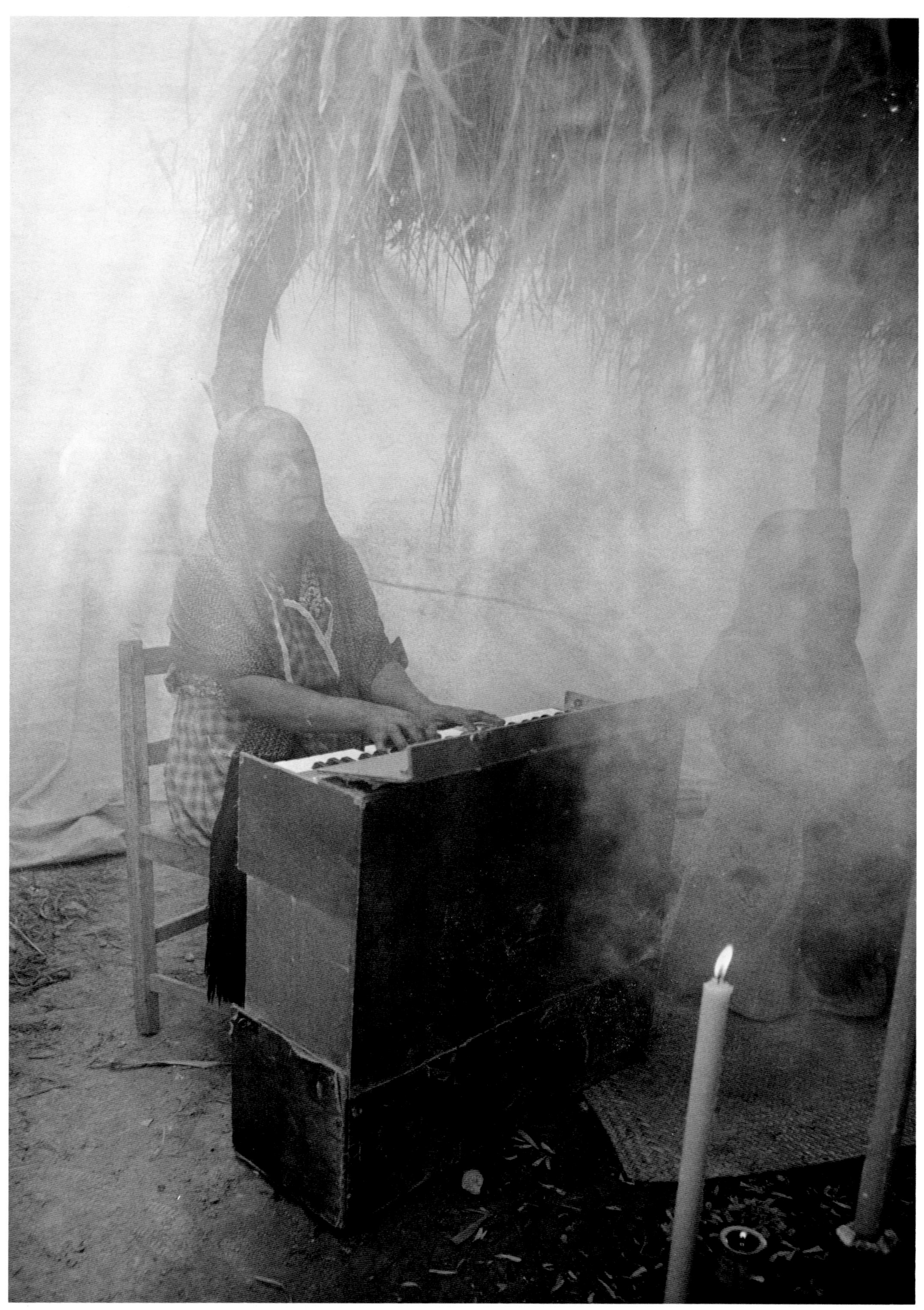

 Cementerio (Cemetery), Chilac, Puebla, 1992

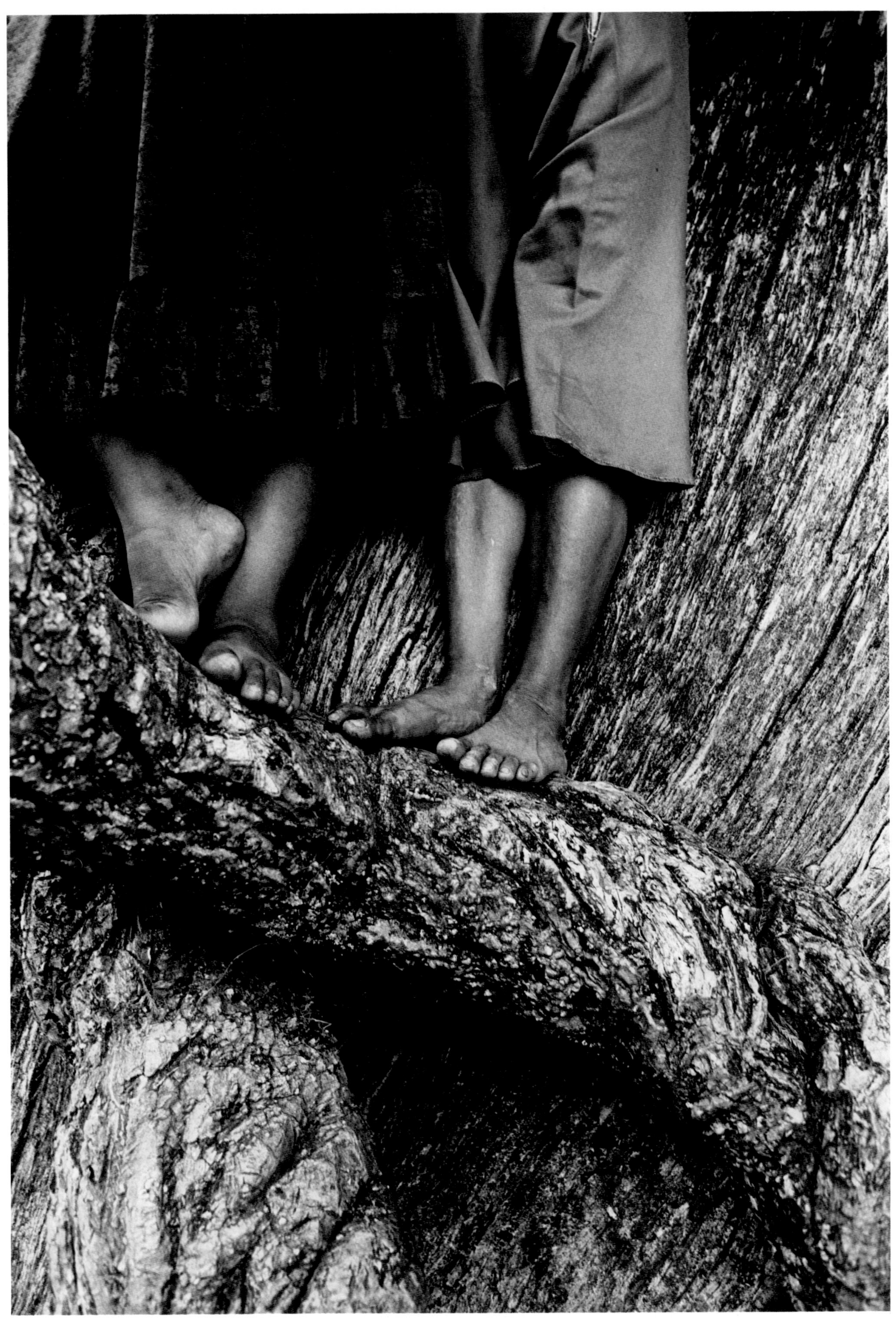

La ascensión (The ascension), Chalma, State of Mexico, 1984

Angelito mexicano (Mexican cherub), Chalma, State of Mexico, 1984

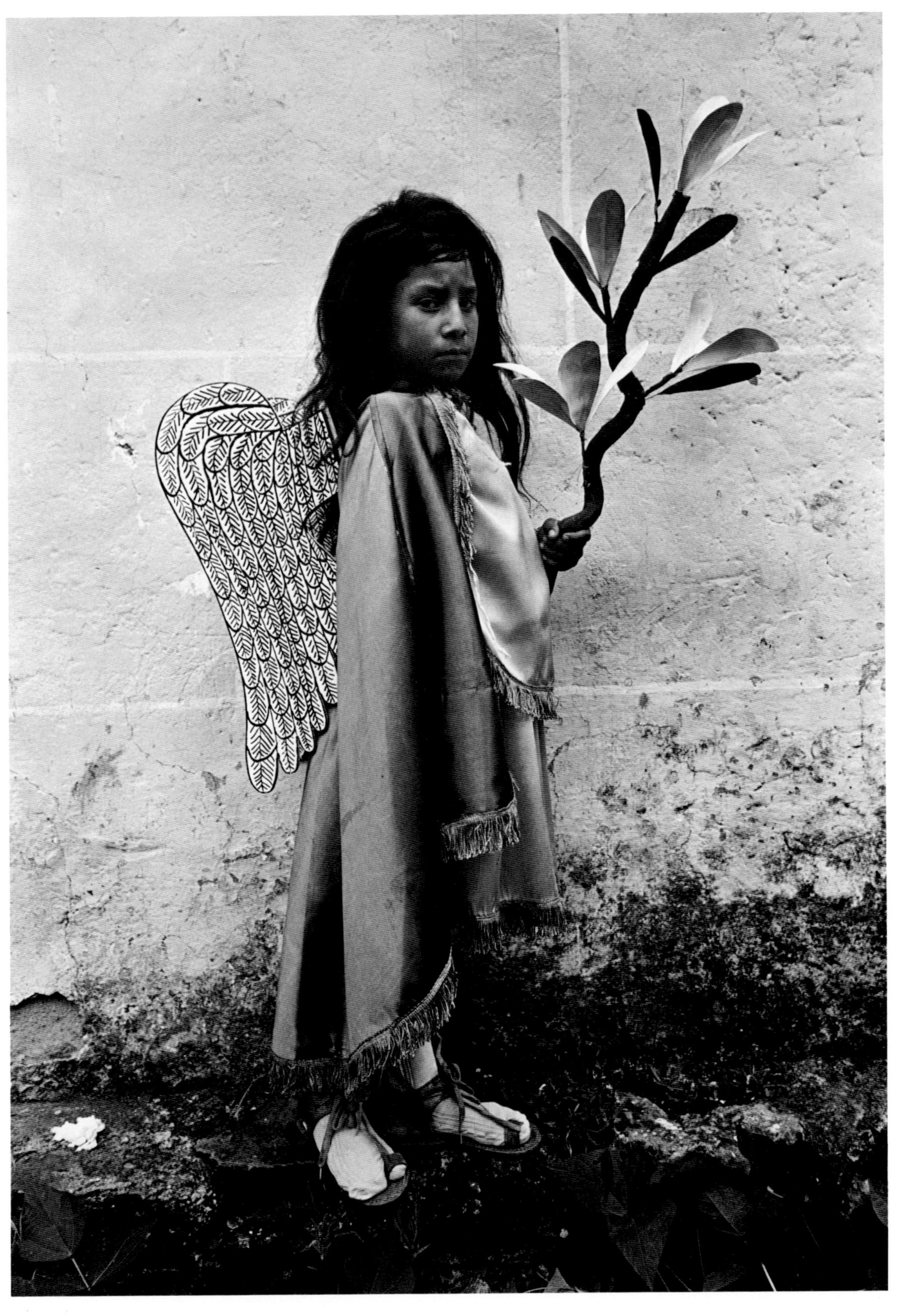

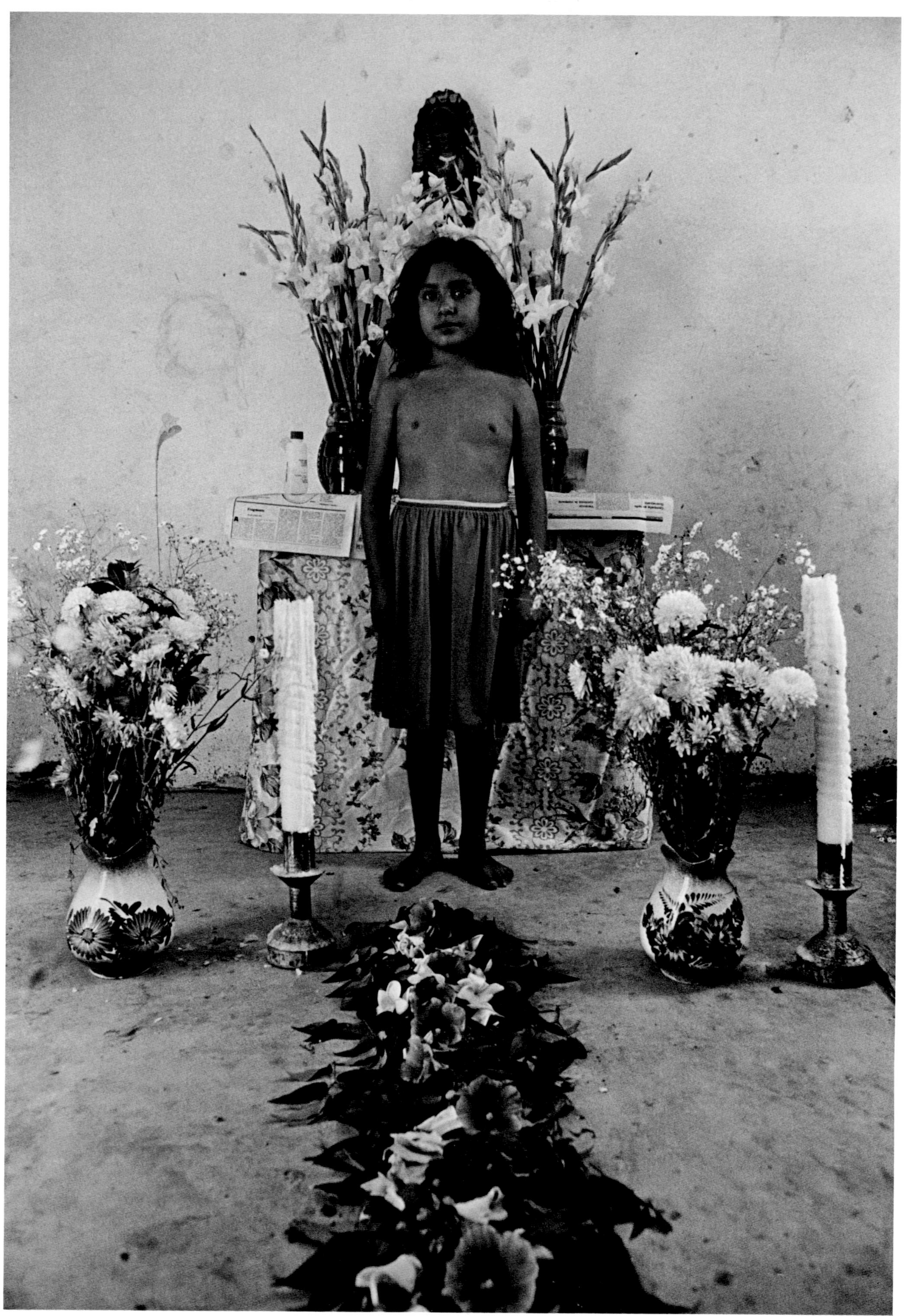

 Nueve días de luto (Nine days of mourning), Juchitán, Oaxaca, 1986

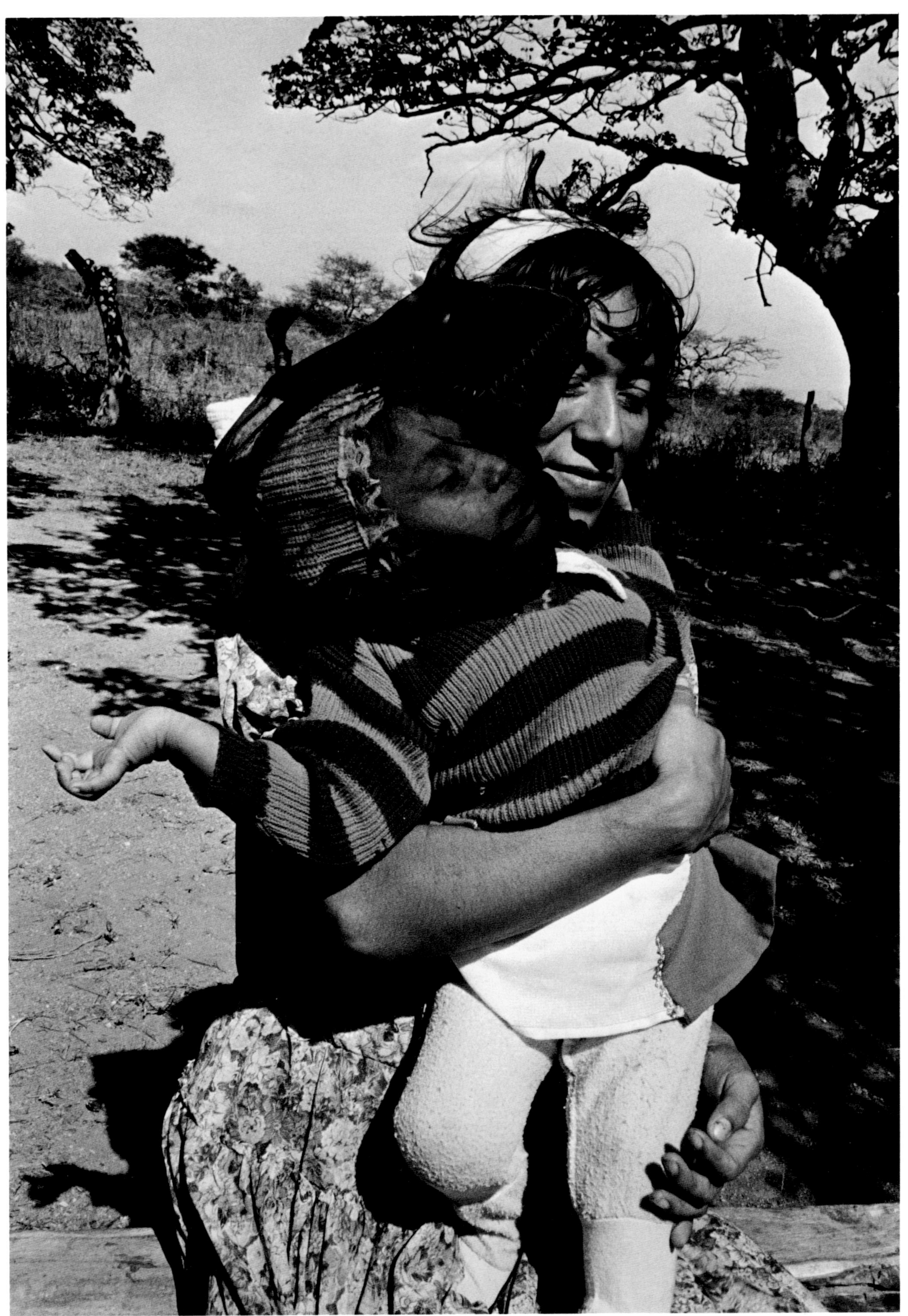

Velo negro para el viento (Black veil for the wind), Juchitán, Oaxaca, 1988

Na' Lupe Pan, Juchitán, Oaxaca, 1986

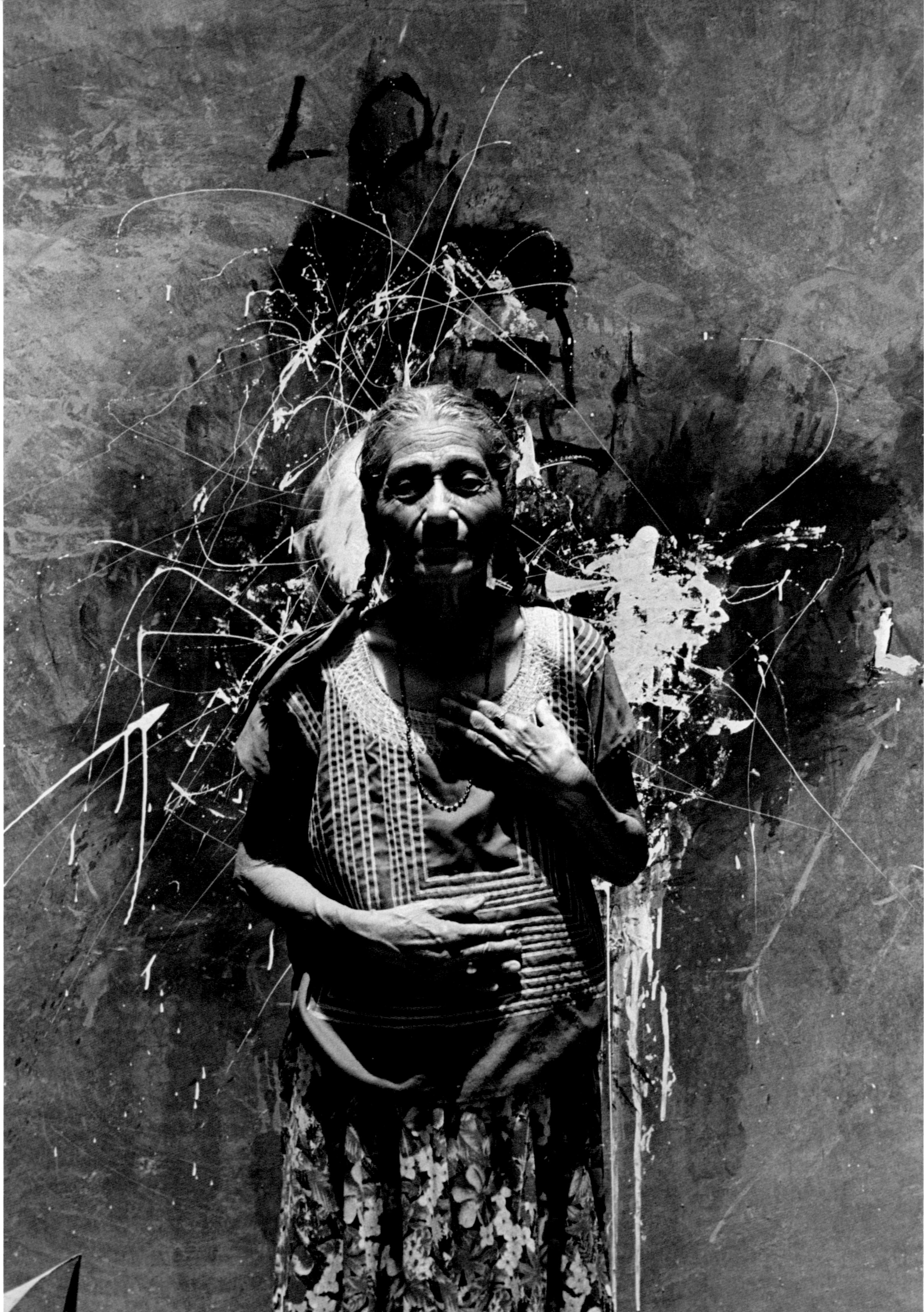

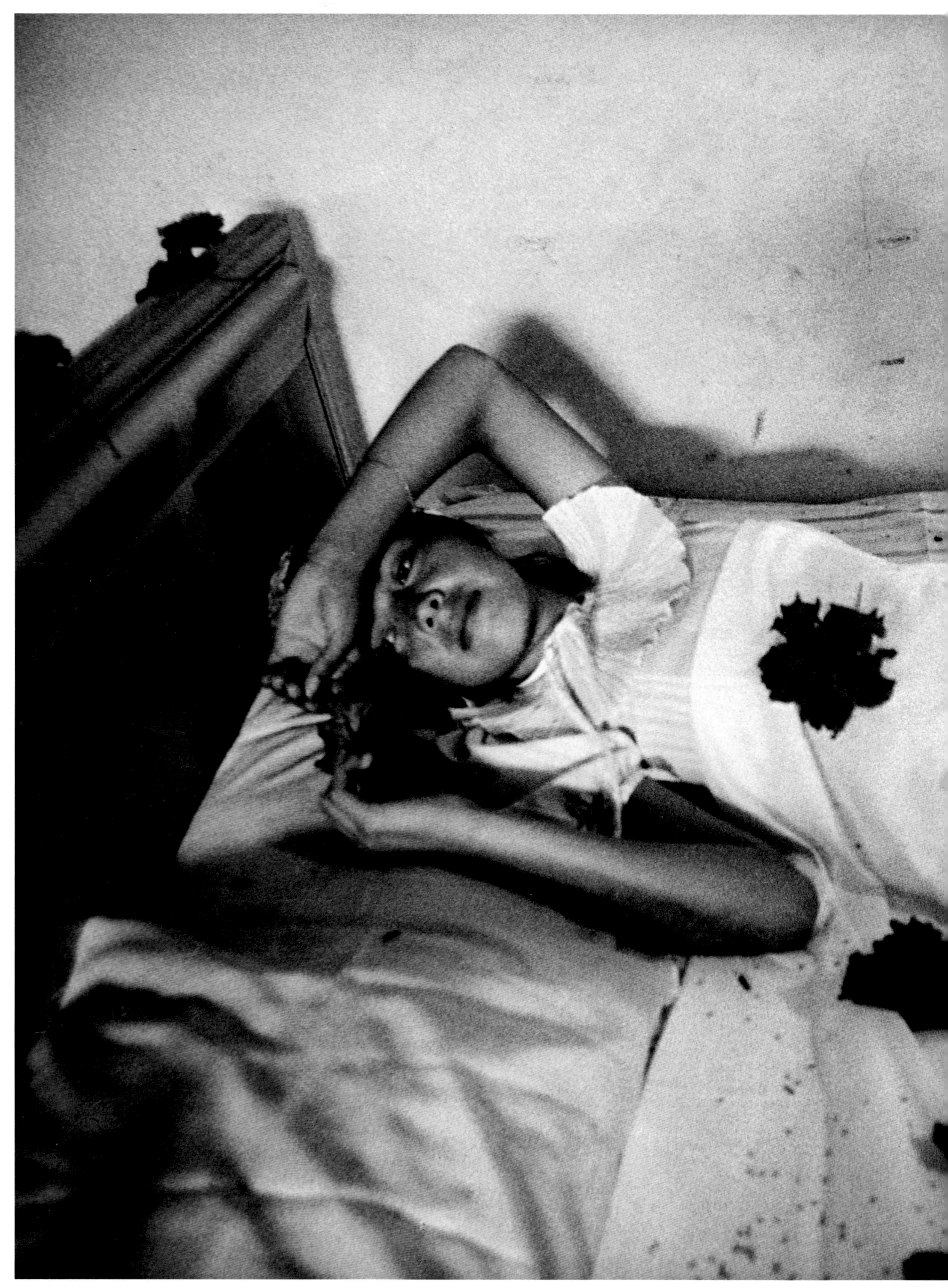

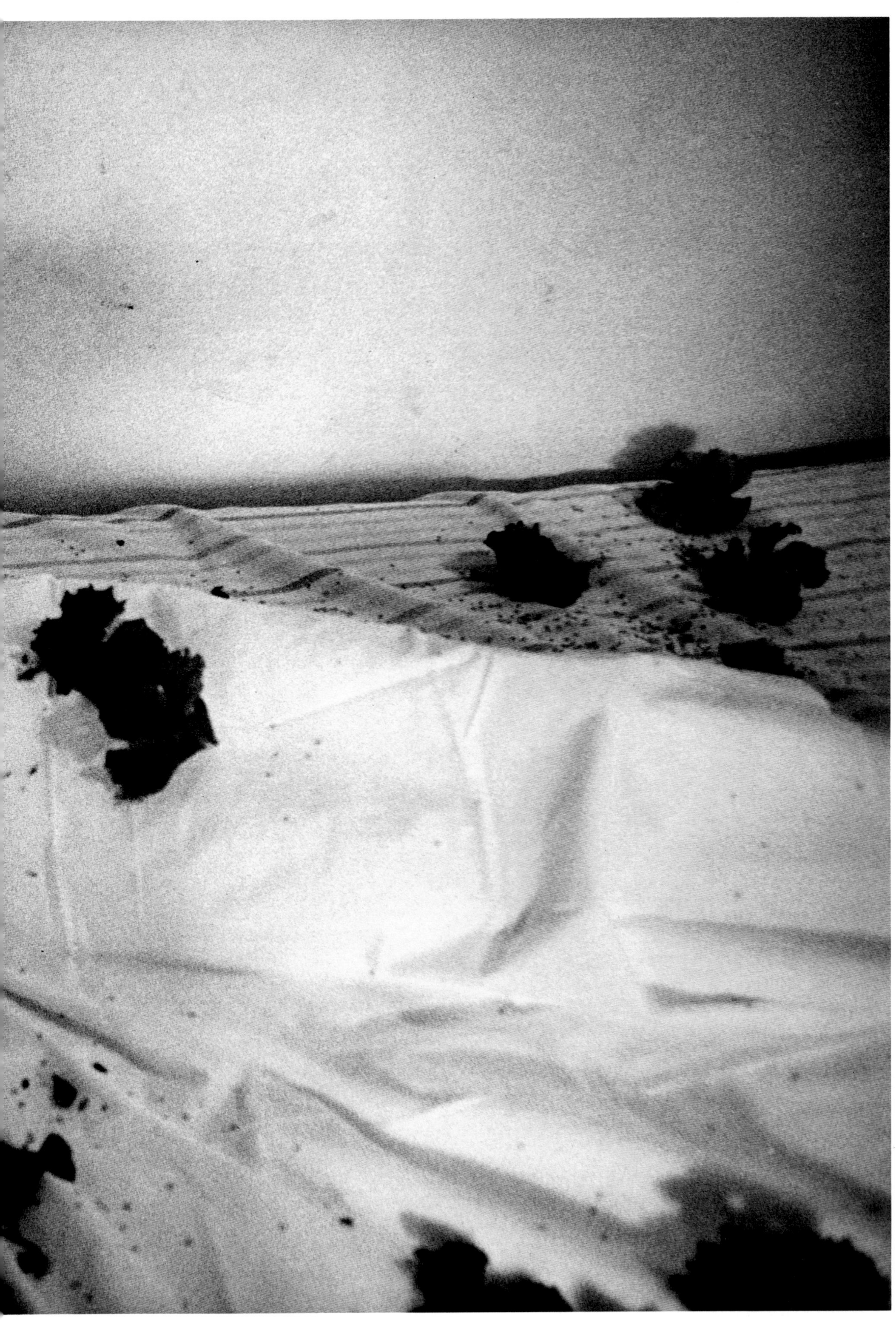

El rapto (The abduction),
Juchitán, Oaxaca, 1986

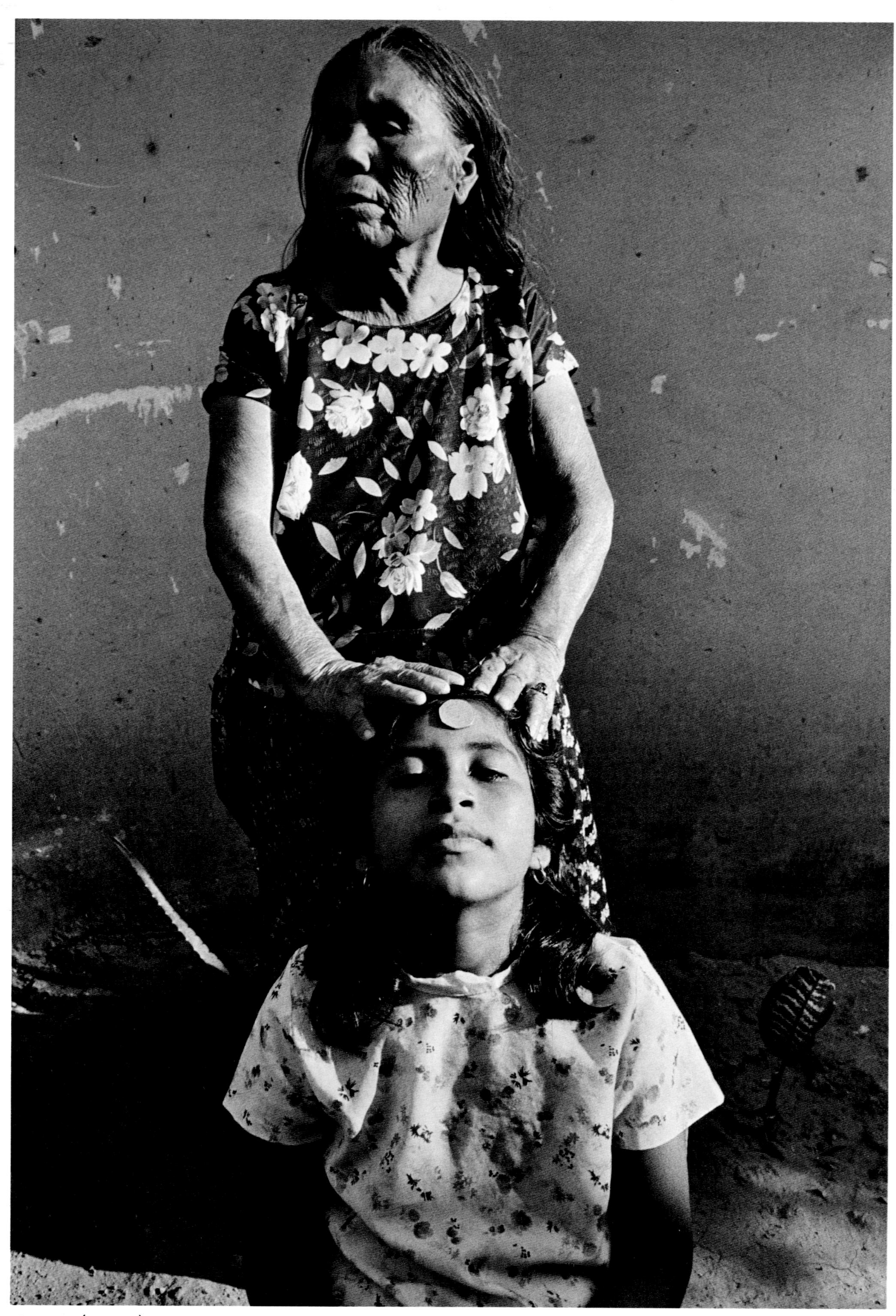

Curación (Healing), Juchitán, Oaxaca, 1988

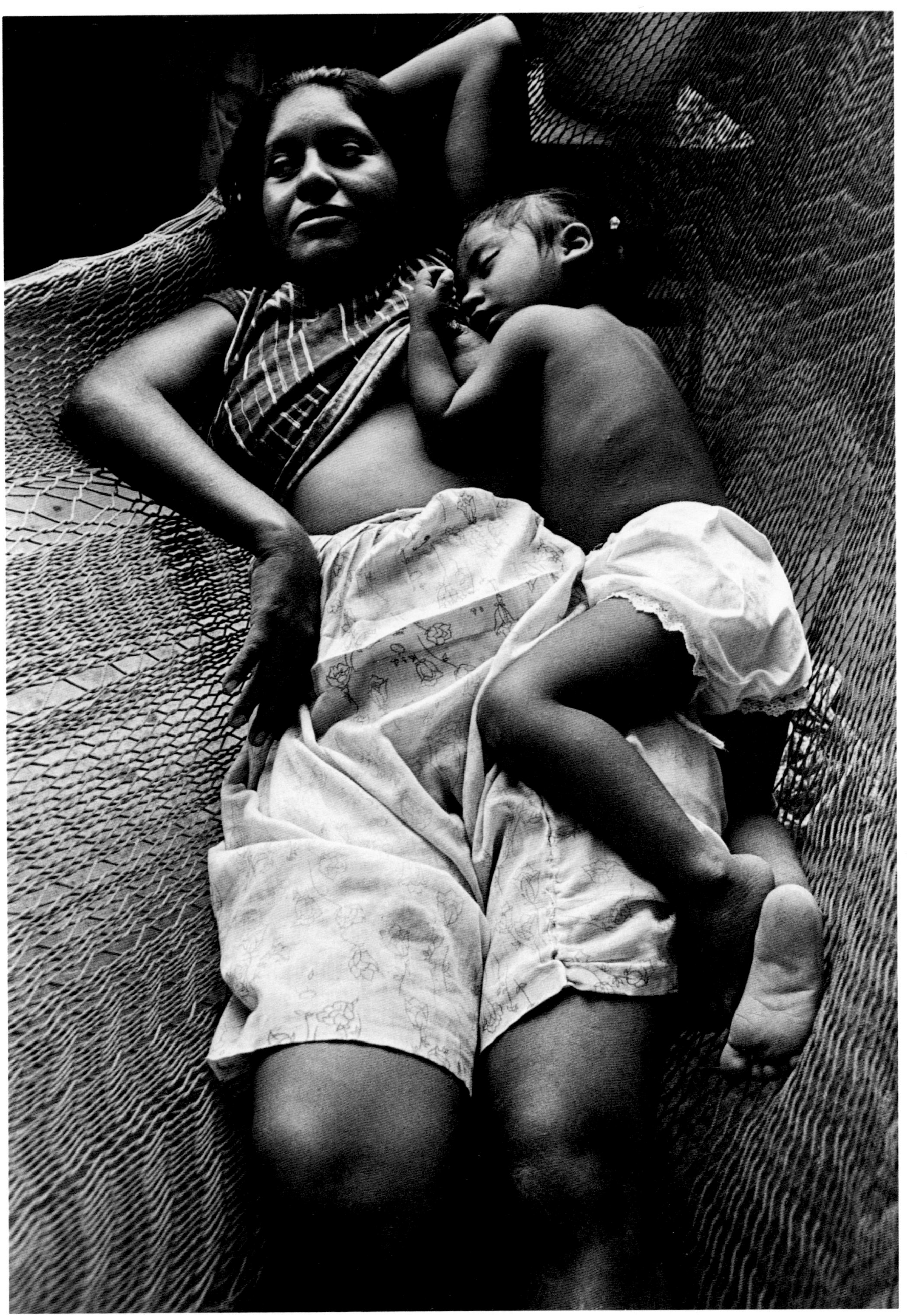

Maternidad (Motherhood), Juchitán, Oaxaca, 1986

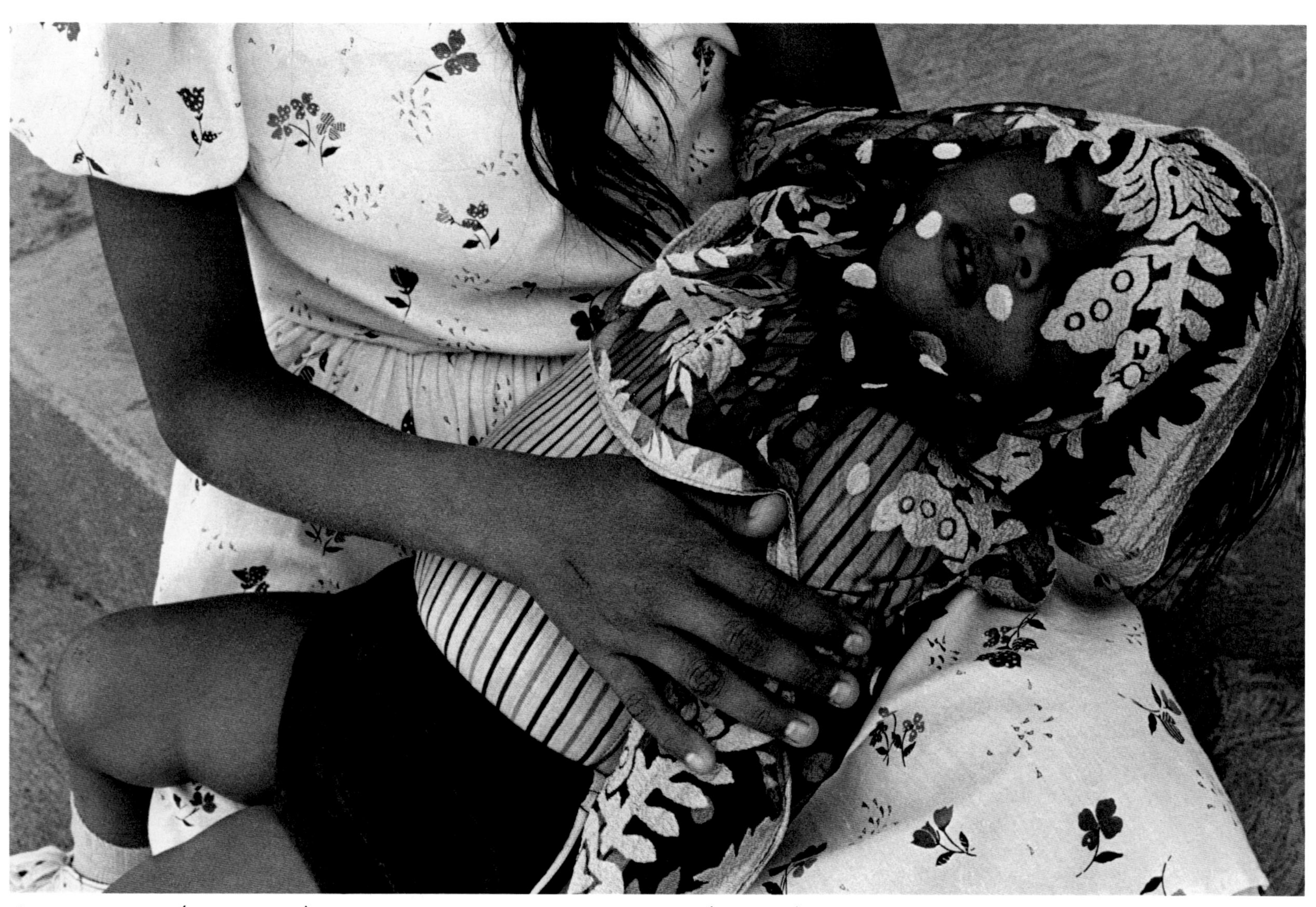

Above: *Jueves santo* (Holy Thursday), Juchitán, Oaxaca, 1986. *Opposite*: *Cementerio* (Cemetery), Juchitán, Oaxaca, 1988

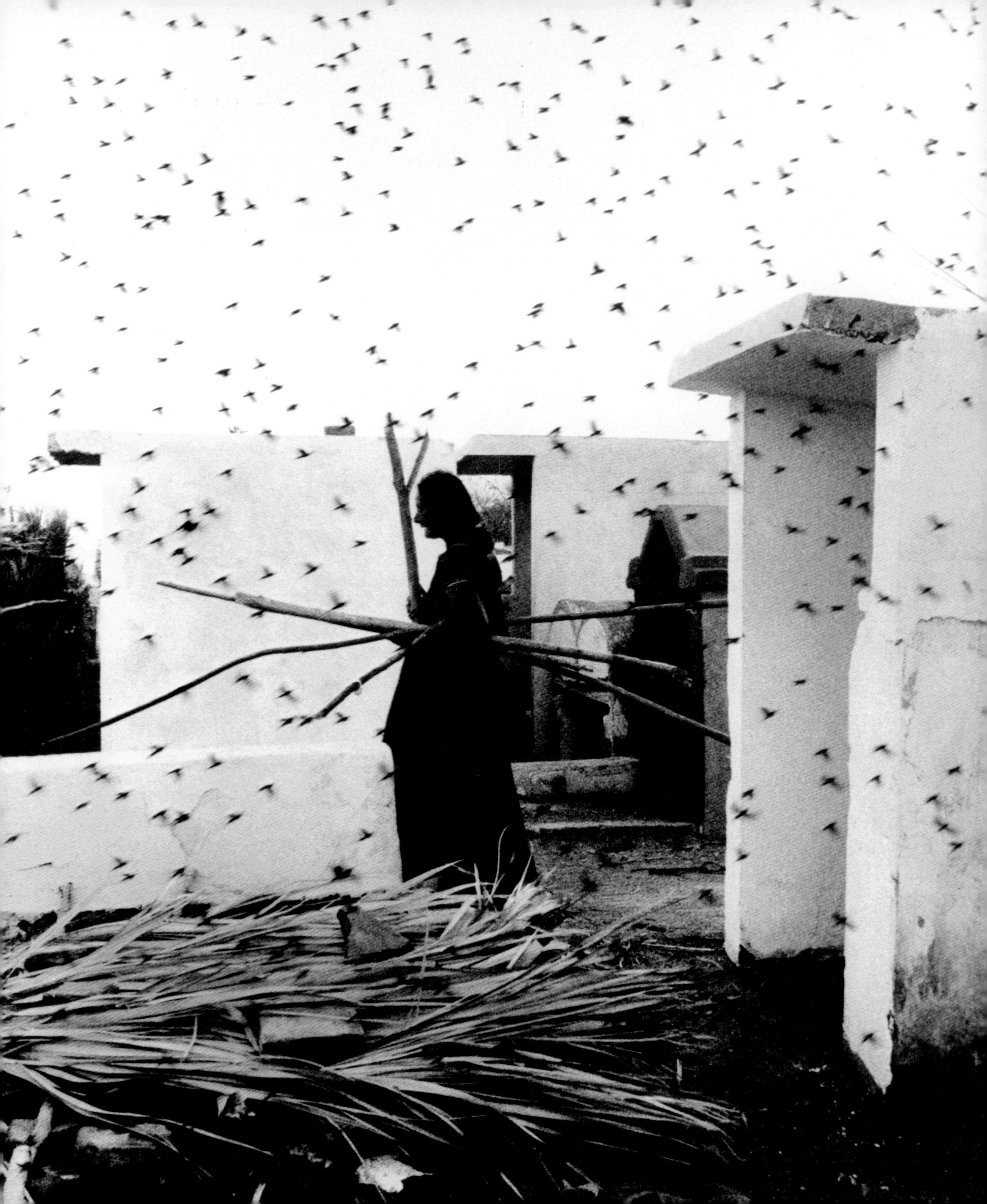

Doña Guadalupe, Juchitán, Oaxaca, 1988

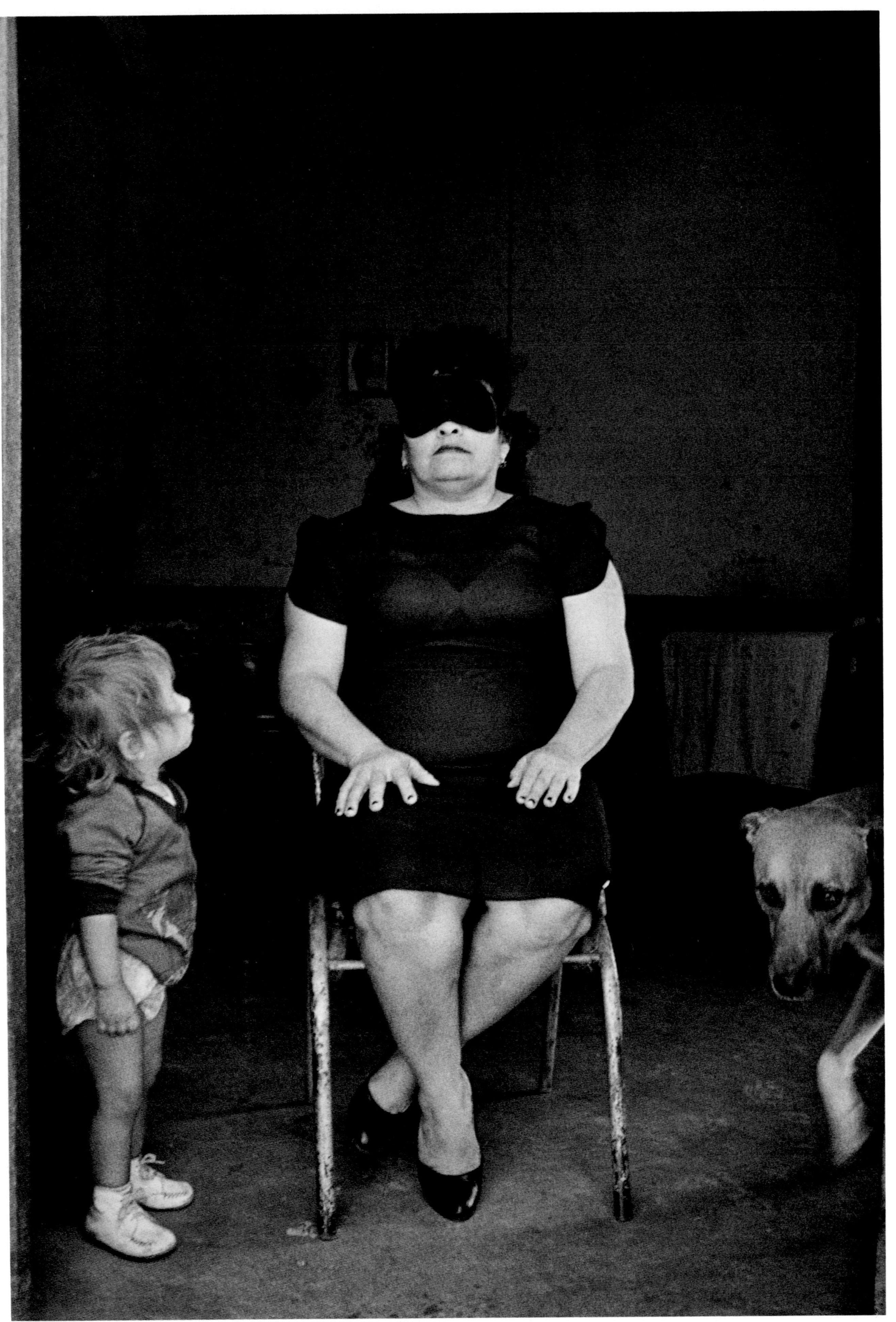

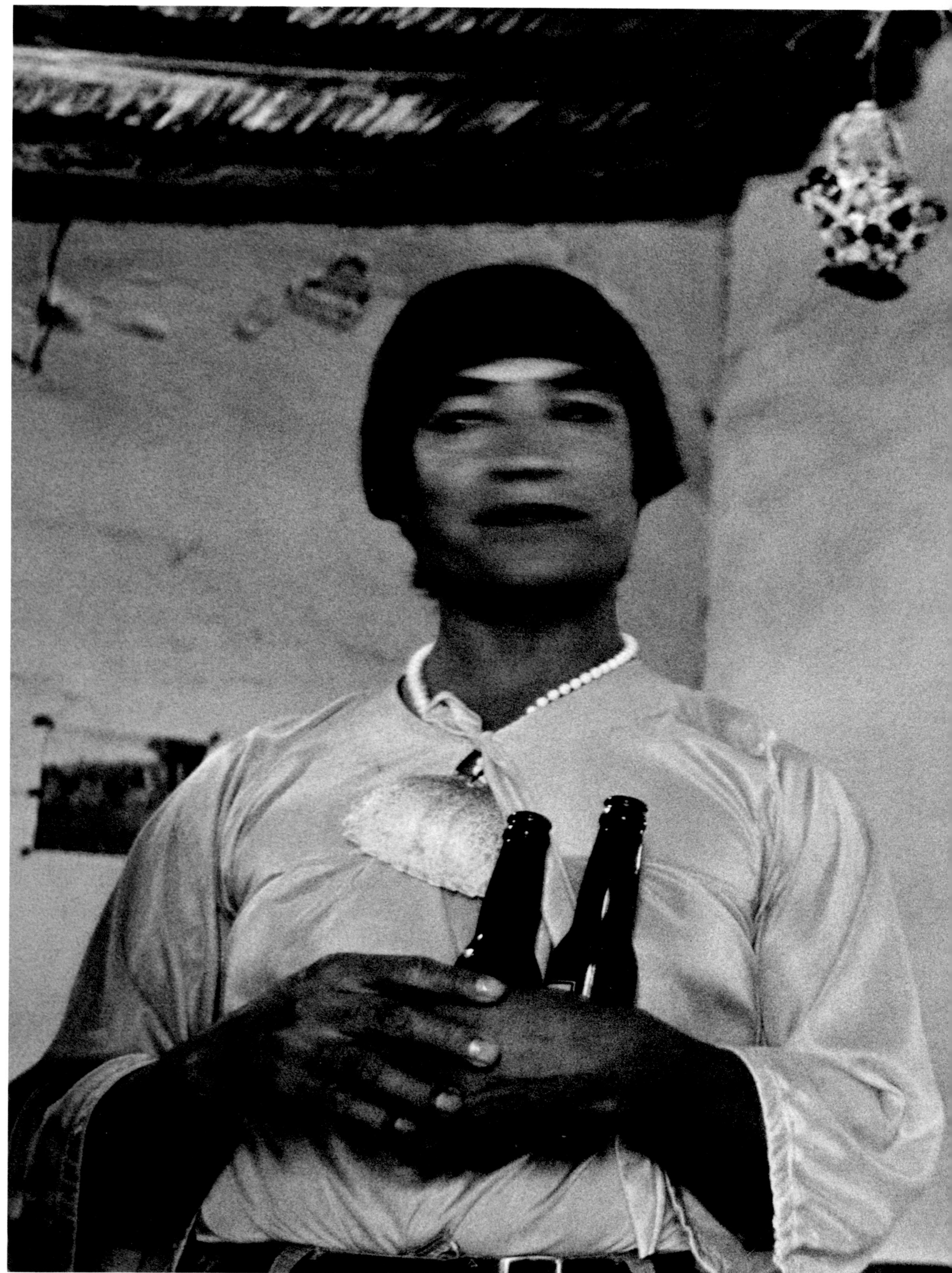

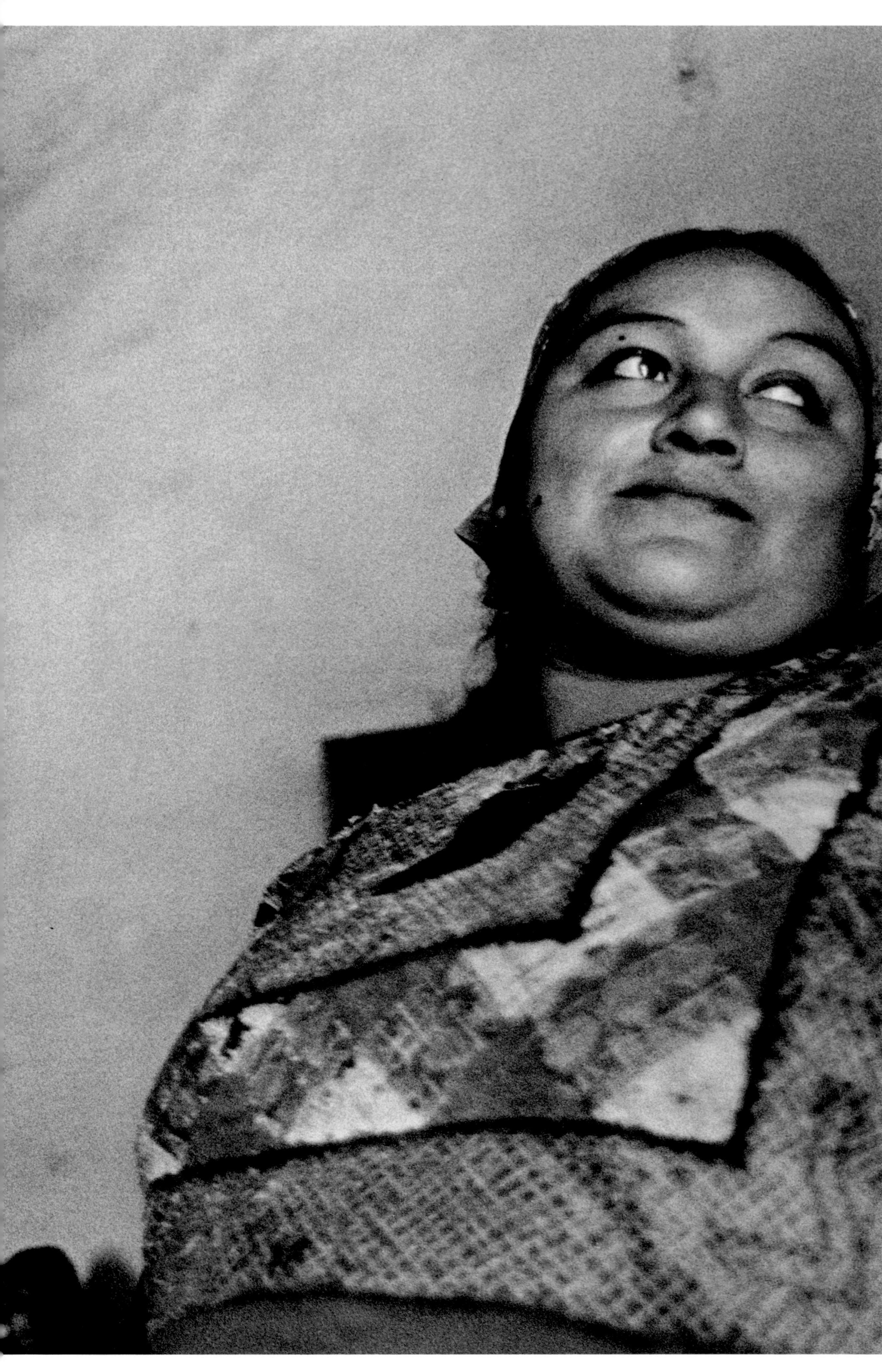

La Cantina (Cantina),
Juchitán, Oaxaca, 1986

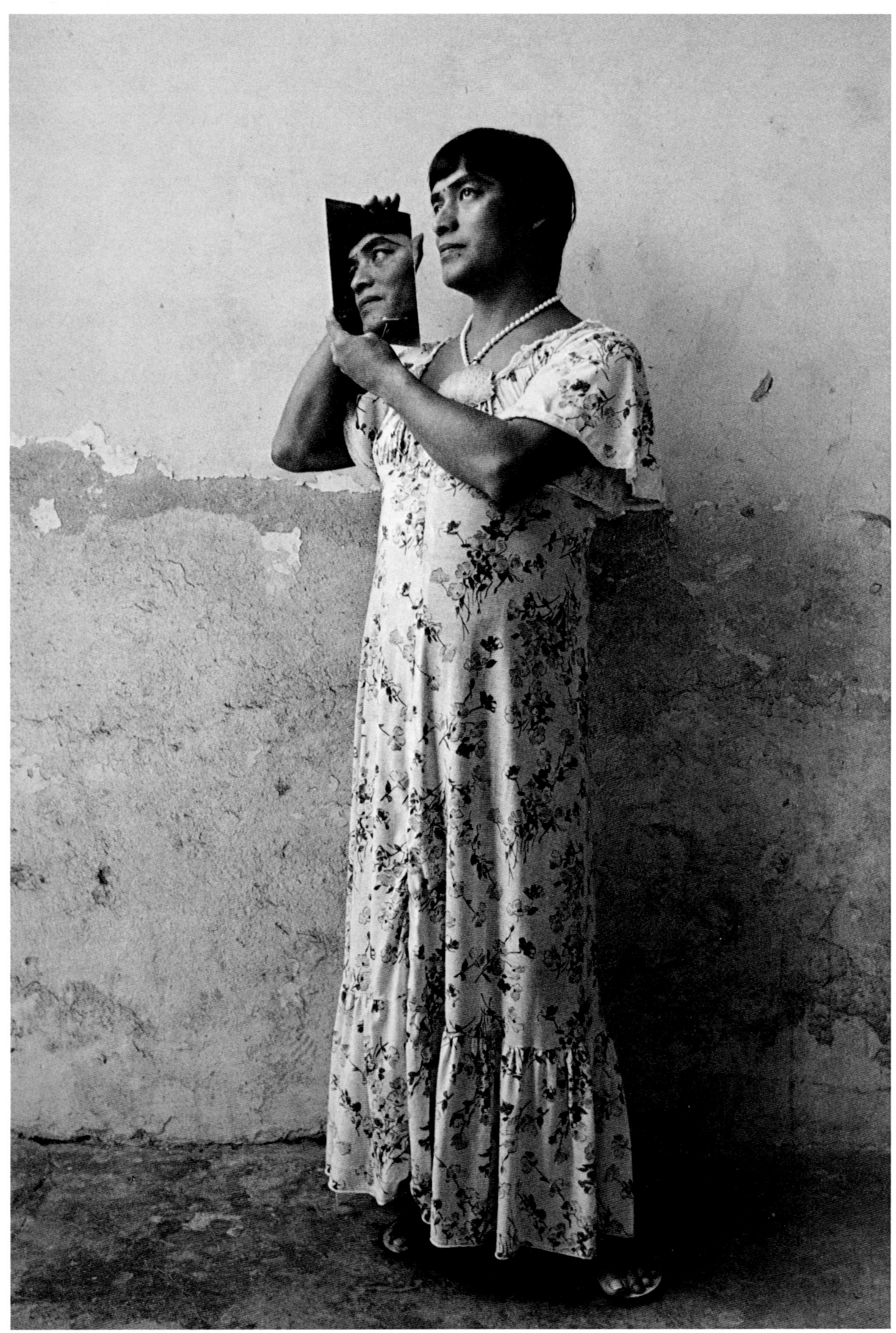

Magnolia, Juchitán, Oaxaca, 1986

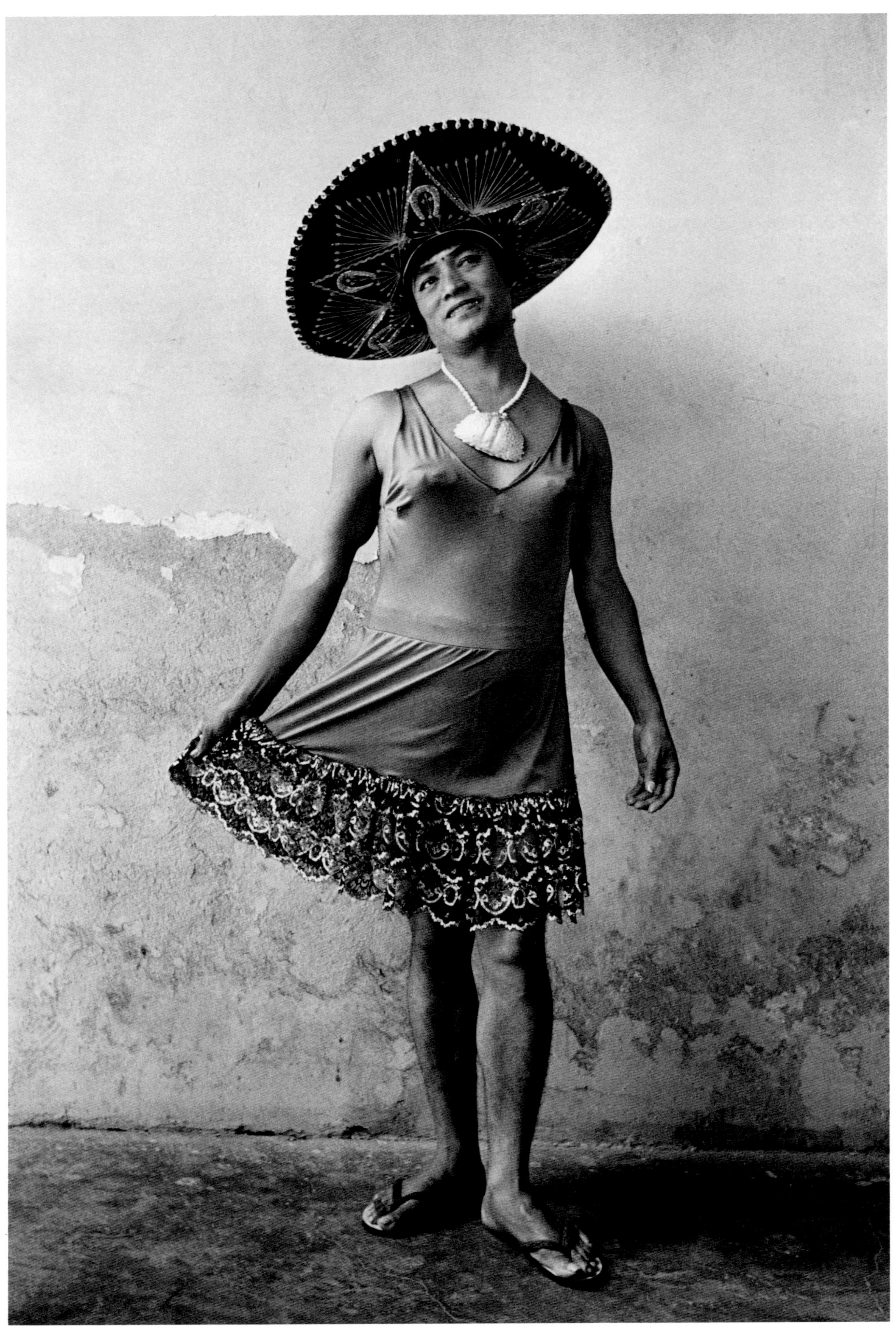

Magnolia, Juchitán, Oaxaca, 1986

Serafina, Juchitán, Oaxaca, 1985

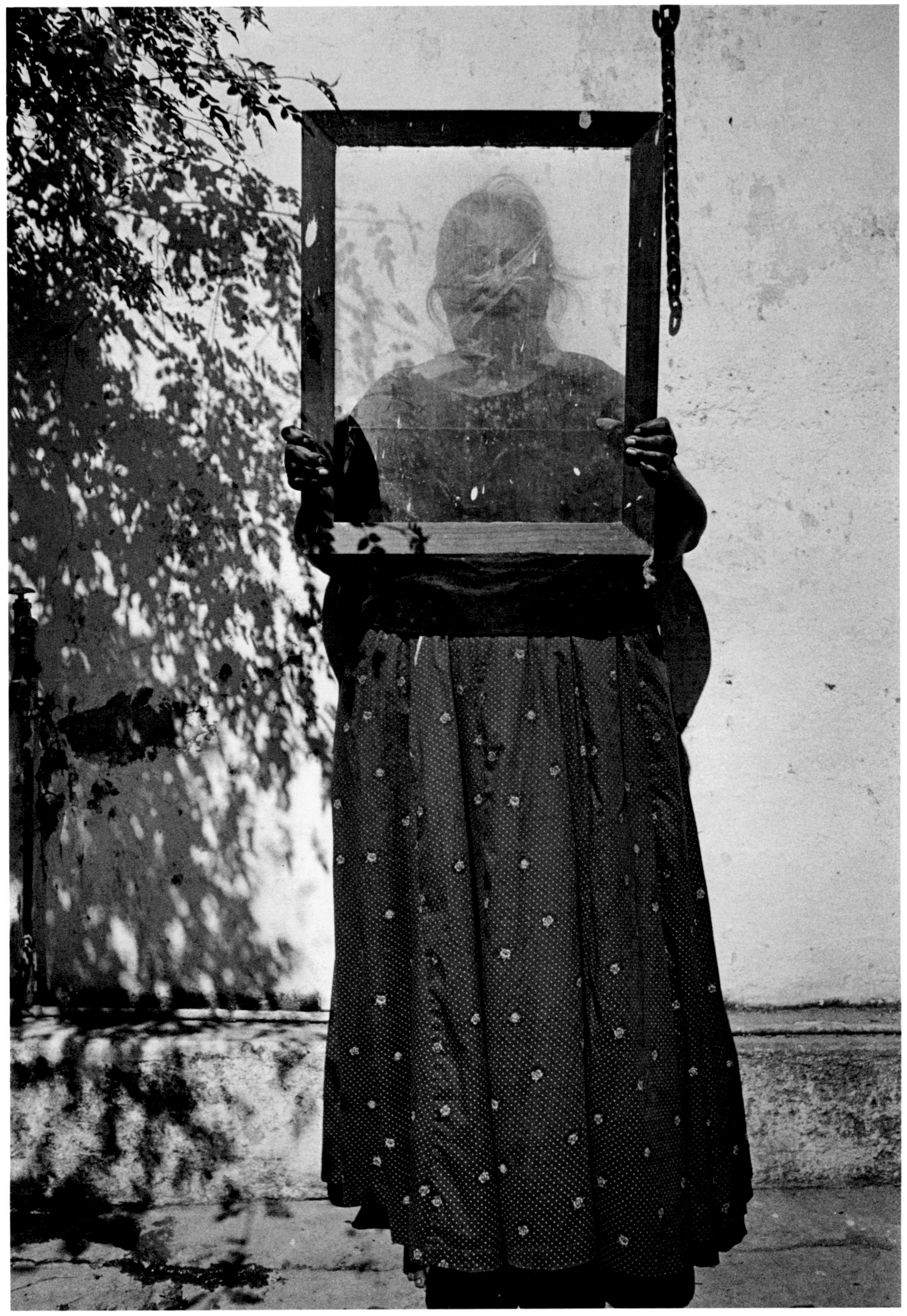

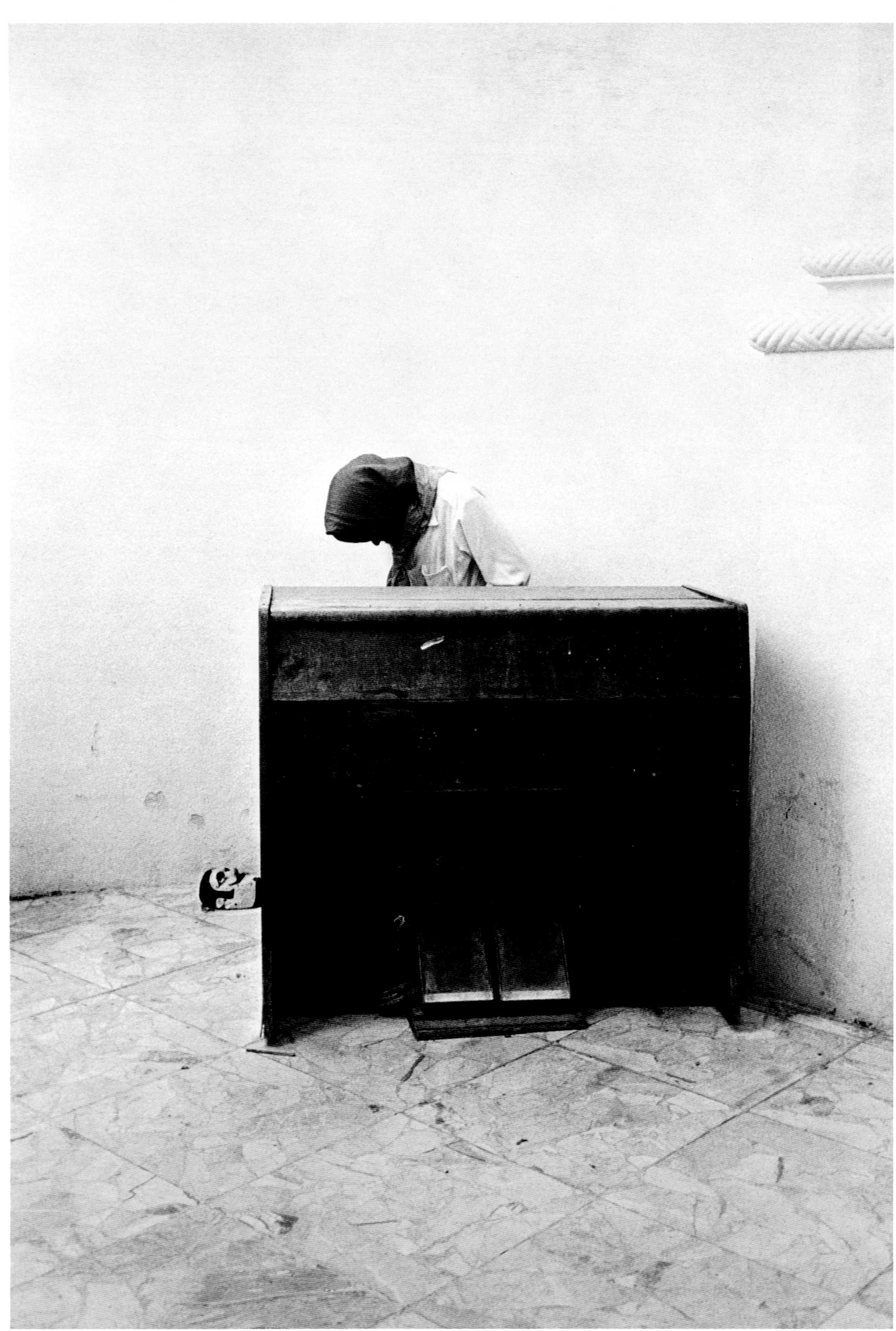

 Danzante (Ritual dancer), Cuetzalan, Puebla, 1993

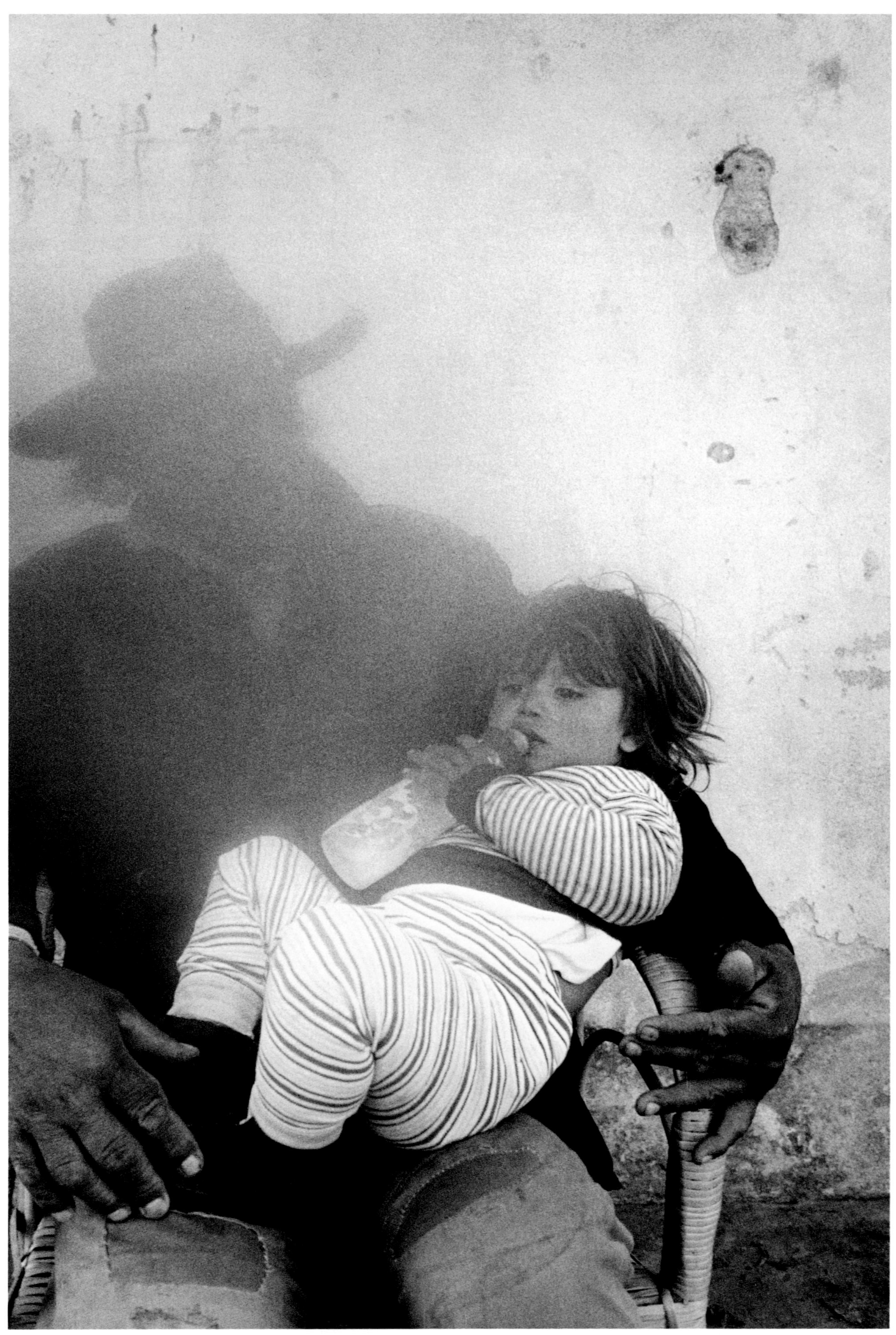

Gaucho, Santa Fe, Argentina, 1988

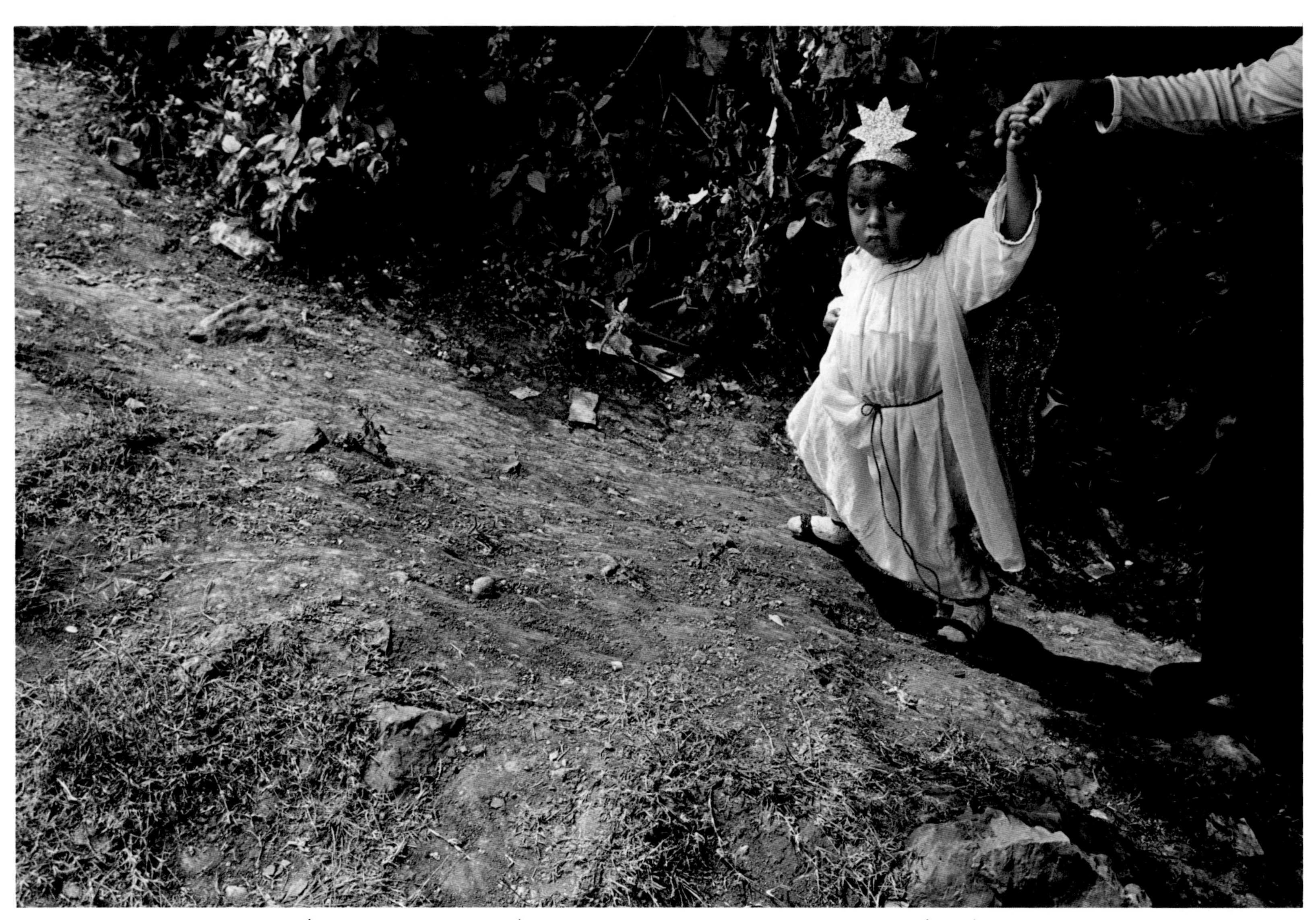

Above: *Autorretrato de la infancia* (Self-portrait of childhood), State of Mexico, Chalma, 1984. *Opposite*: *Jano* (Janus), Ocumichu, Michoacán, 1980

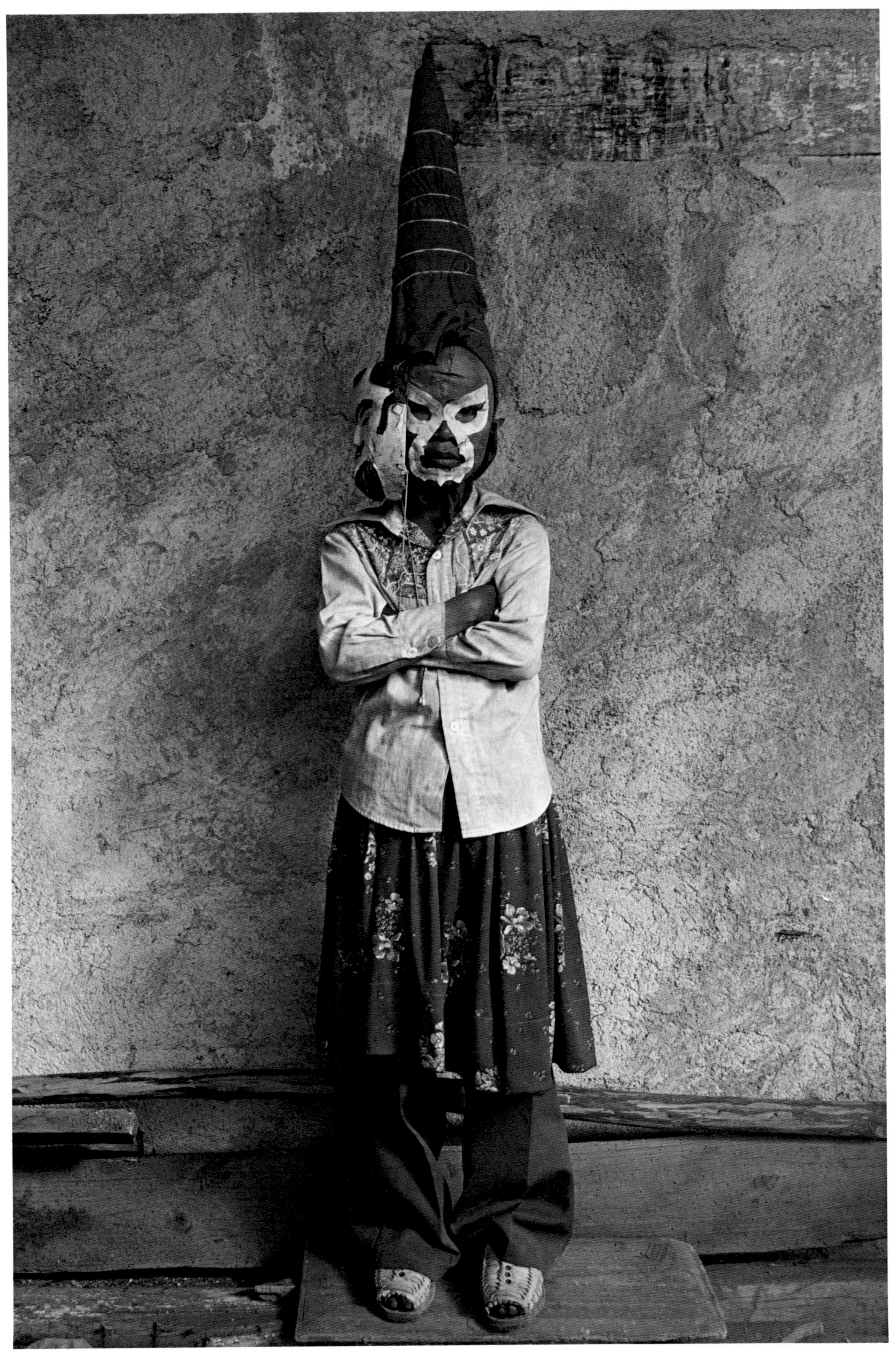

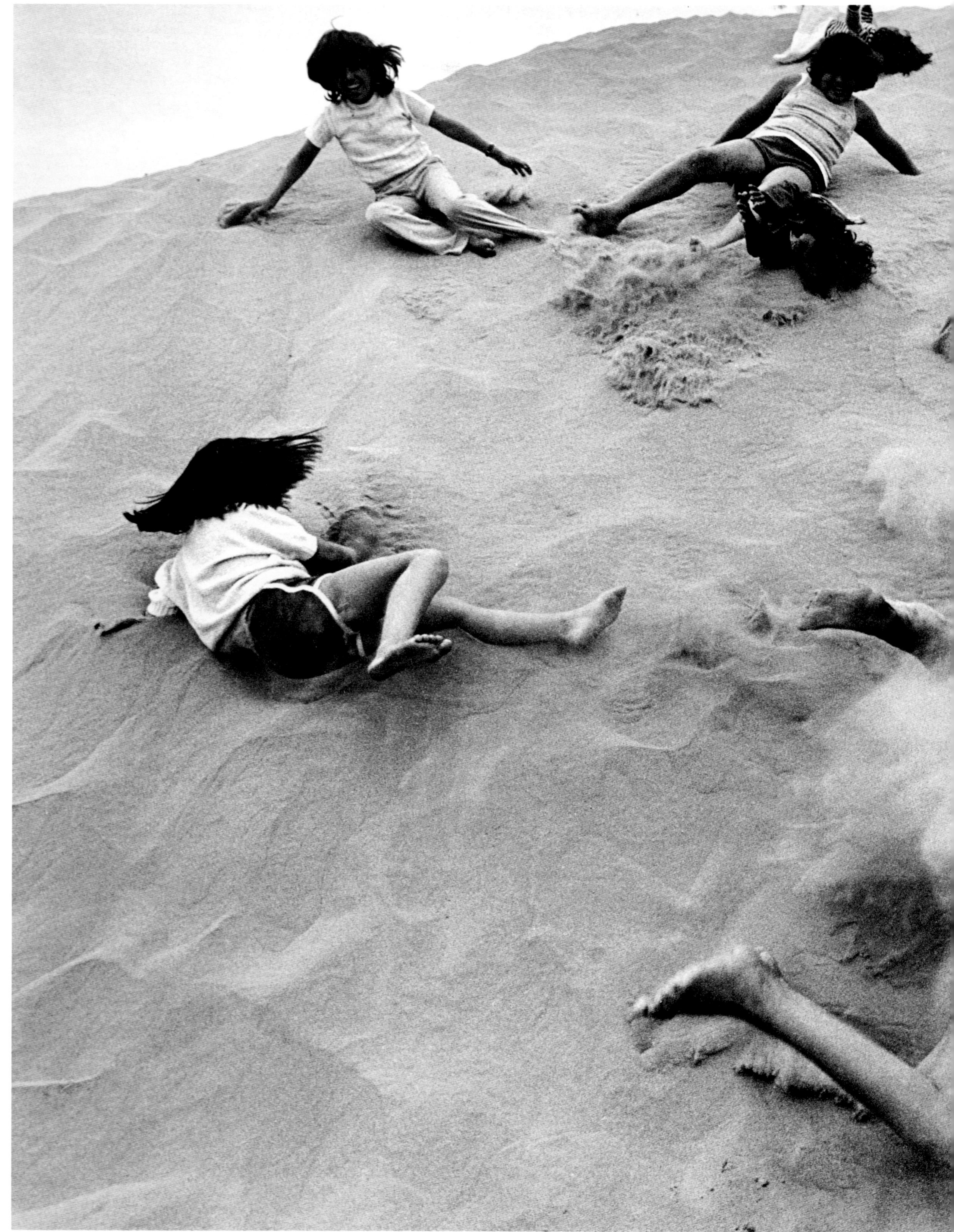

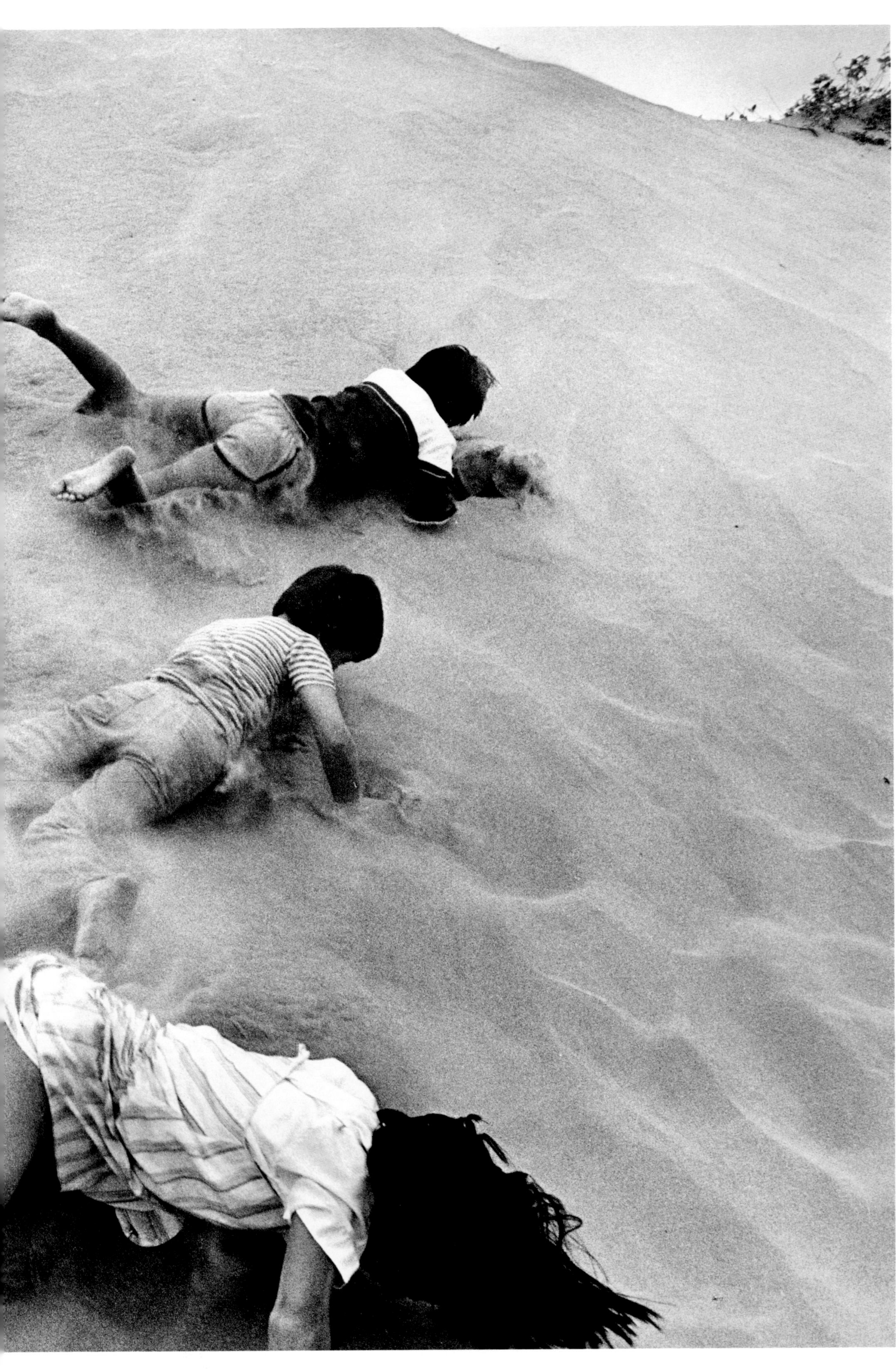

Primer día del verano
(First day of summer),
Veracruz, 1982

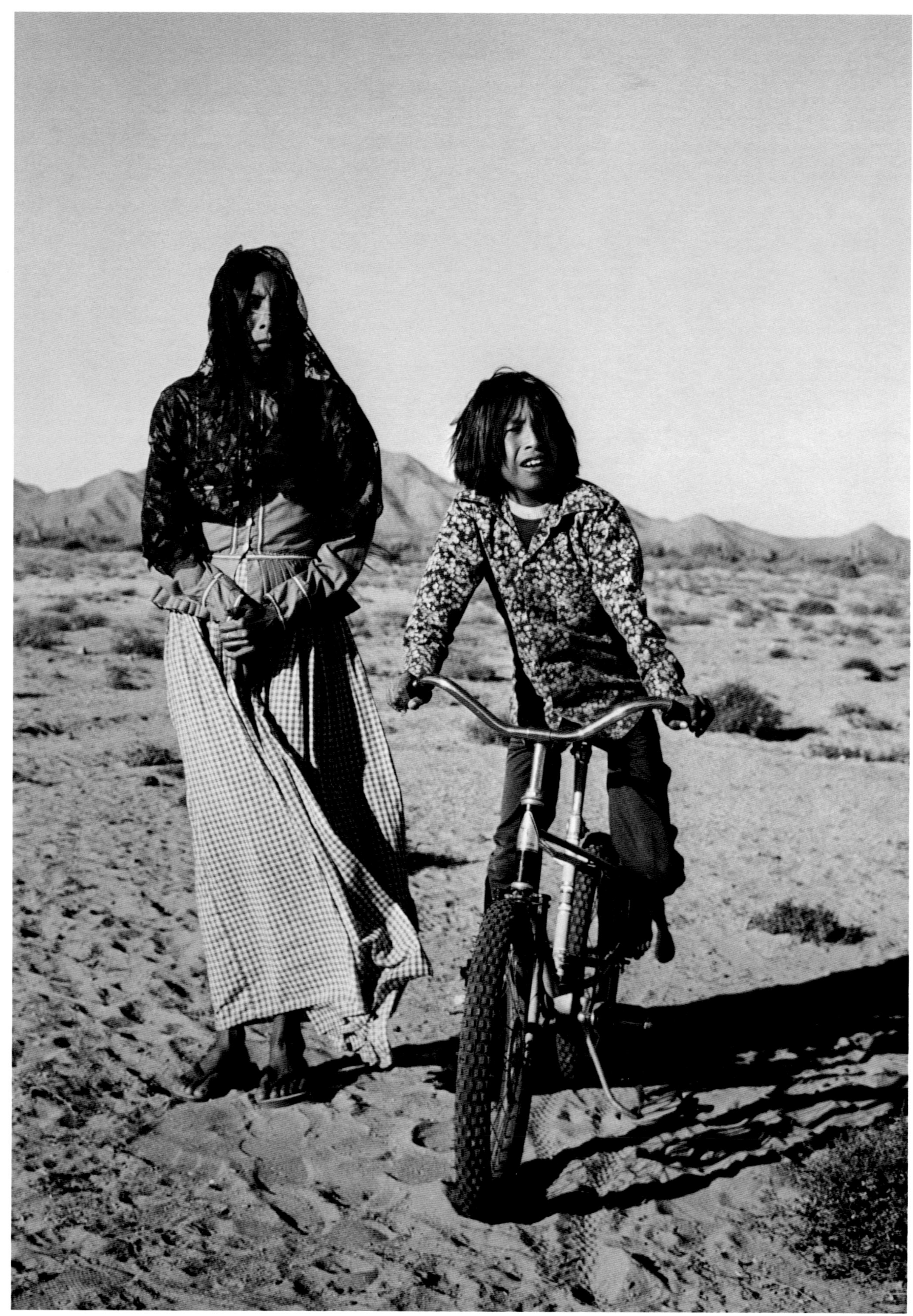

Desierto de Sonora (Sonora Desert), 1979

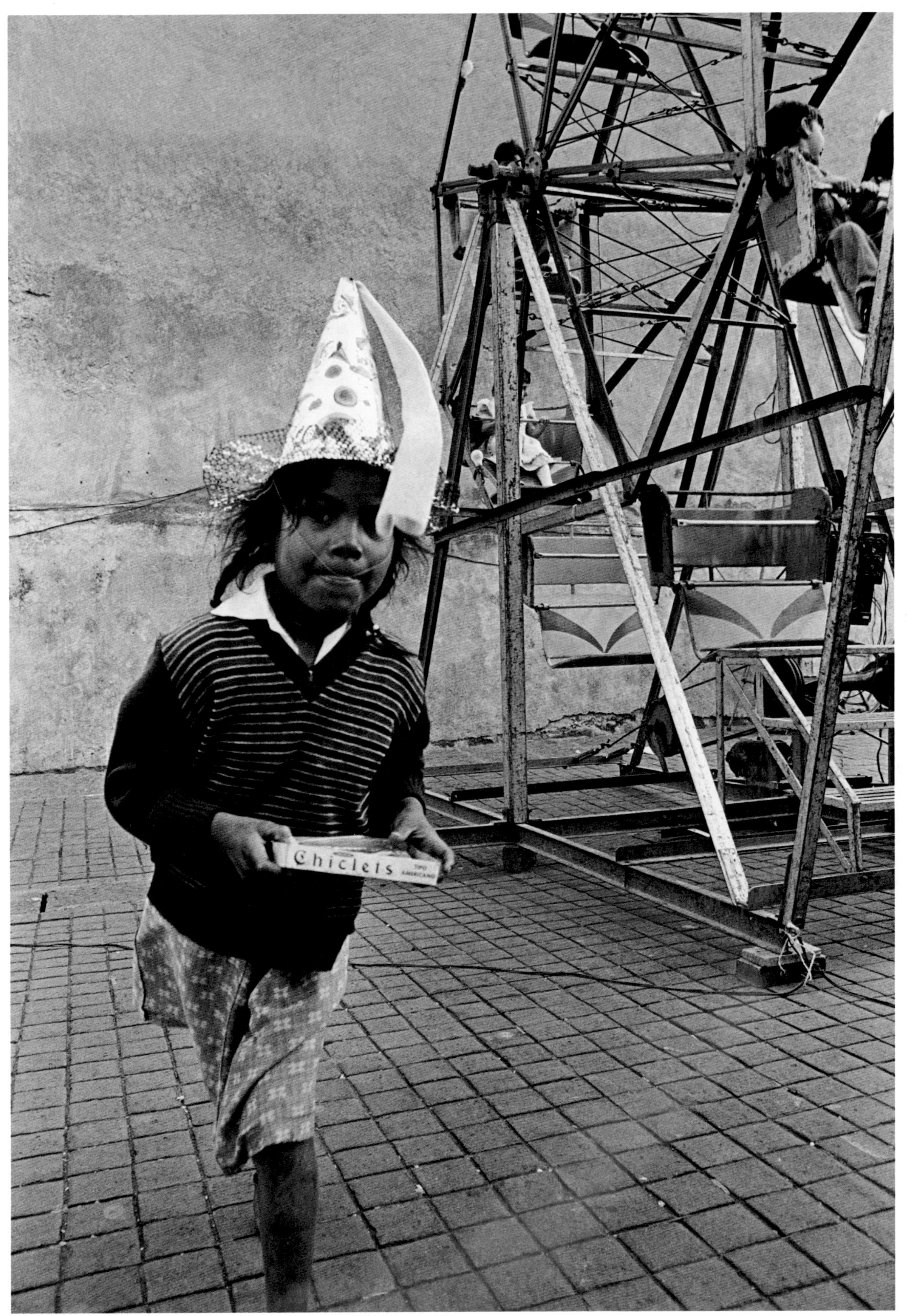

Feria (Fair), Coyoacán, Mexico City, 1983

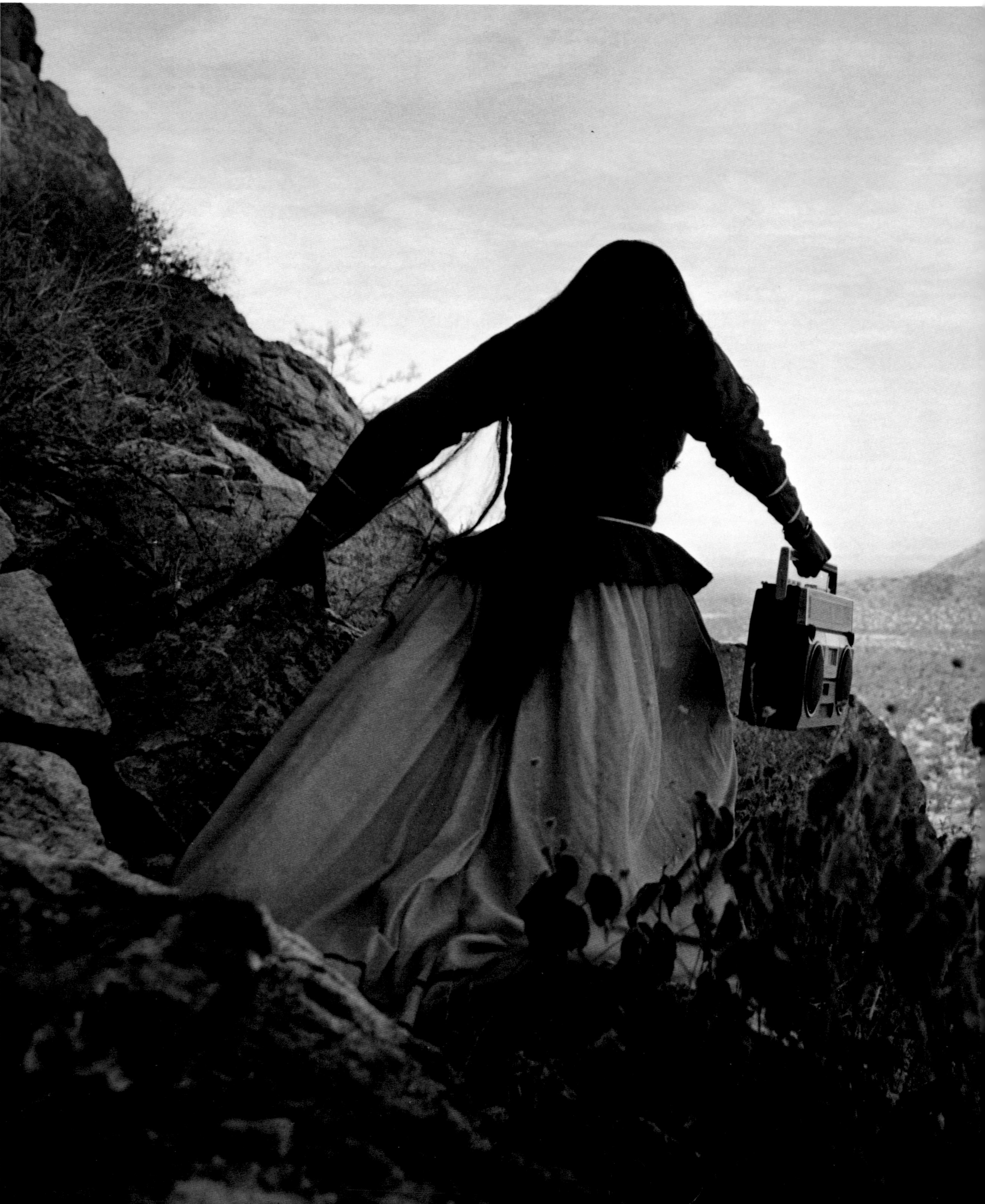

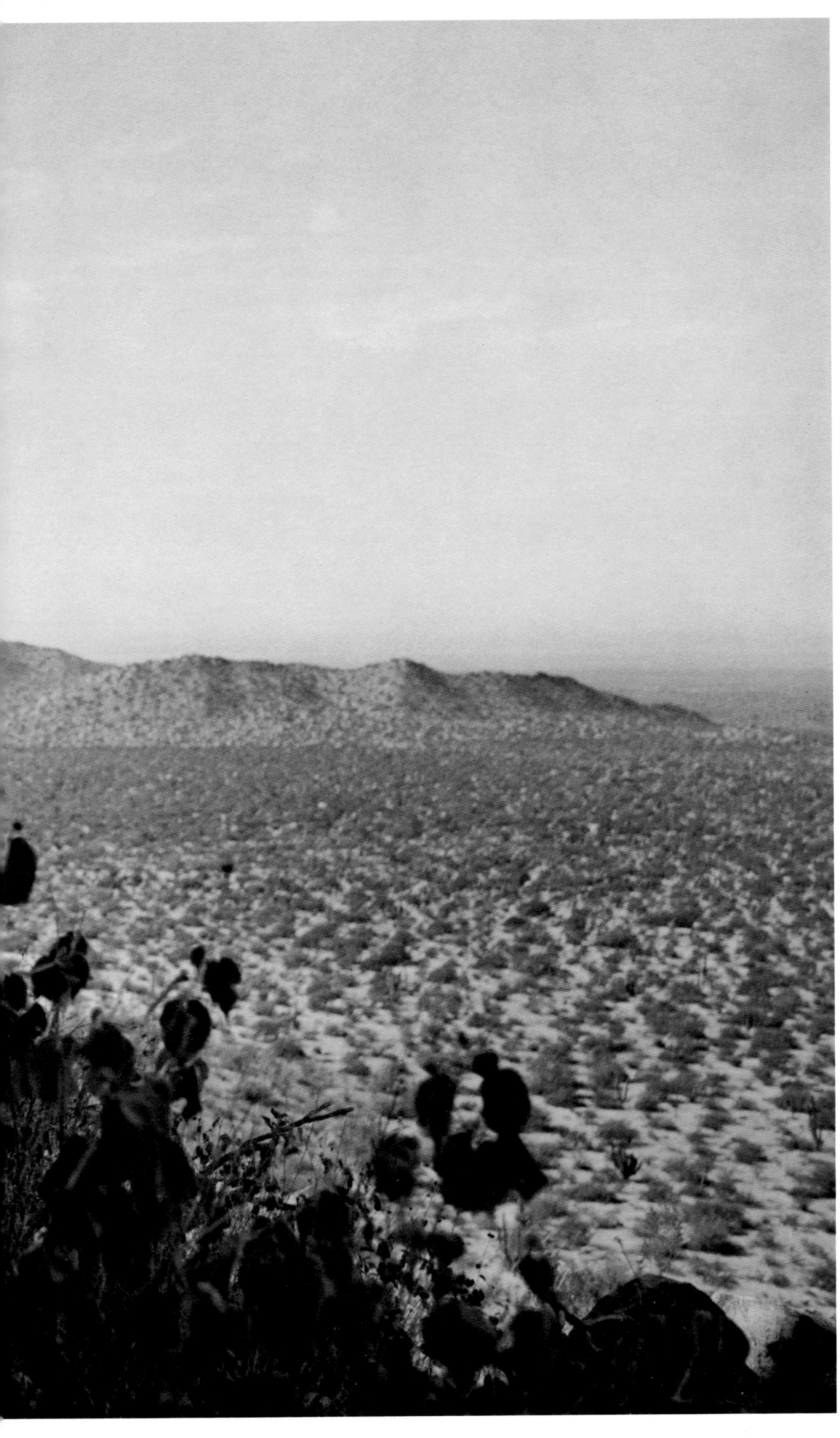

Mujer ángel (Angel woman), Sonora Desert, 1979

Marcha política (Political rally), Juchitán, Oaxaca, 1984

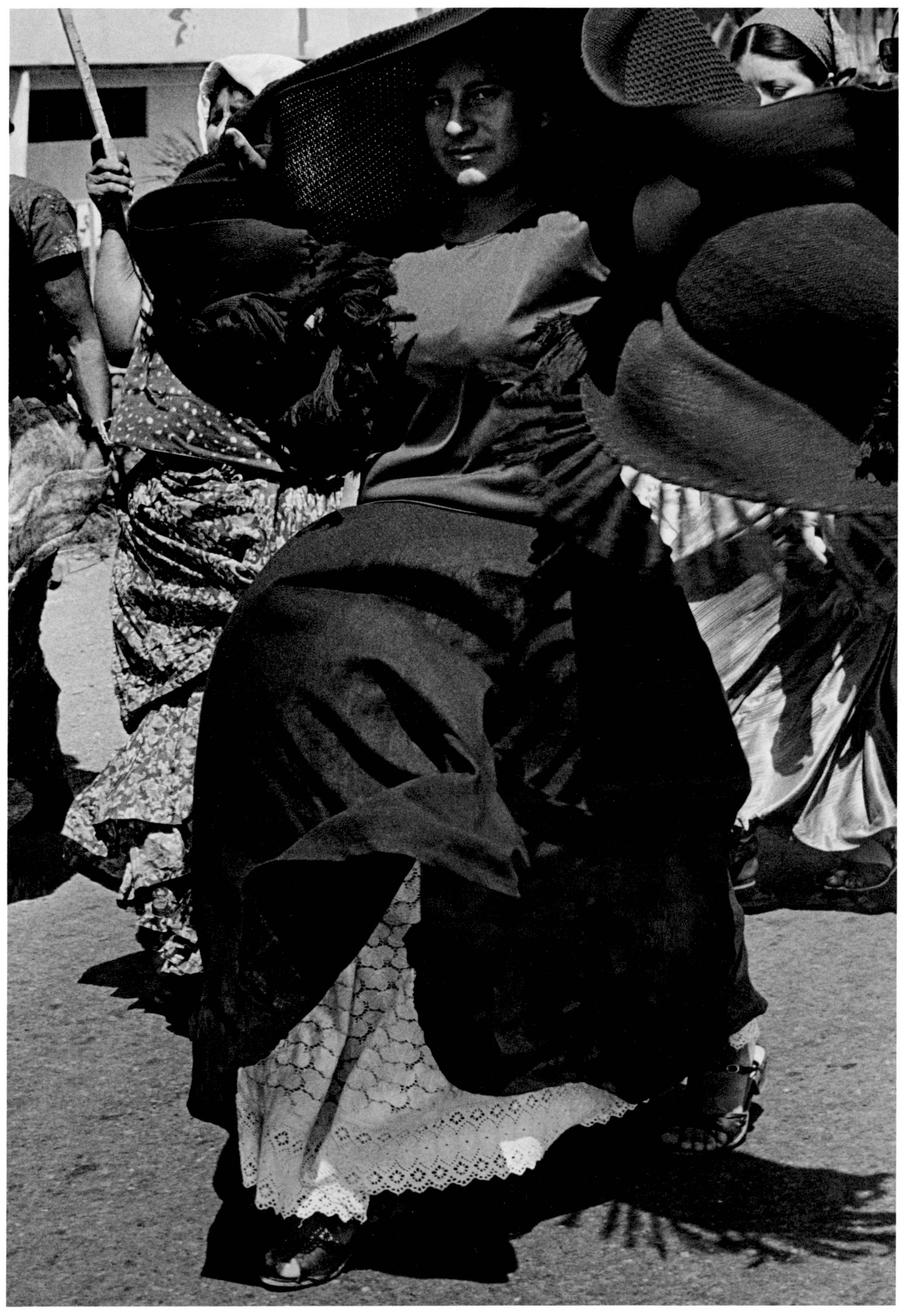

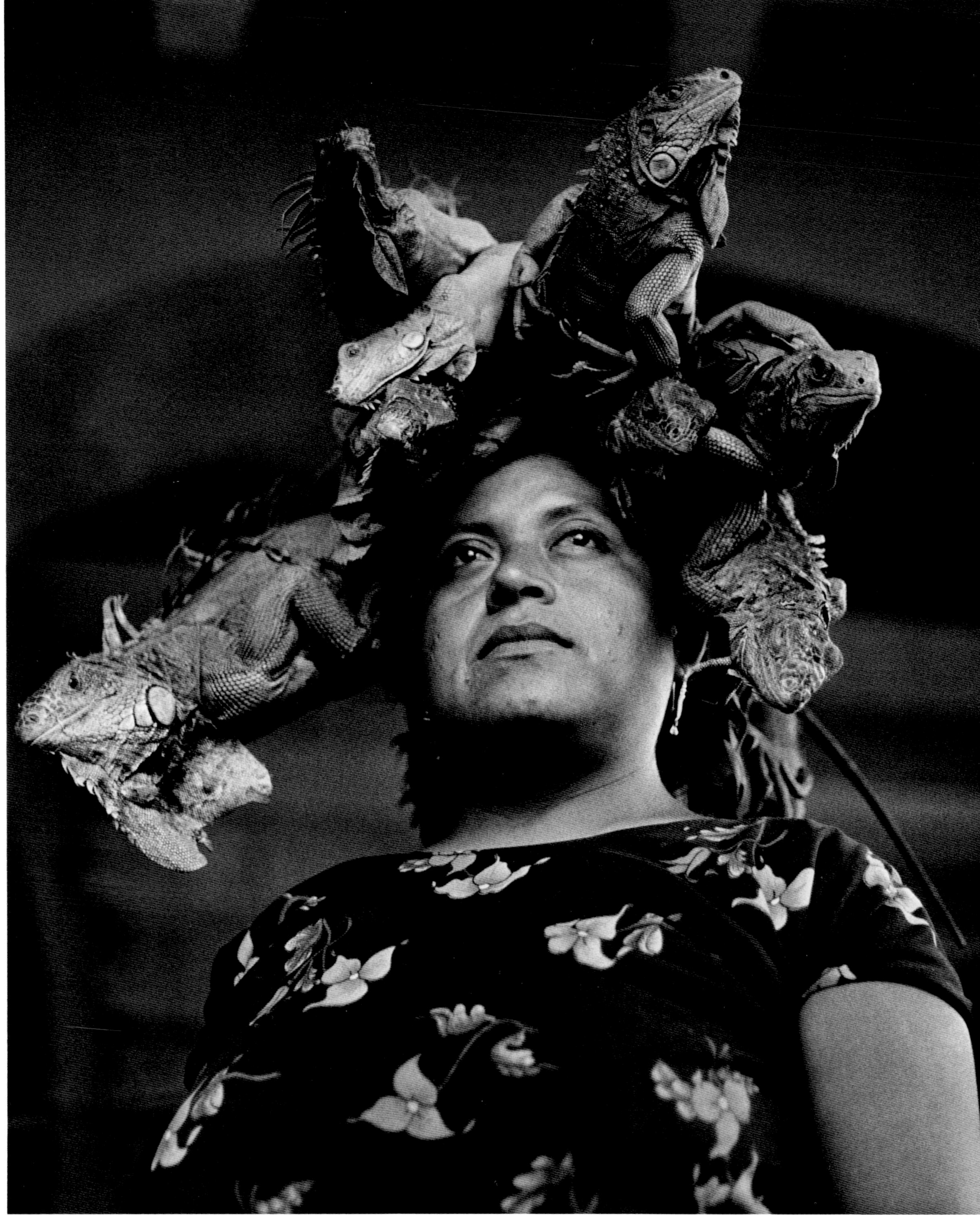

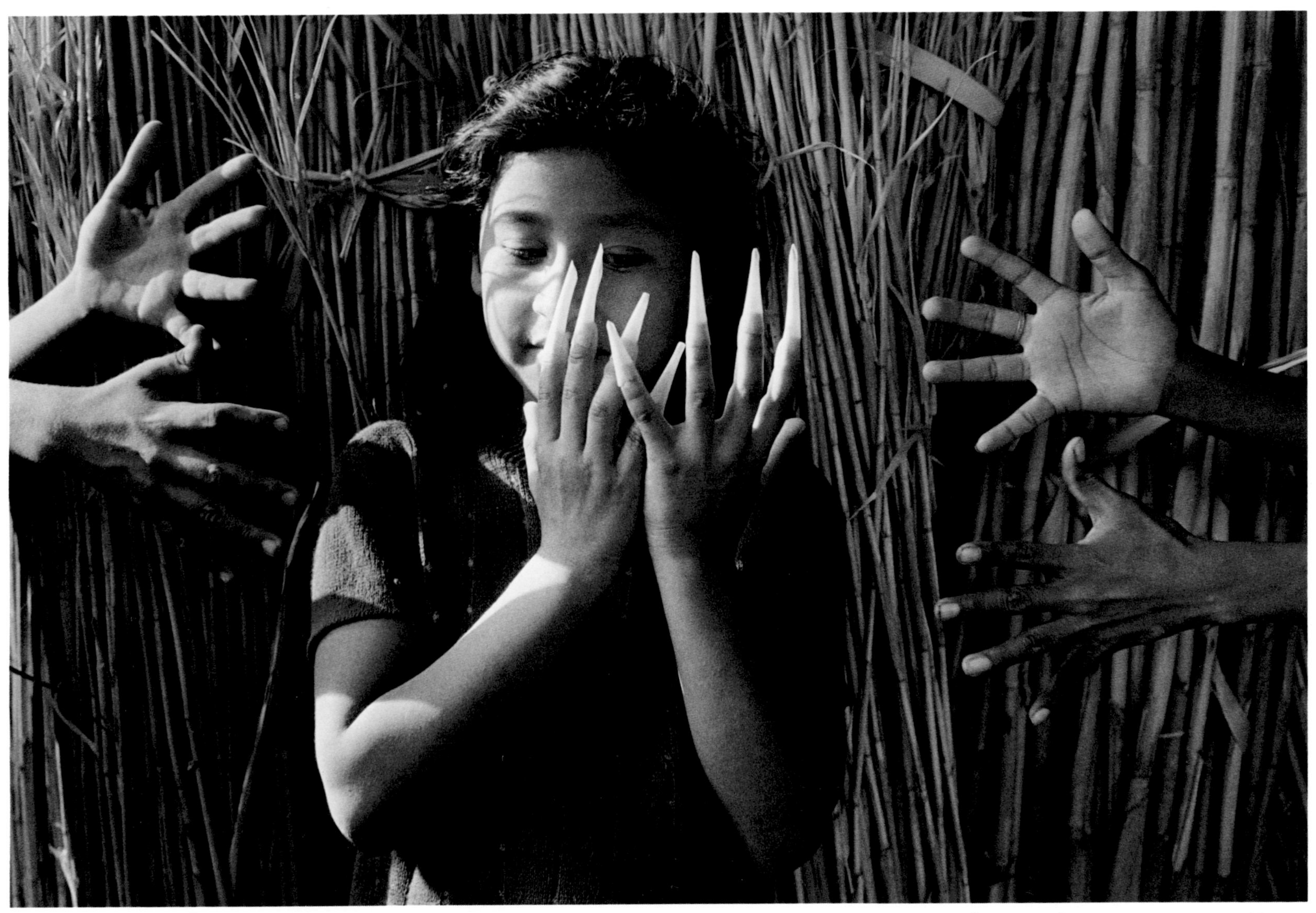

Opposite: *Nuestra Señora de las Iguanas* (Our Lady of the Iguanas), Juchitán, Oaxaca, 1979. *Above*: *Juego de manos* (Hand play), Juchitán, Oaxaca, 1988

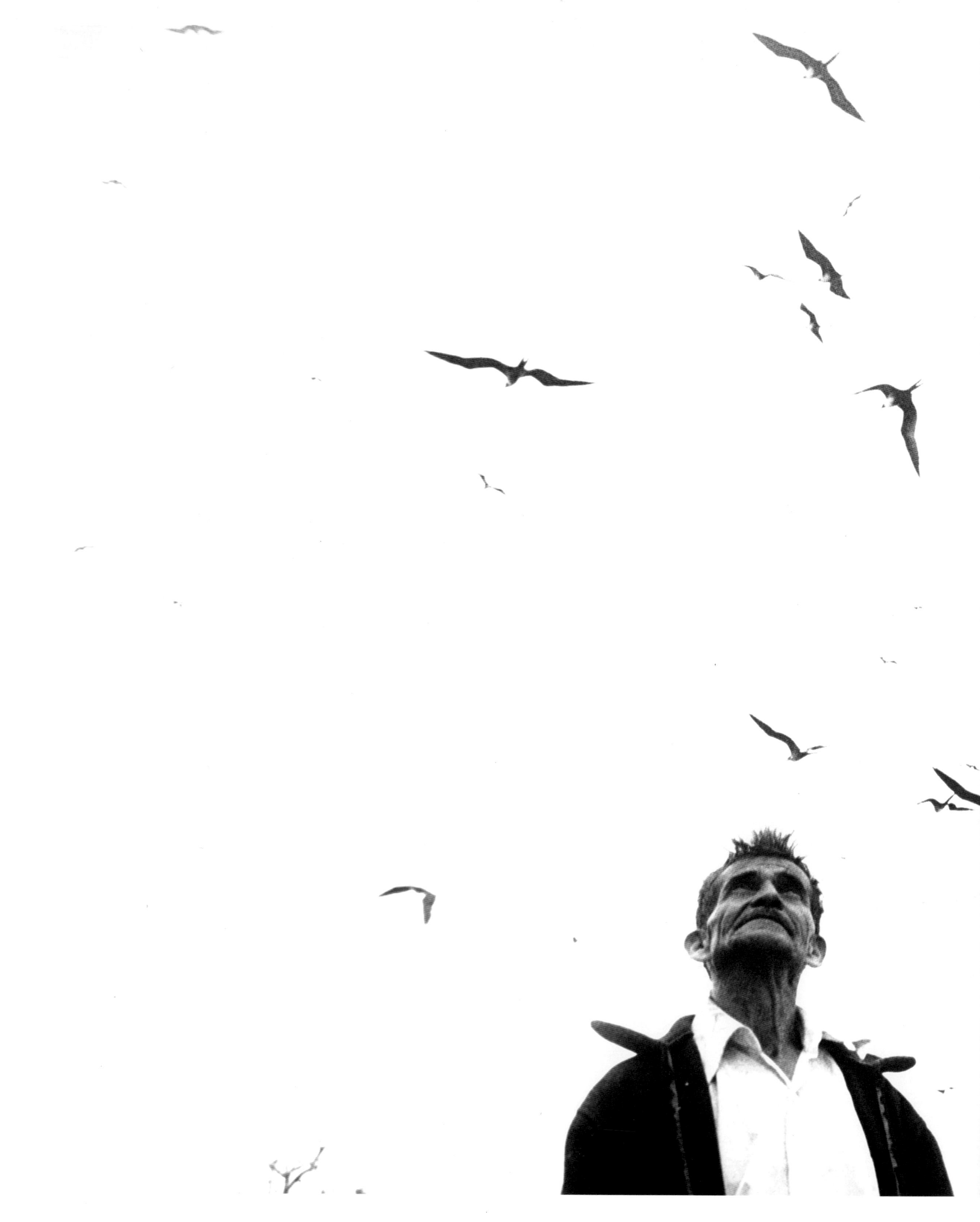

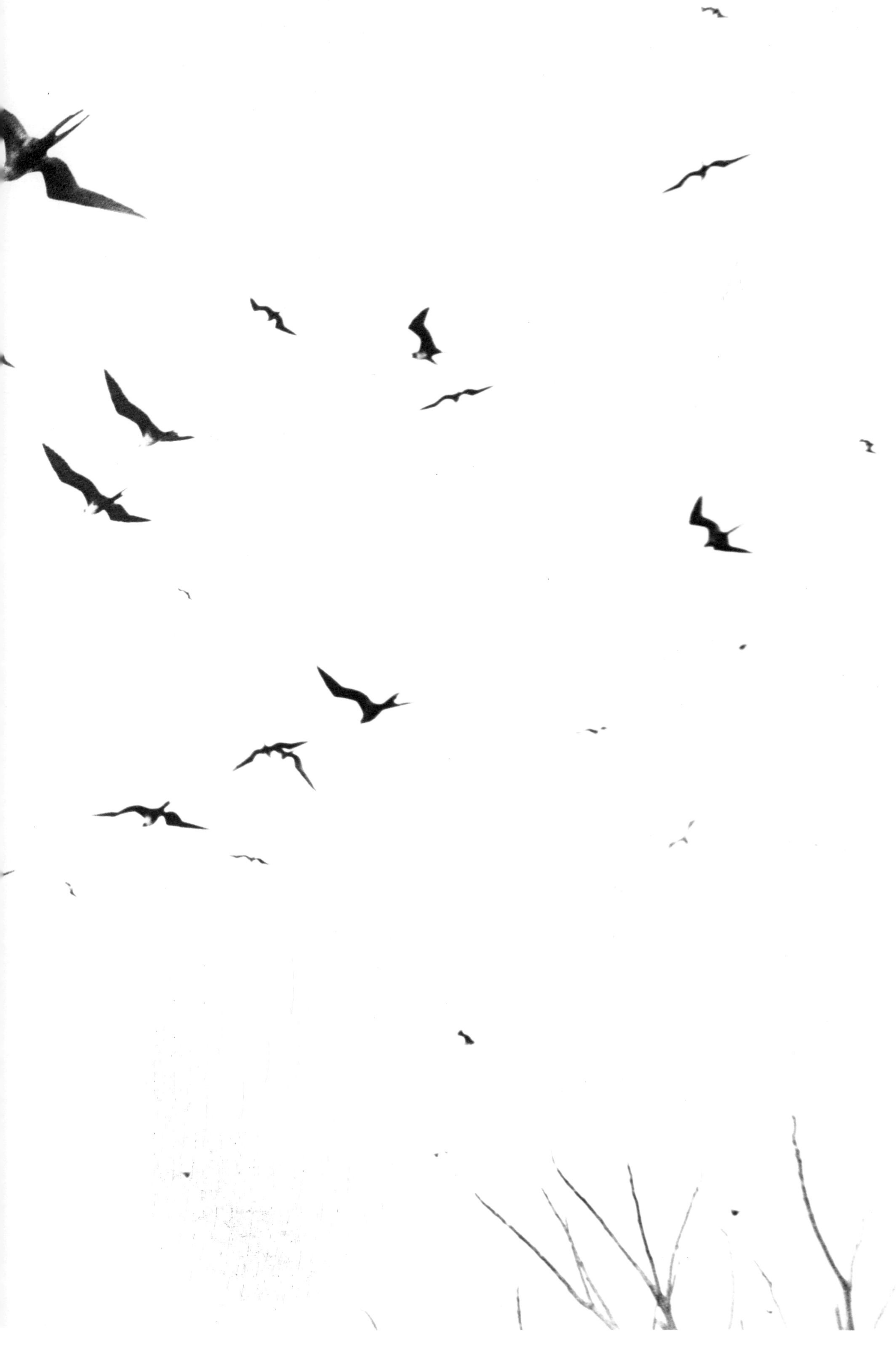

Señor de los pájaros
(Lord of the birds),
Nayarit, 1985

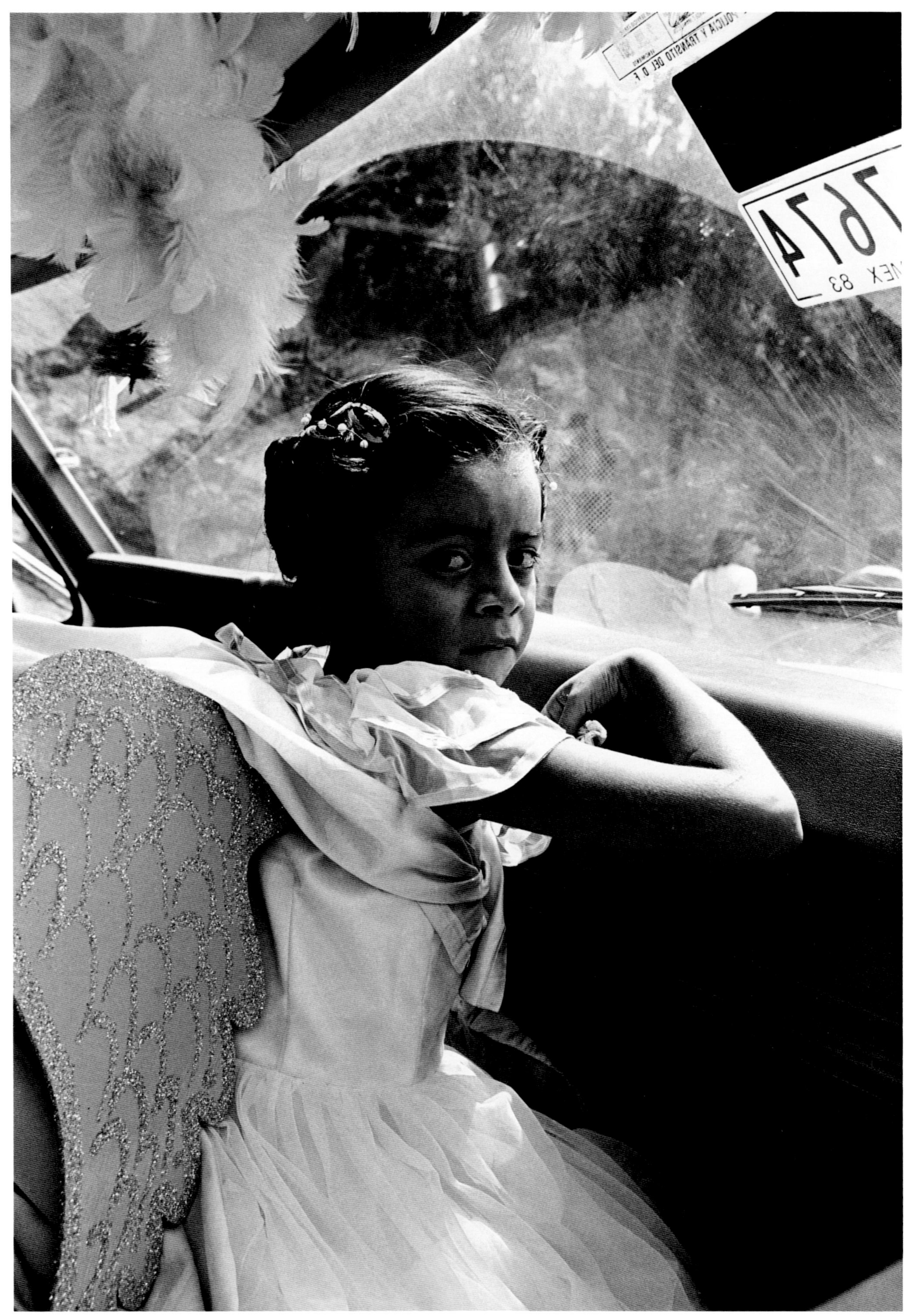

 7674, Chalmita, State of Mexico, 1984

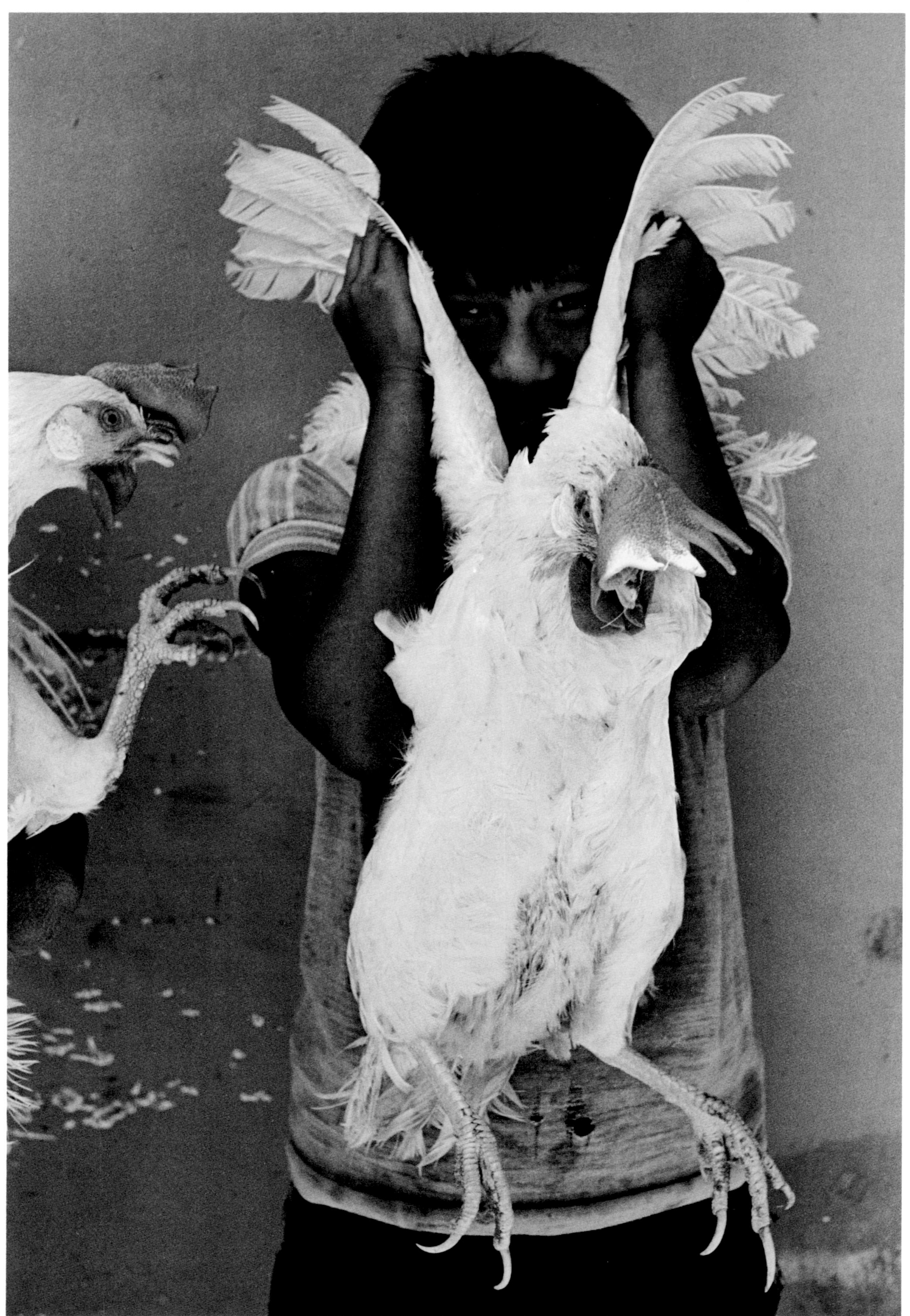

El gallo (The rooster), Juchitán, Oaxaca, 1986

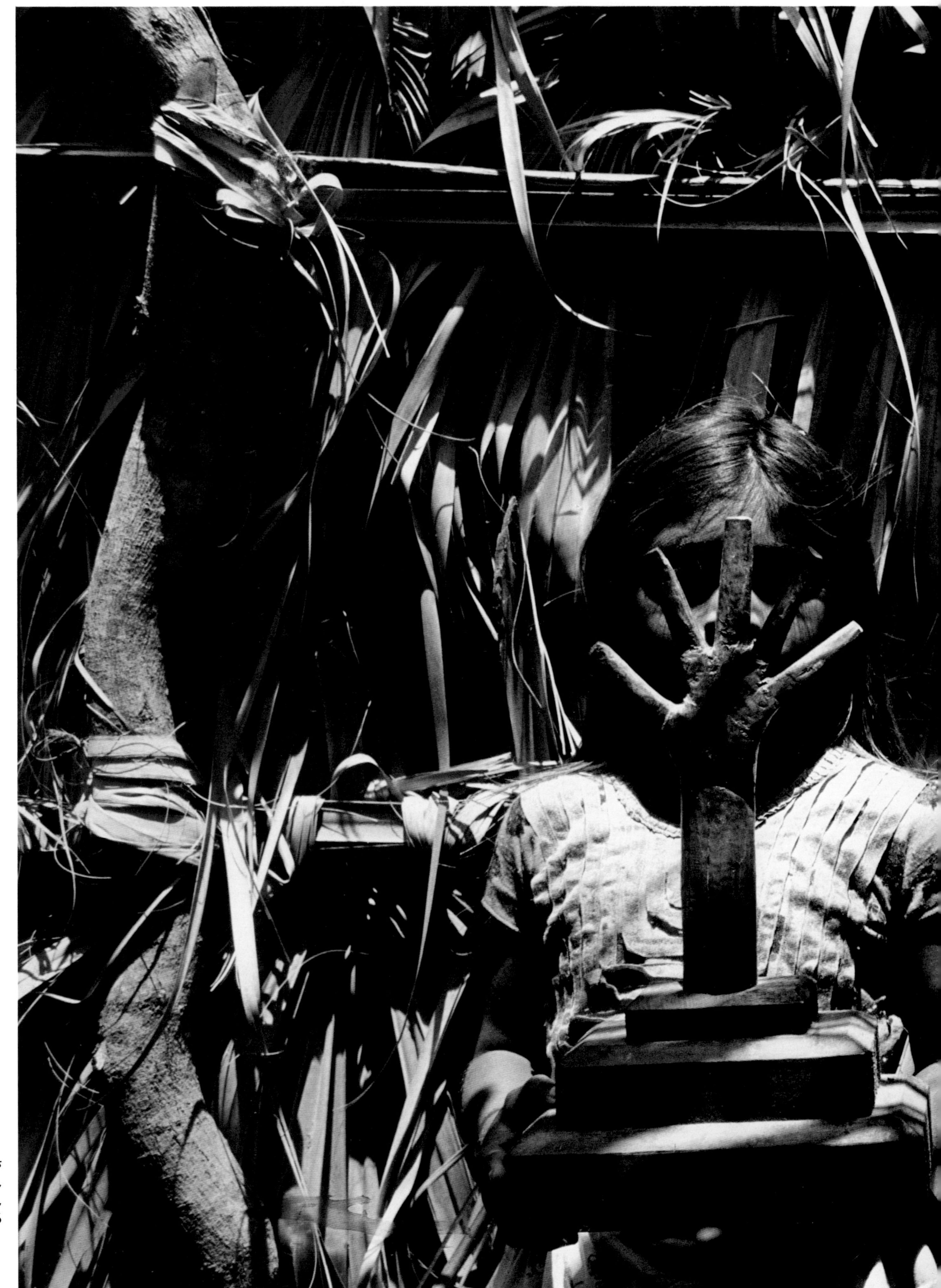

Manos poderosas
(Powerful hands),
Juchitán, Oaxaca,
1986

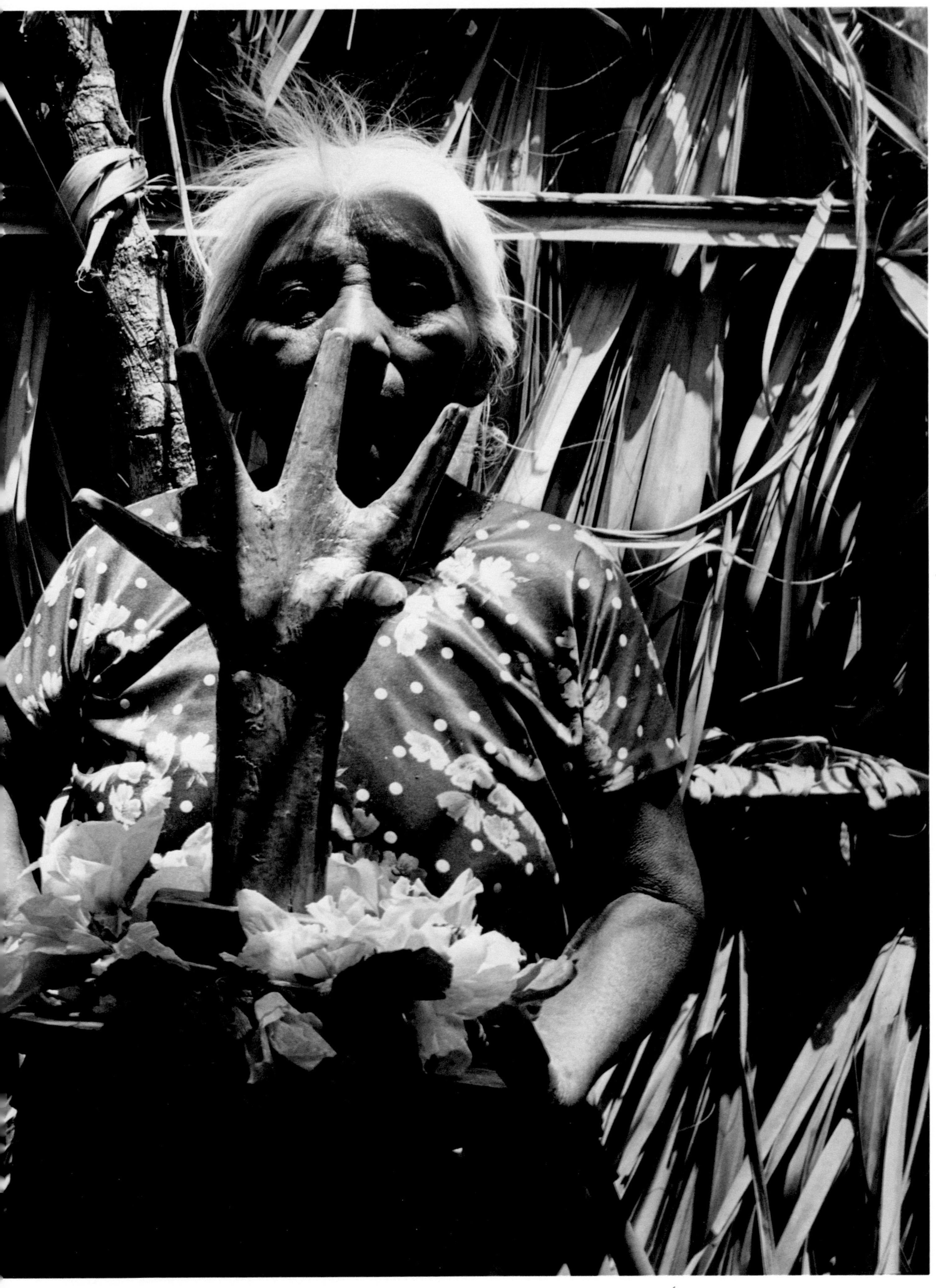

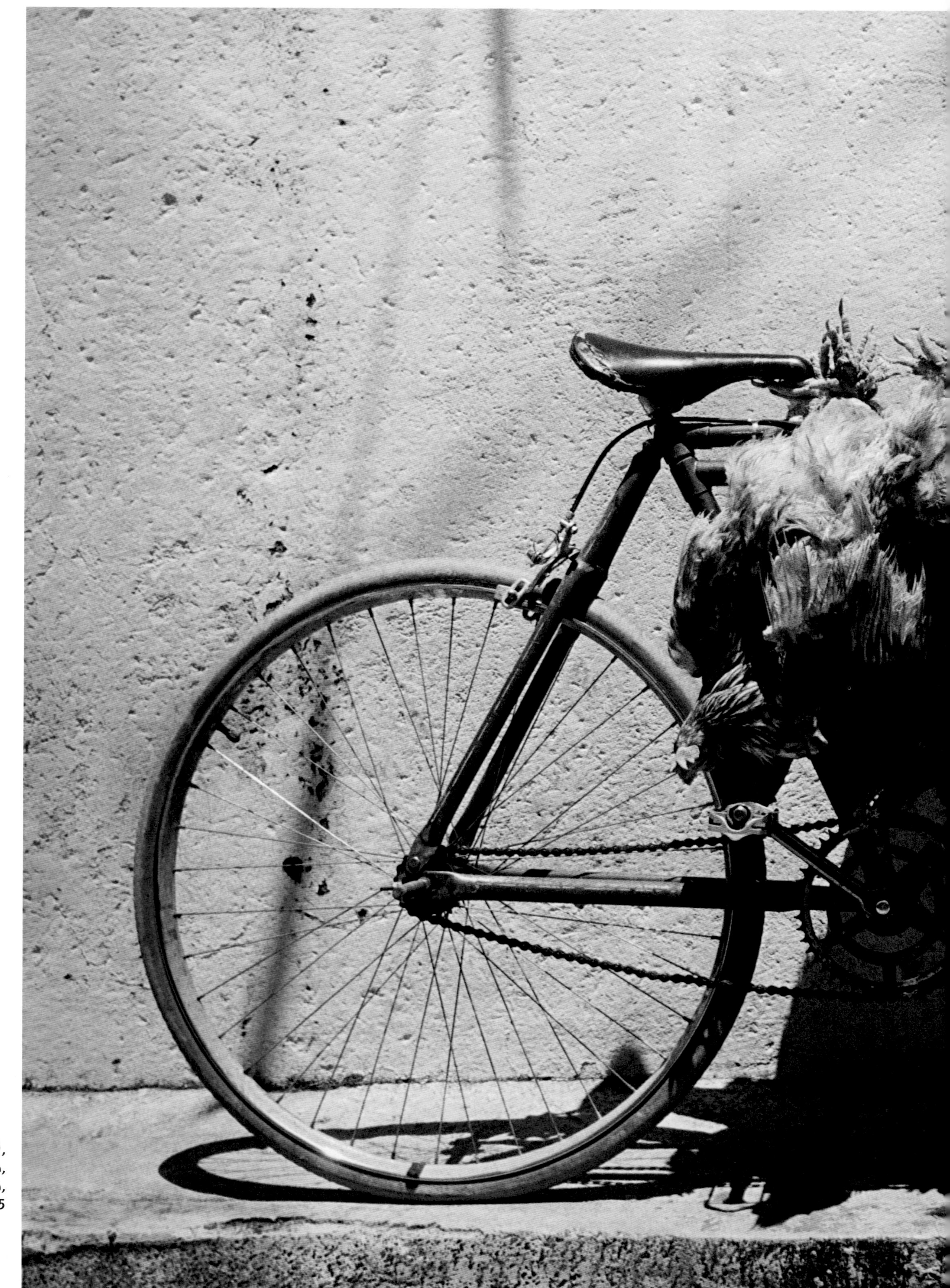

El viaje (Travel),
Tlaxcala,
State of Tlaxcala,
1995

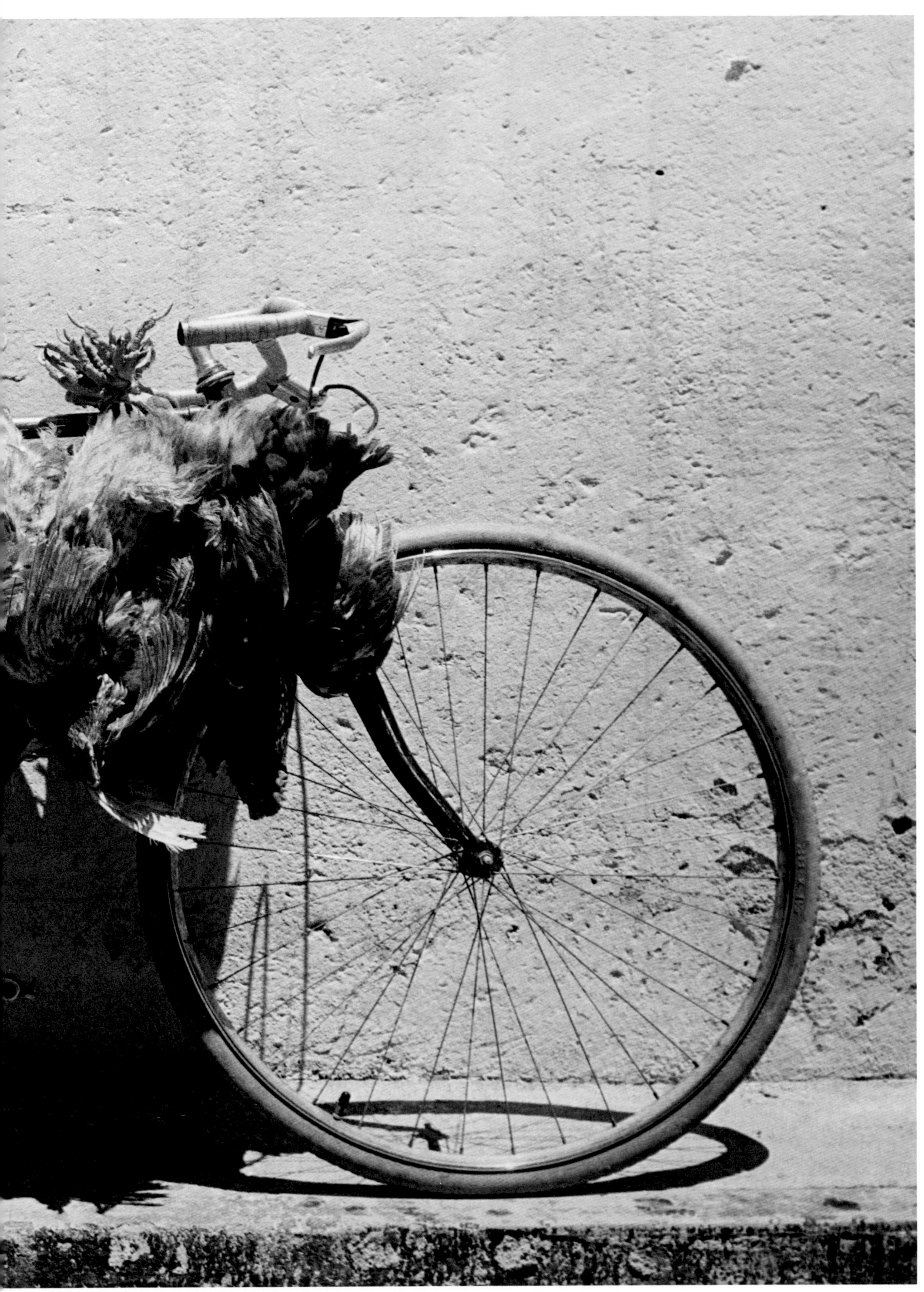

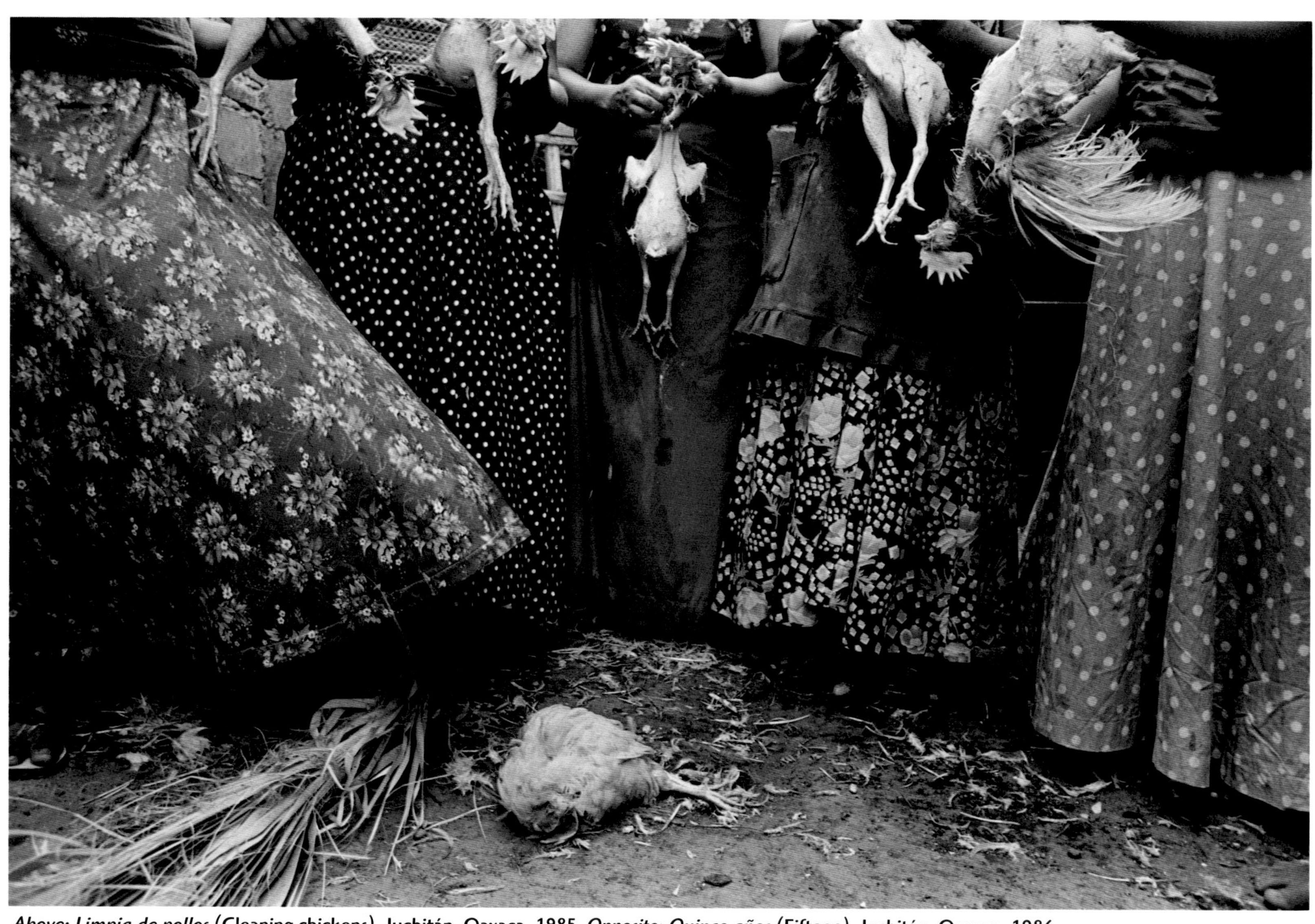

Above: *Limpia de pollos* (Cleaning chickens), Juchitán, Oaxaca, 1985. *Opposite*: *Quince años* (Fifteen), Juchitán, Oaxaca, 1986

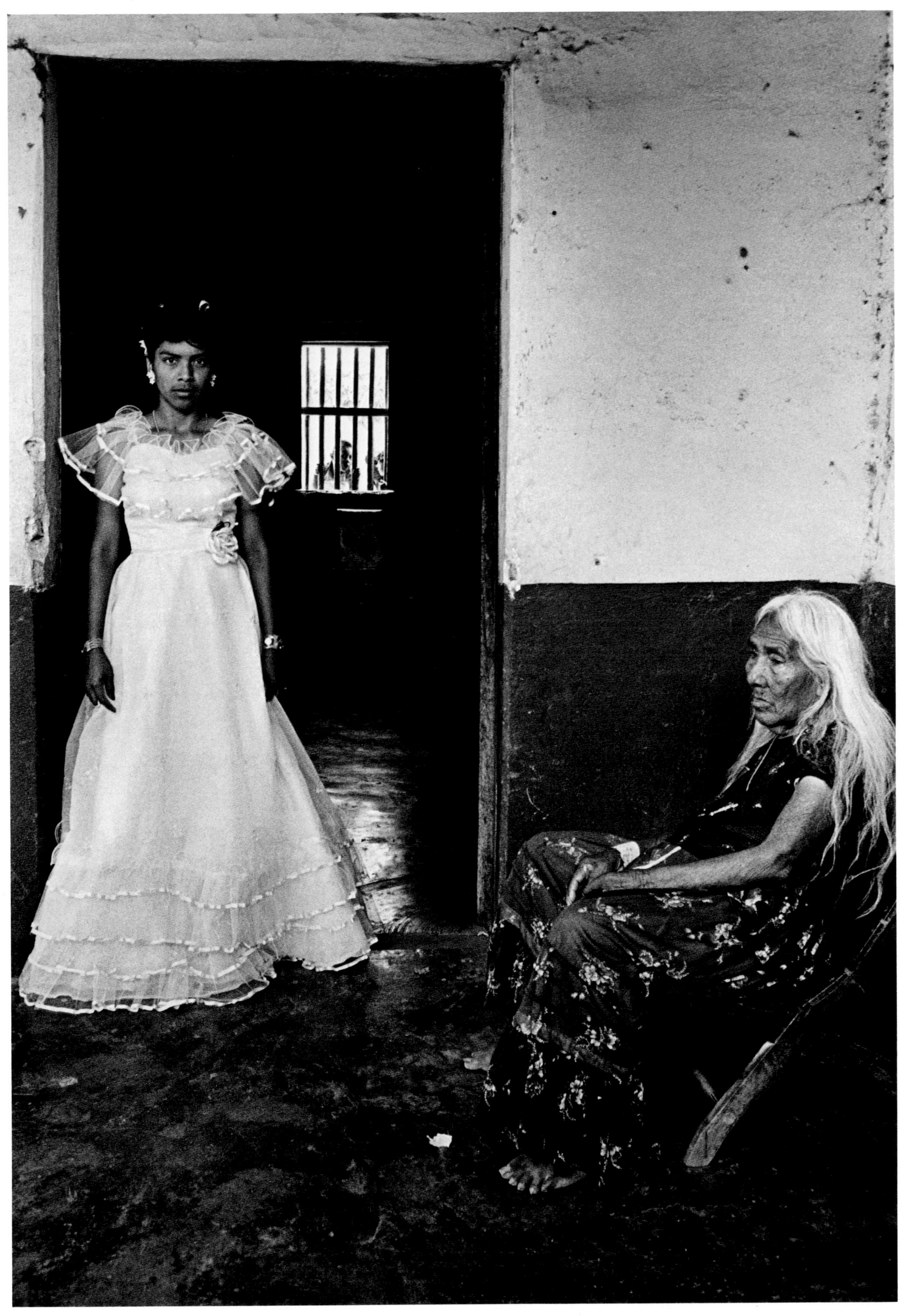

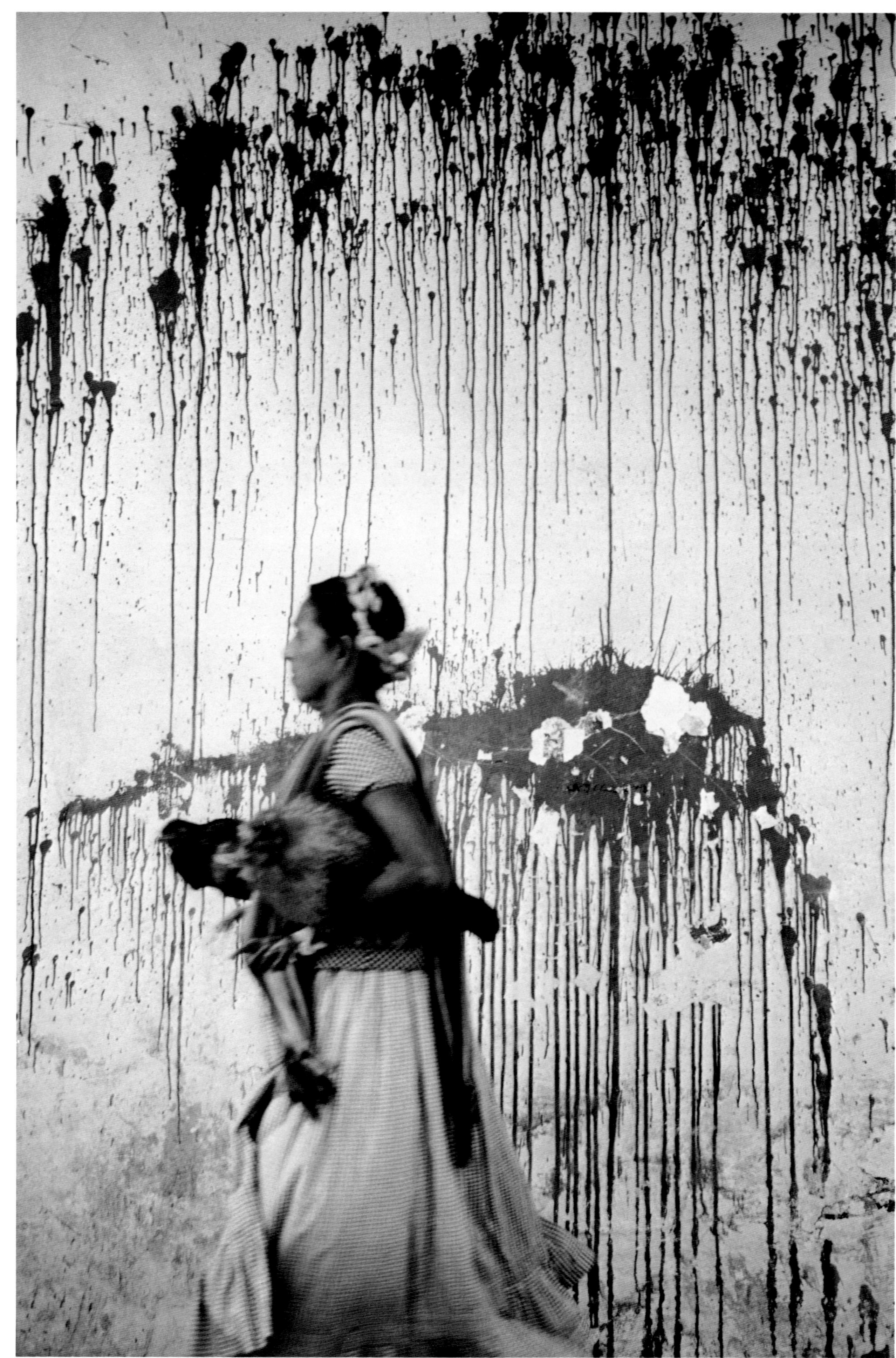

 Los pollos (Chickens), Juchitán, Oaxaca, 1979

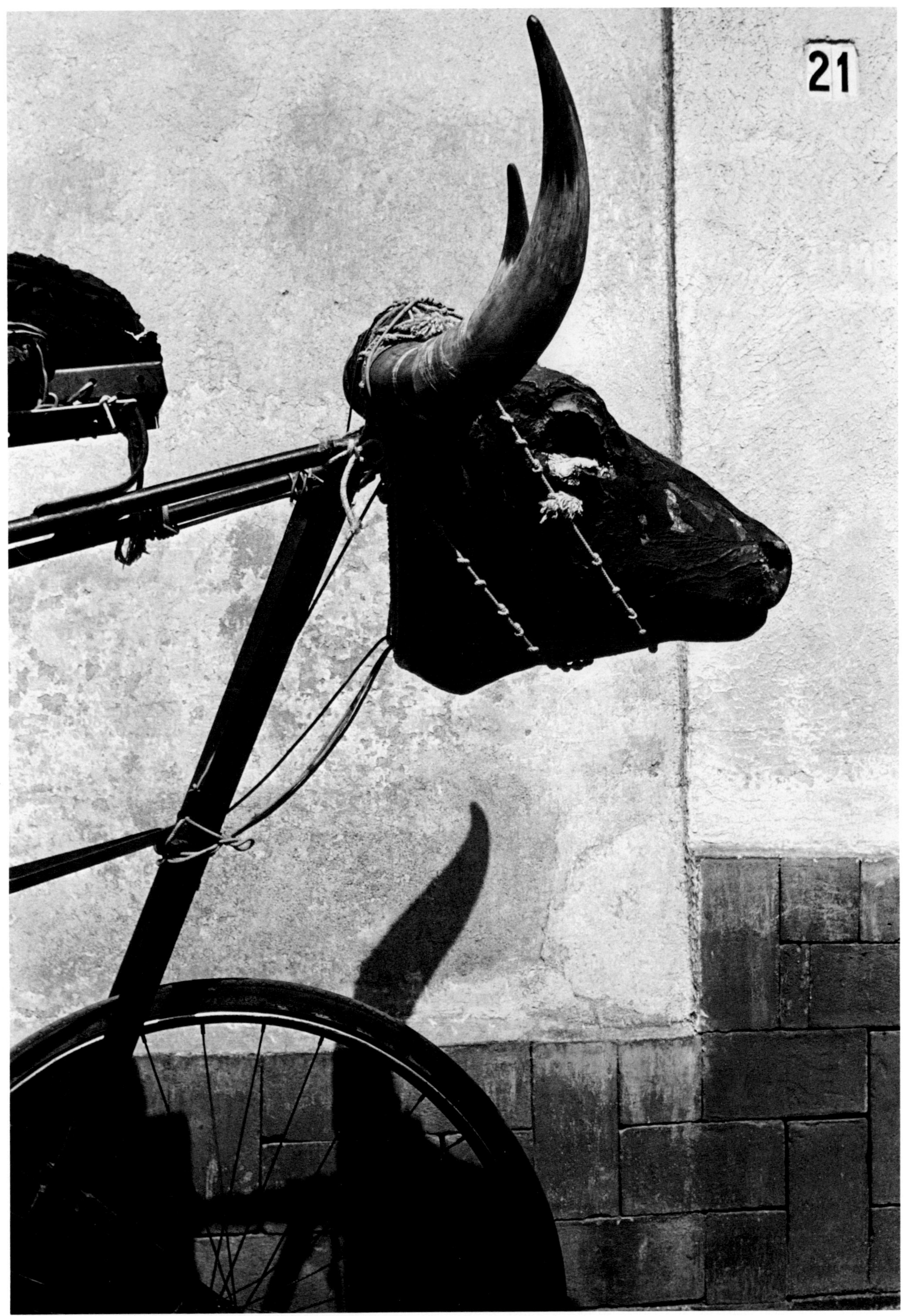

Torito (Young bull), Coyoacán, Mexico City, 1983

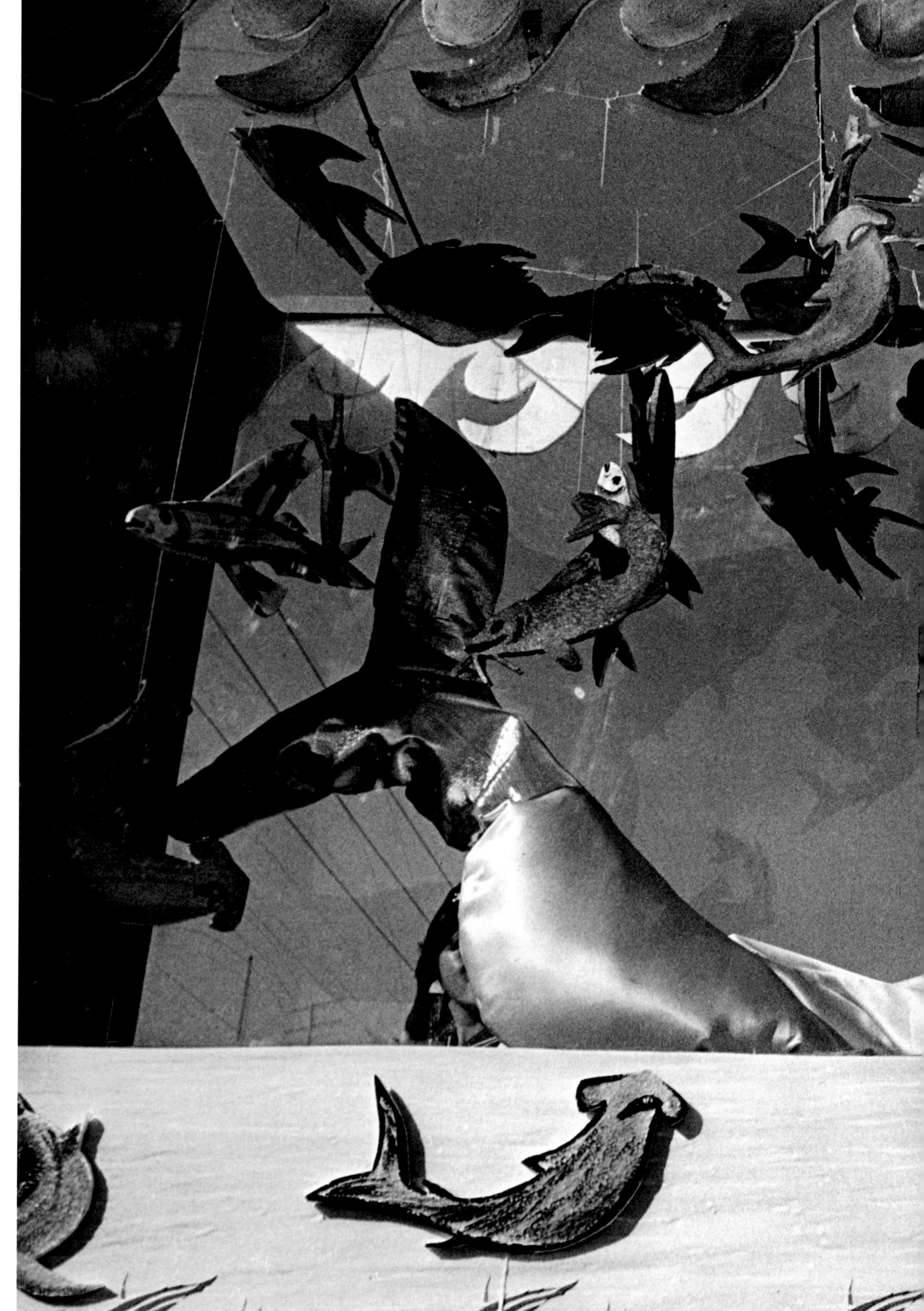

Sirena
(Mermaid),
Capulhuac,
State of Mexico,
1985

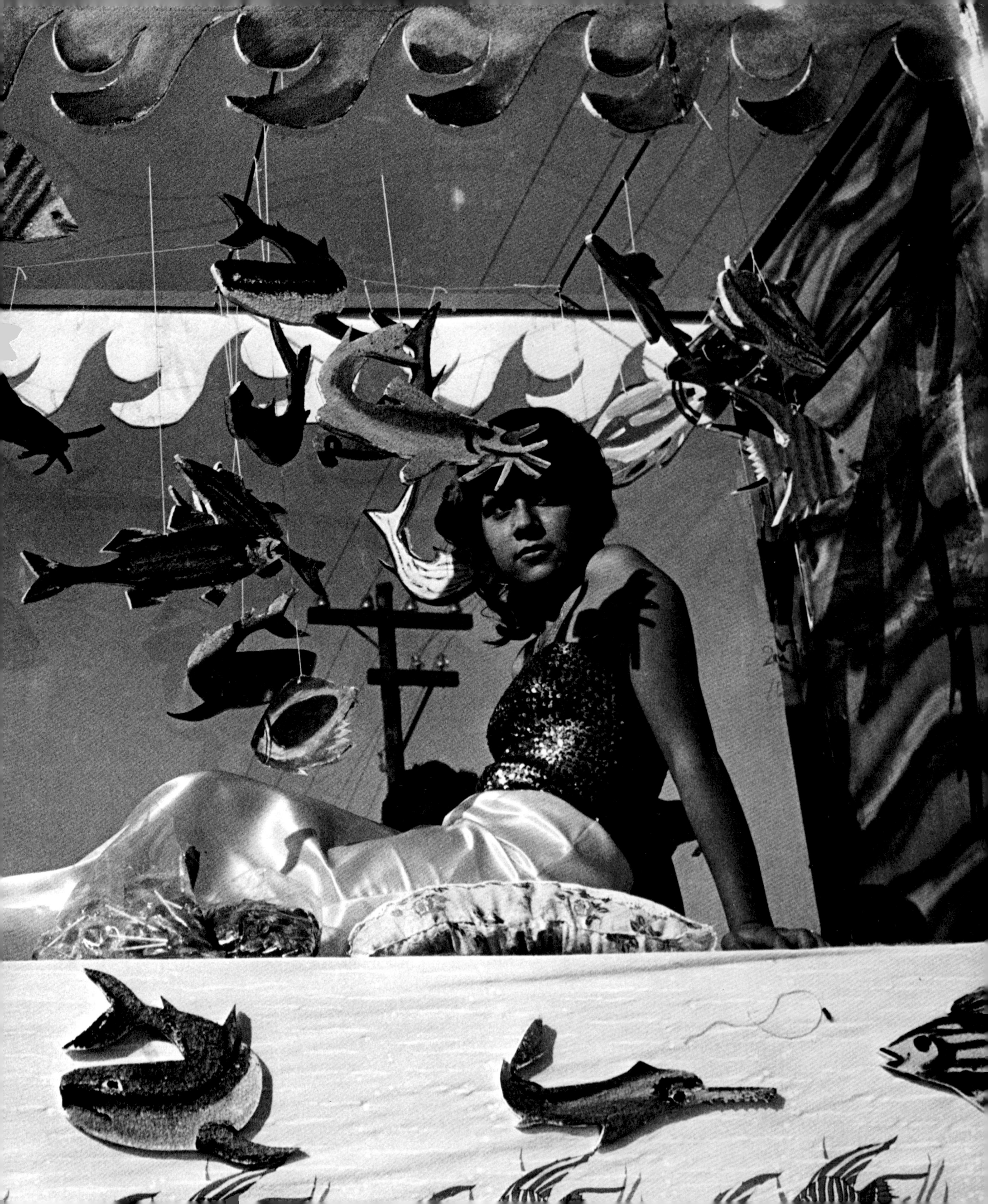

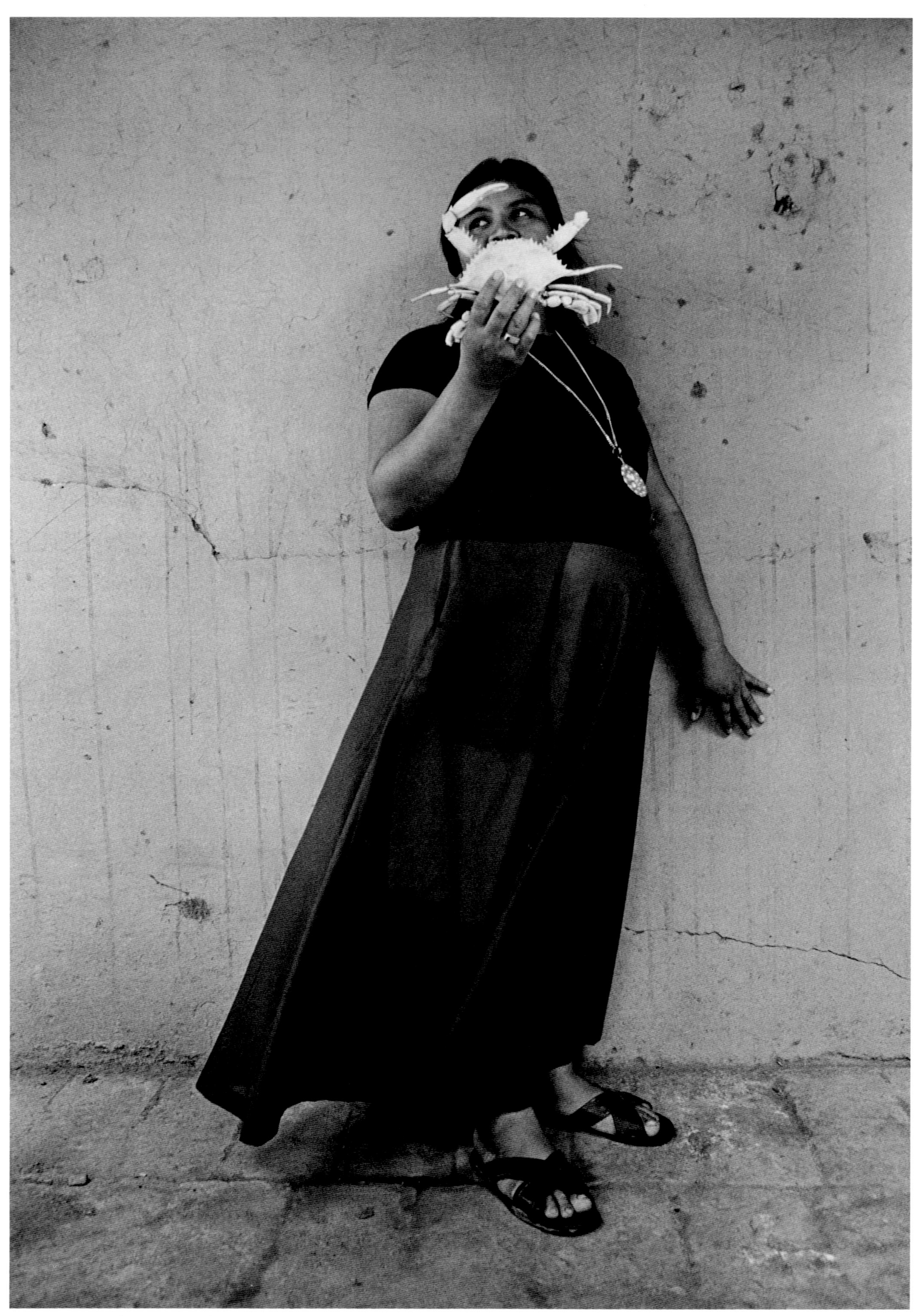

 Mujer cangrejo (Crab woman), Juchitán, Oaxaca, 1985

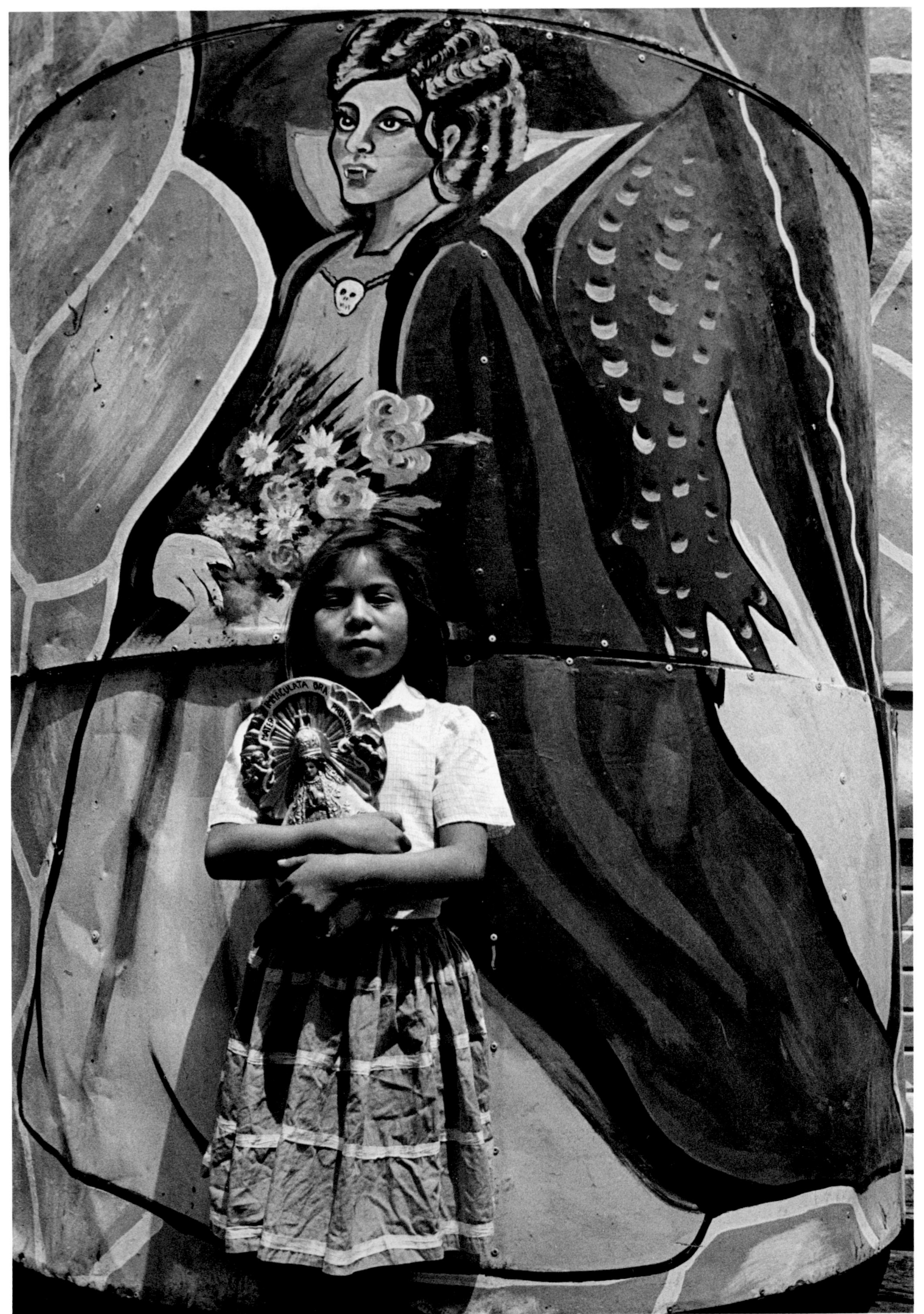

Immaculata, Xochimilco, Federal District, 1984

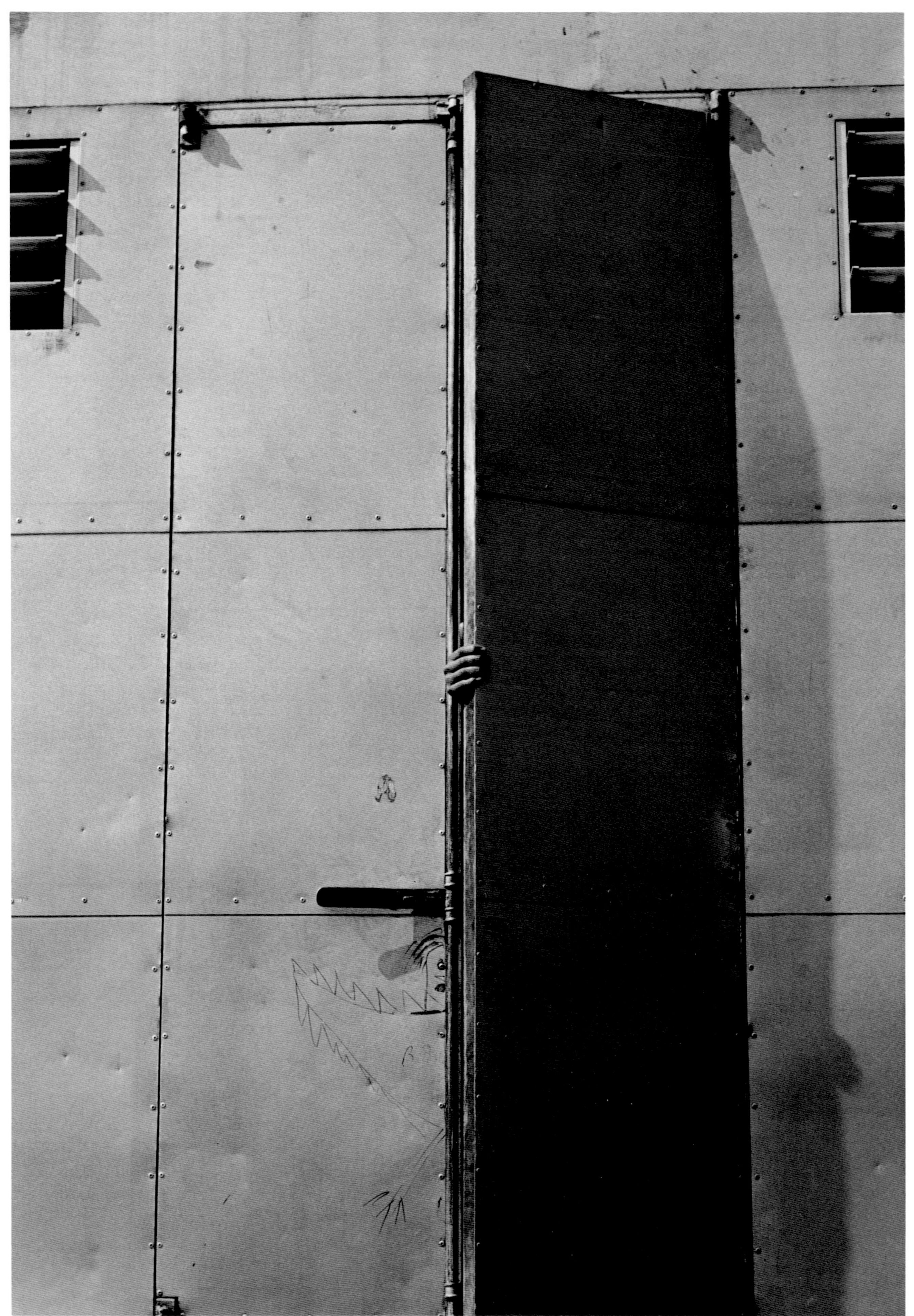

 Camión de carne (Butcher truck), Mexico City, 1973

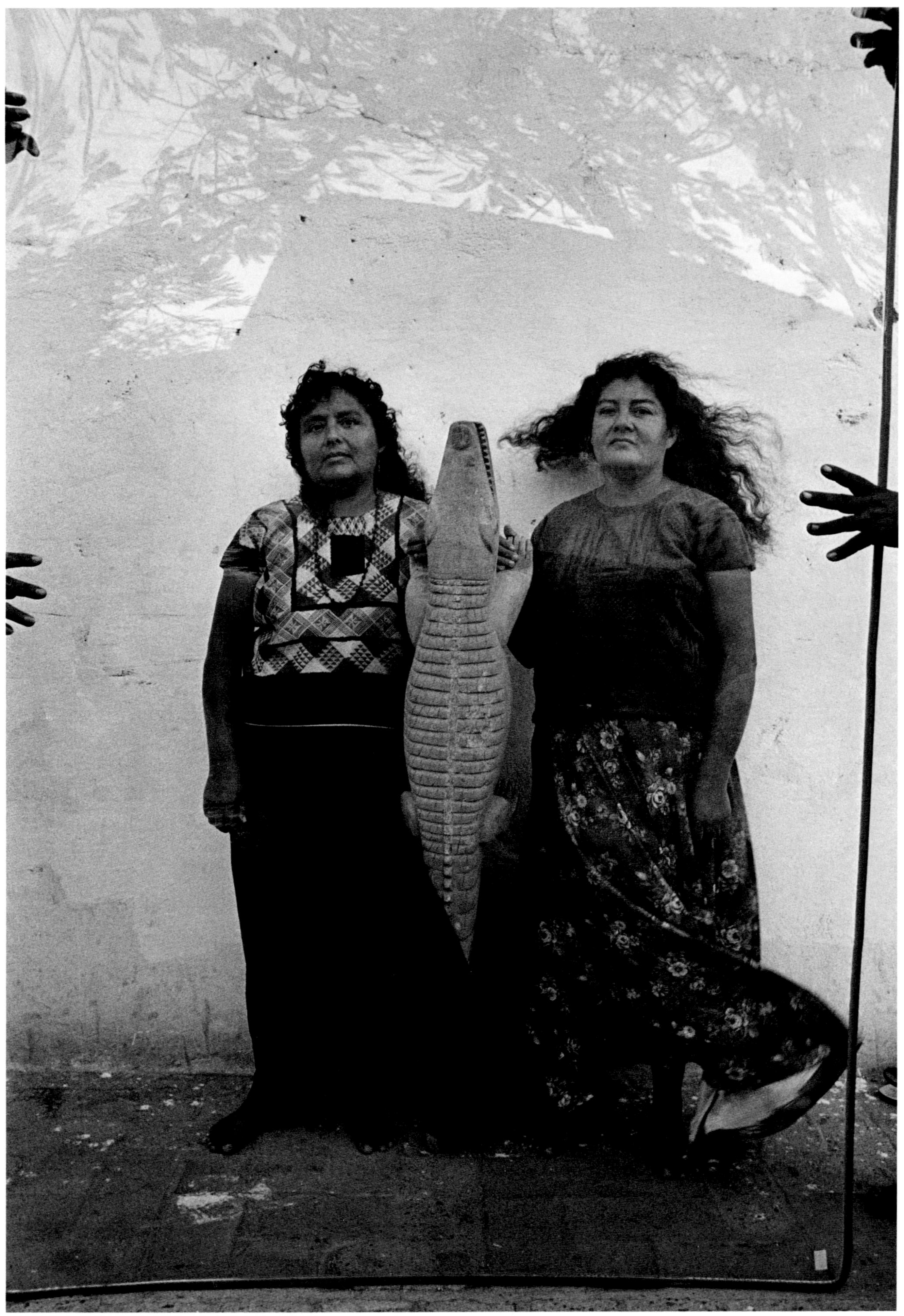

Lagarto (Alligator), Juchitán, Oaxaca, 1986

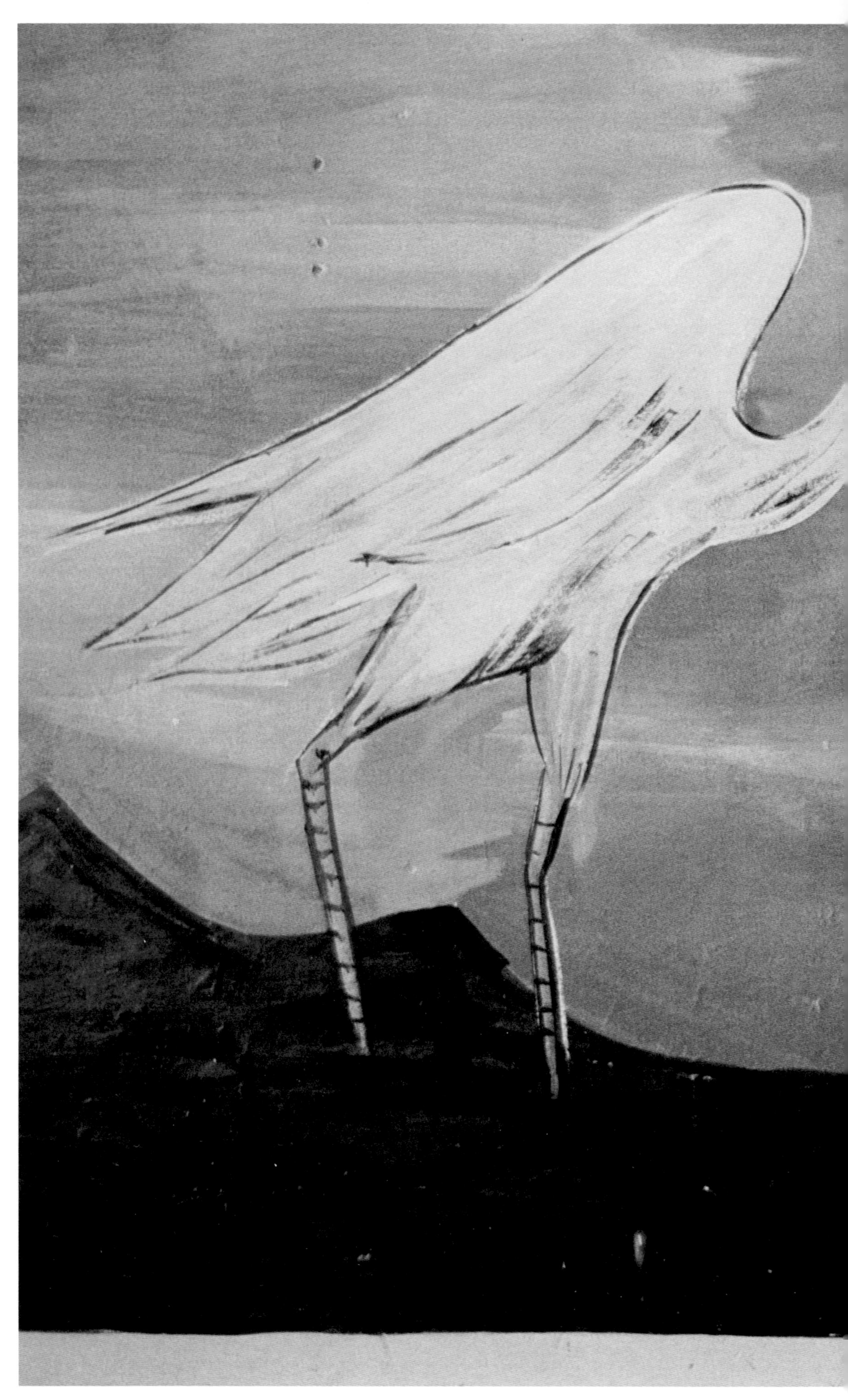

Tehuantepec, Oaxaca, 1985

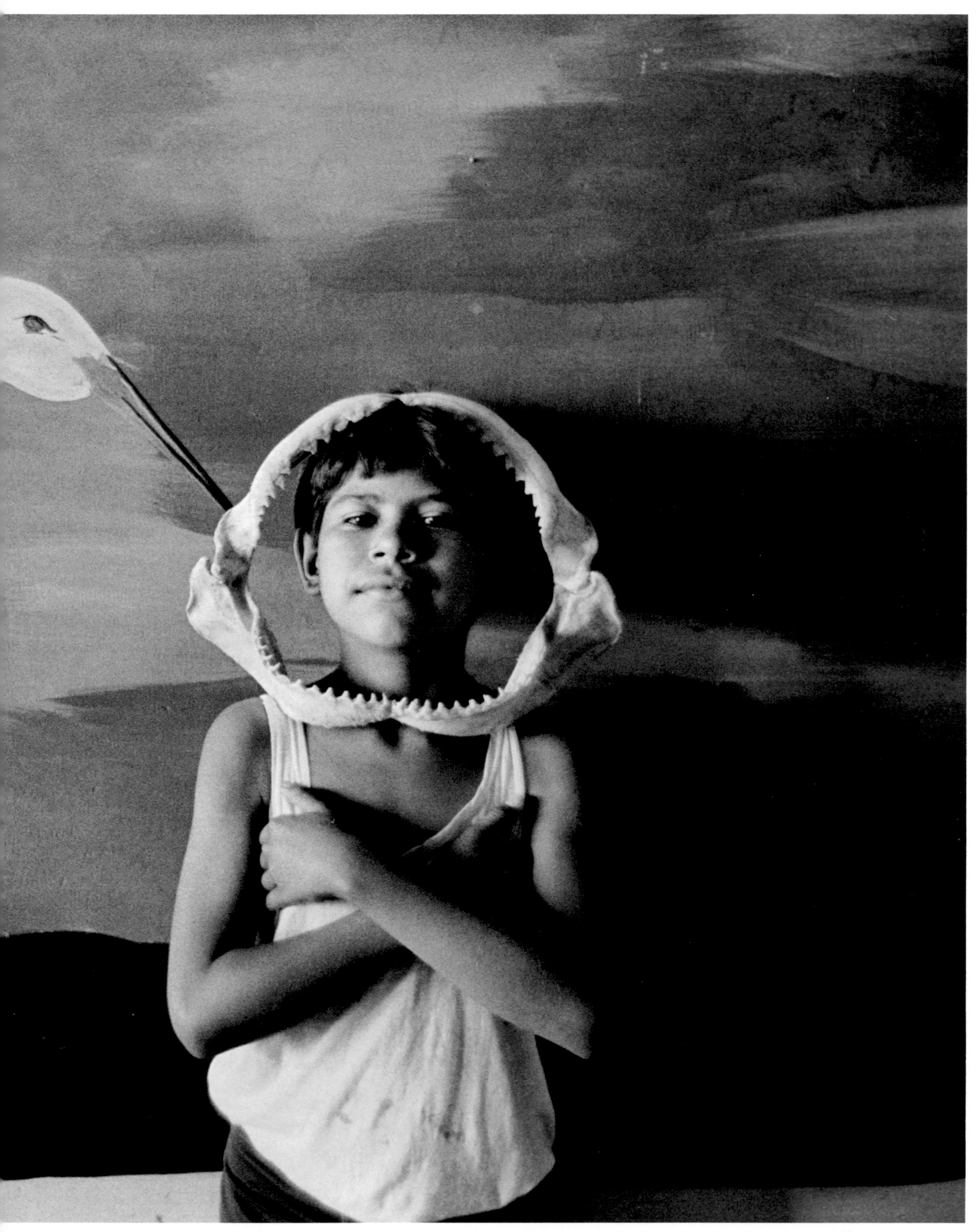

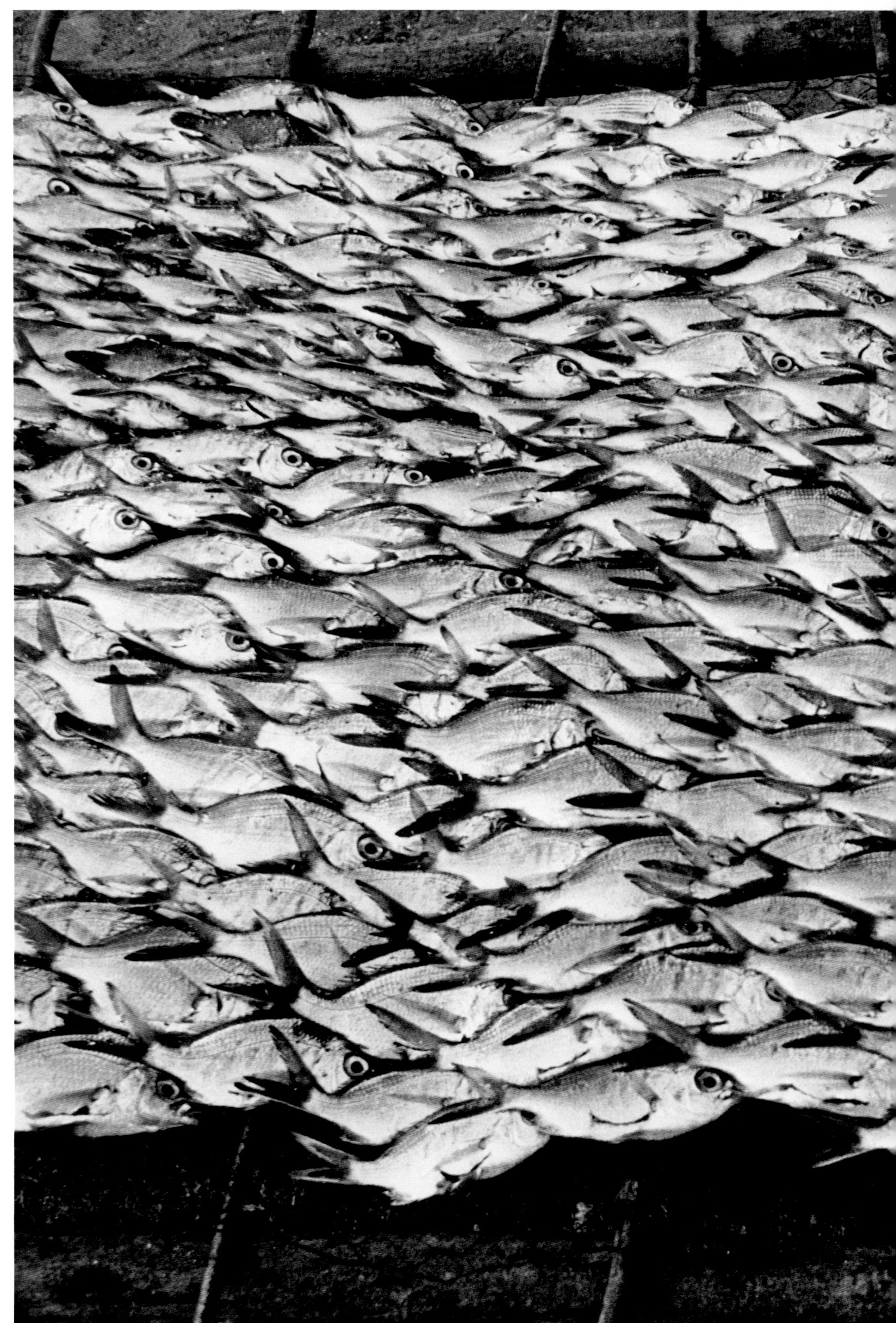

Pescaditos de Oaxaca
(Fish from Oaxaca),
Oaxaca, 1992

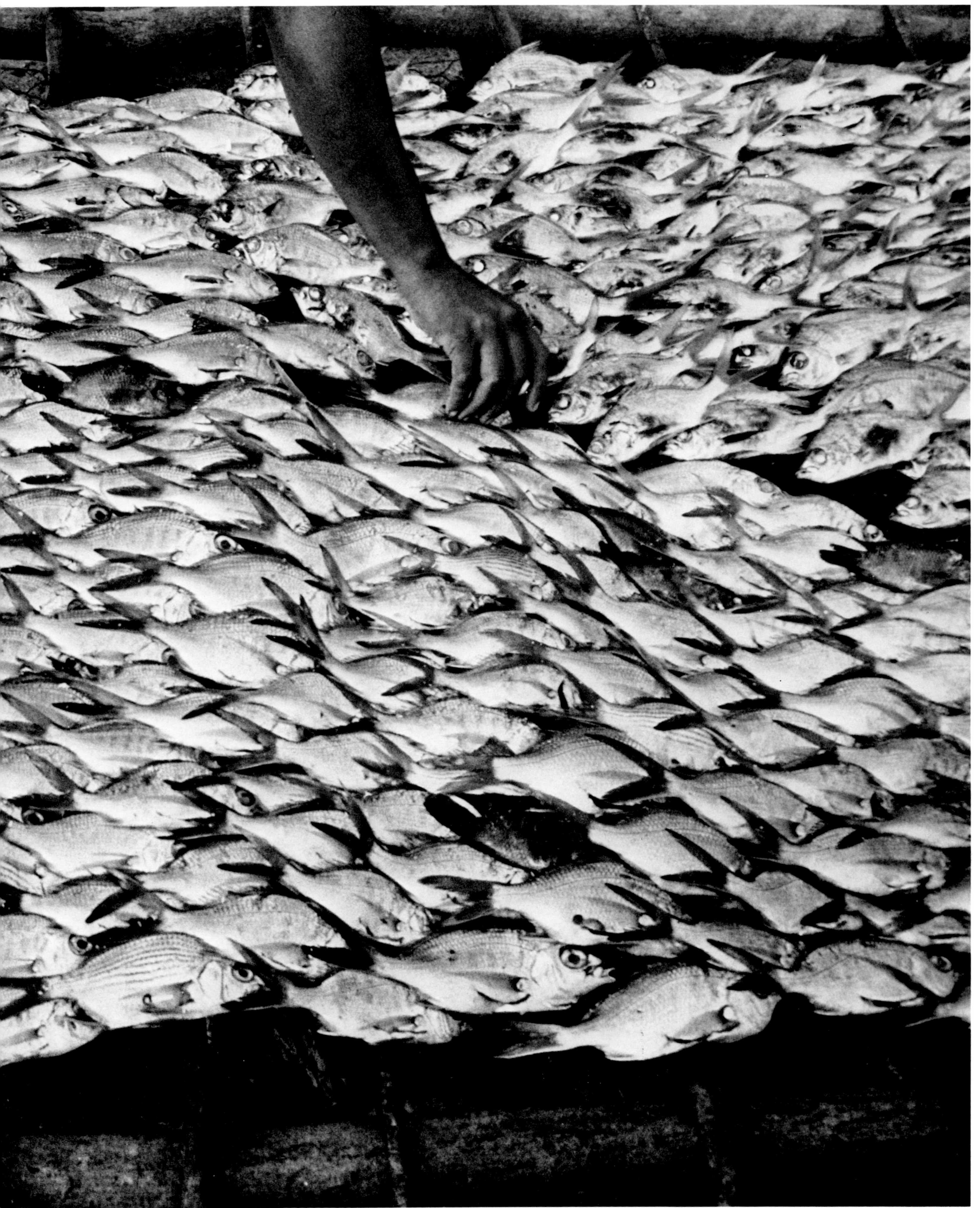

Cuatro pescaditos (Four fish), Juchitán, Oaxaca, 1986

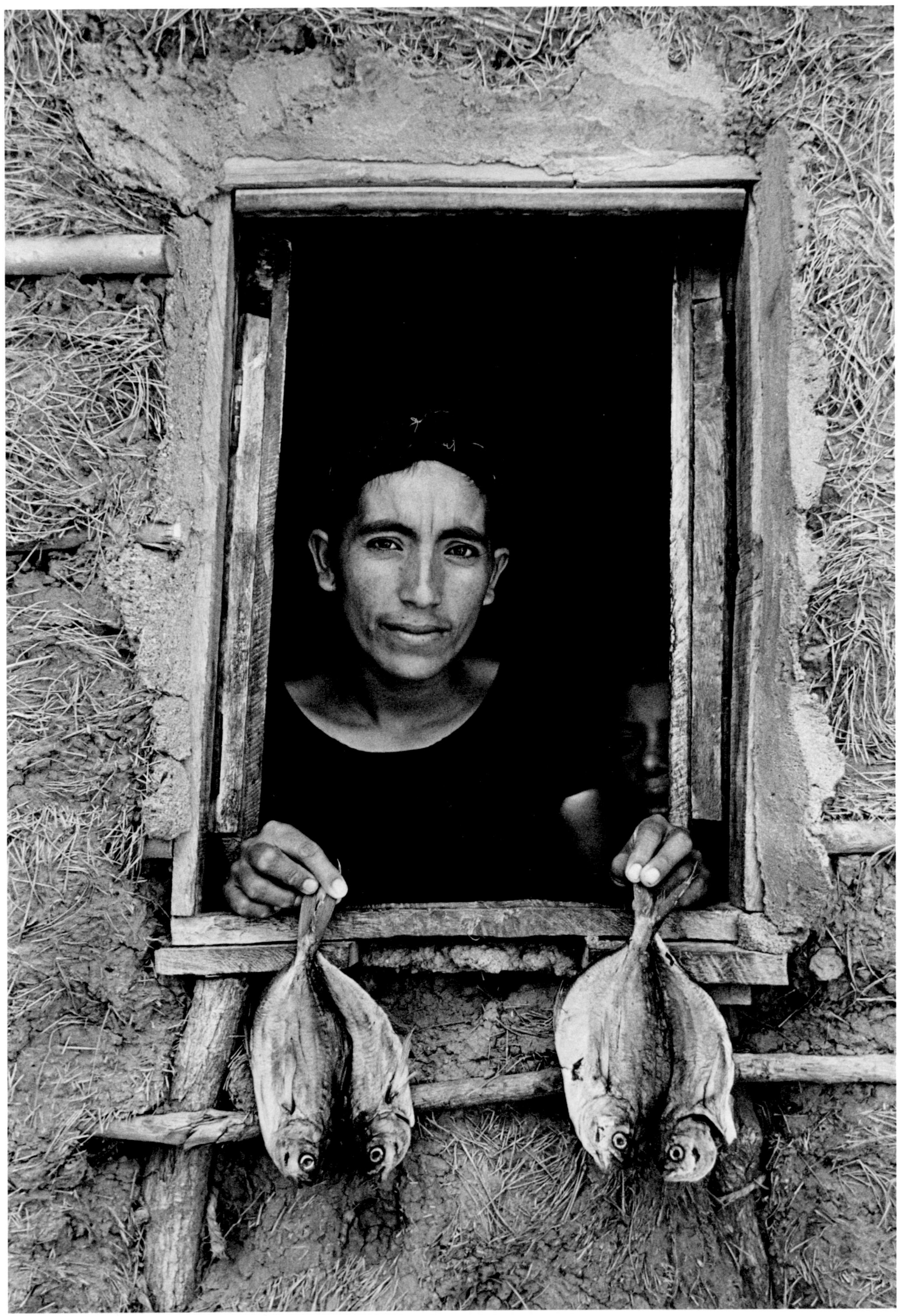

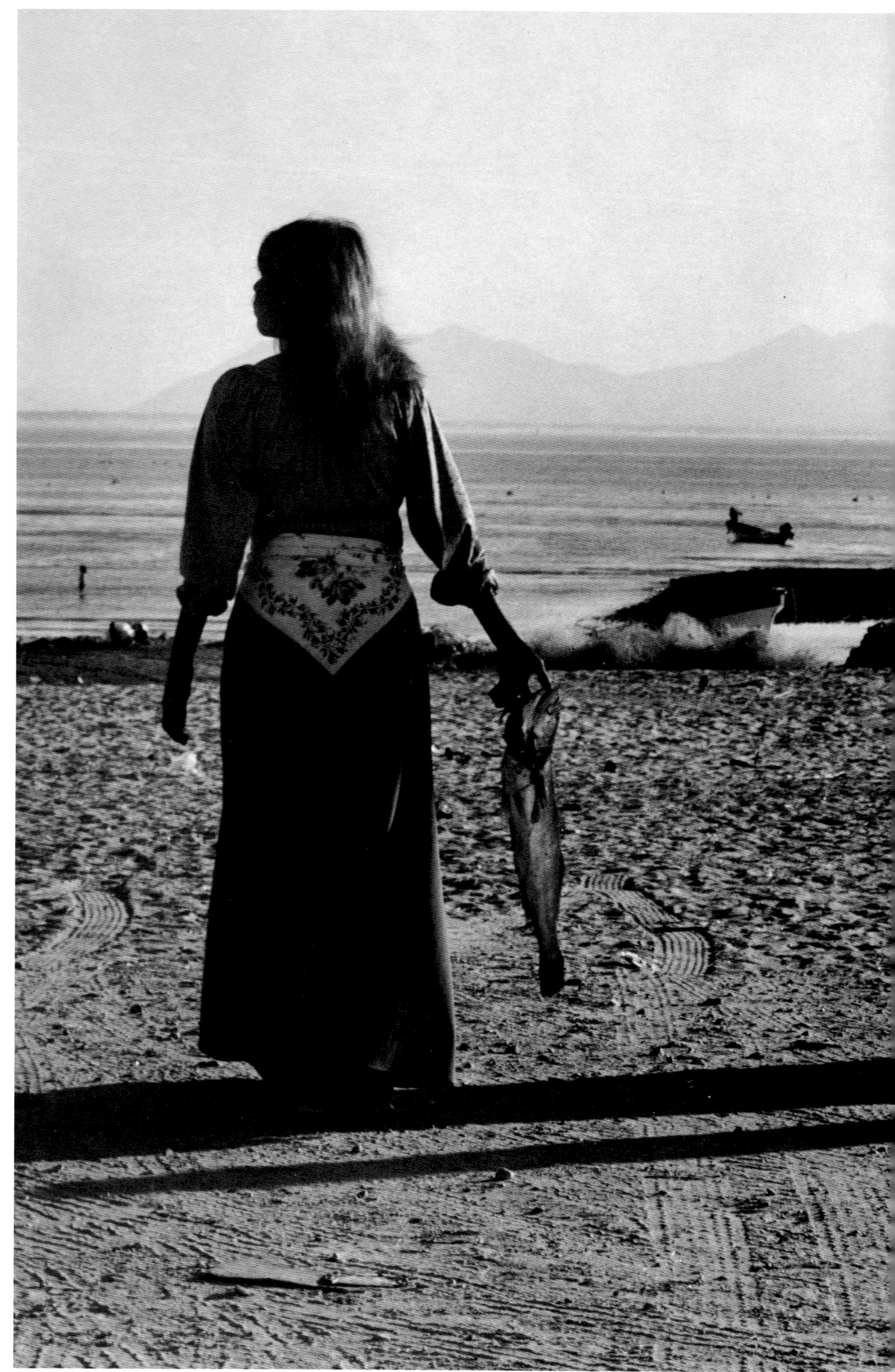

Mujeres seris (Seri women),
Sonora Desert, 1979

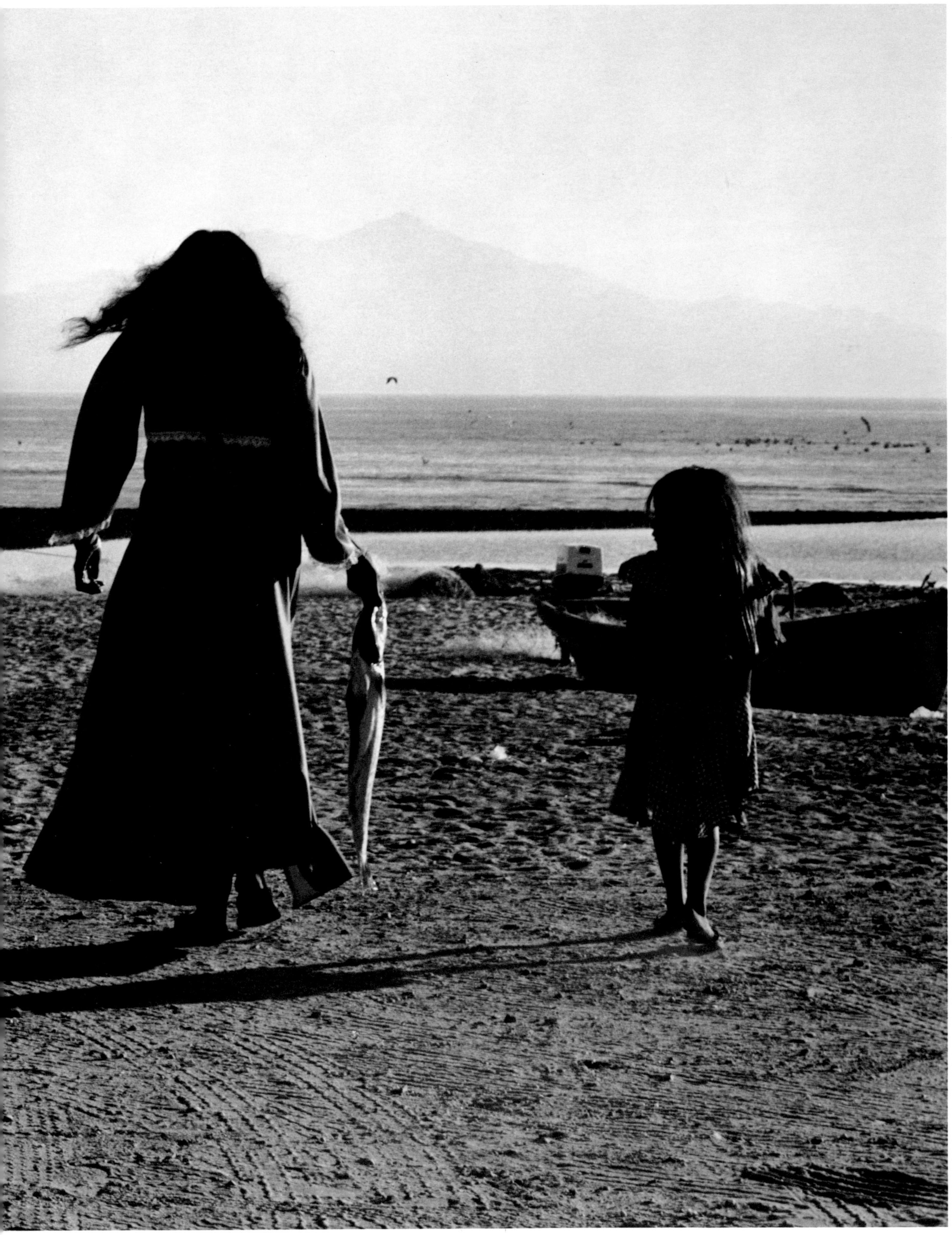

Cholos, White Fence, East Los Angeles, 1986

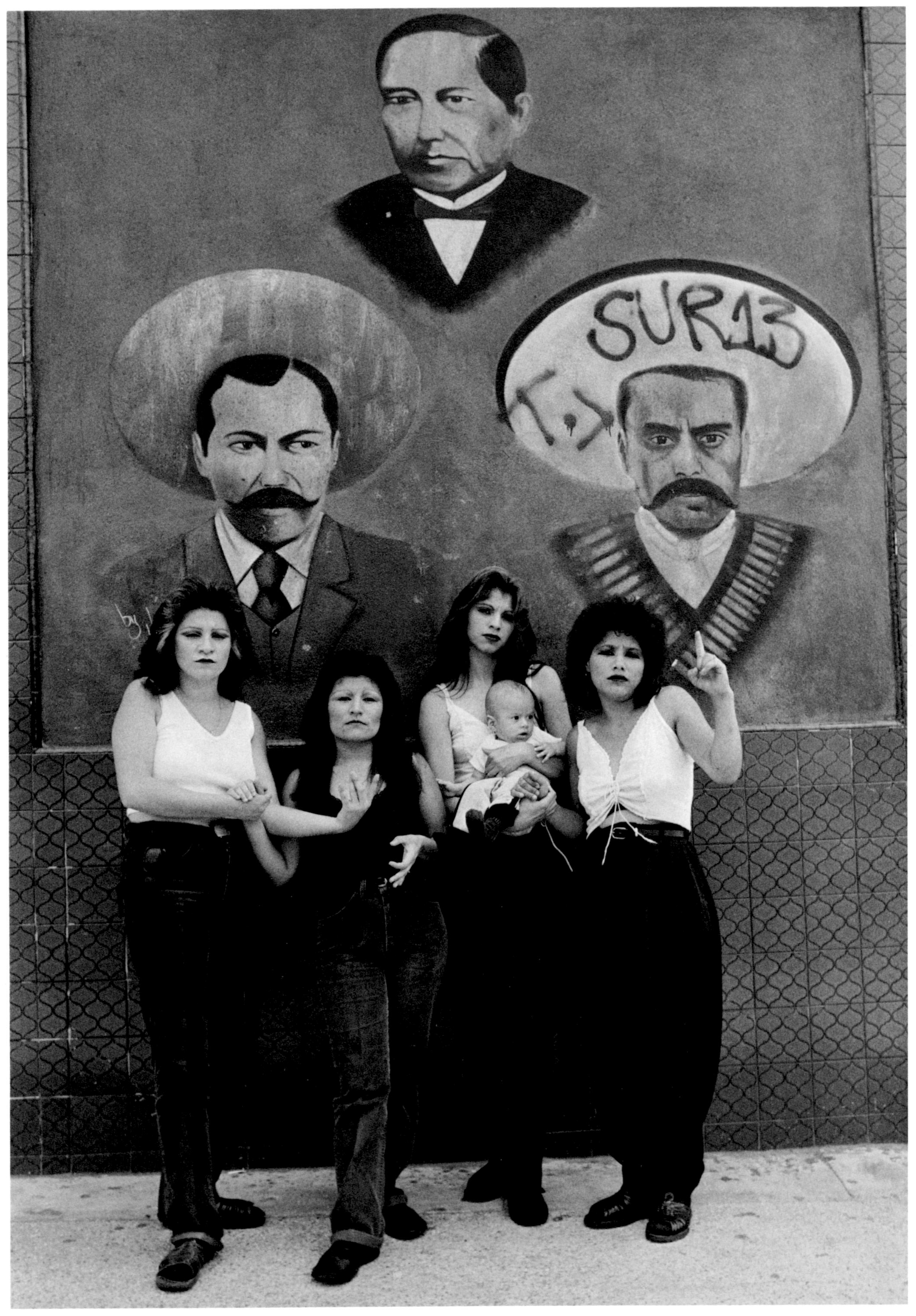
SUR13

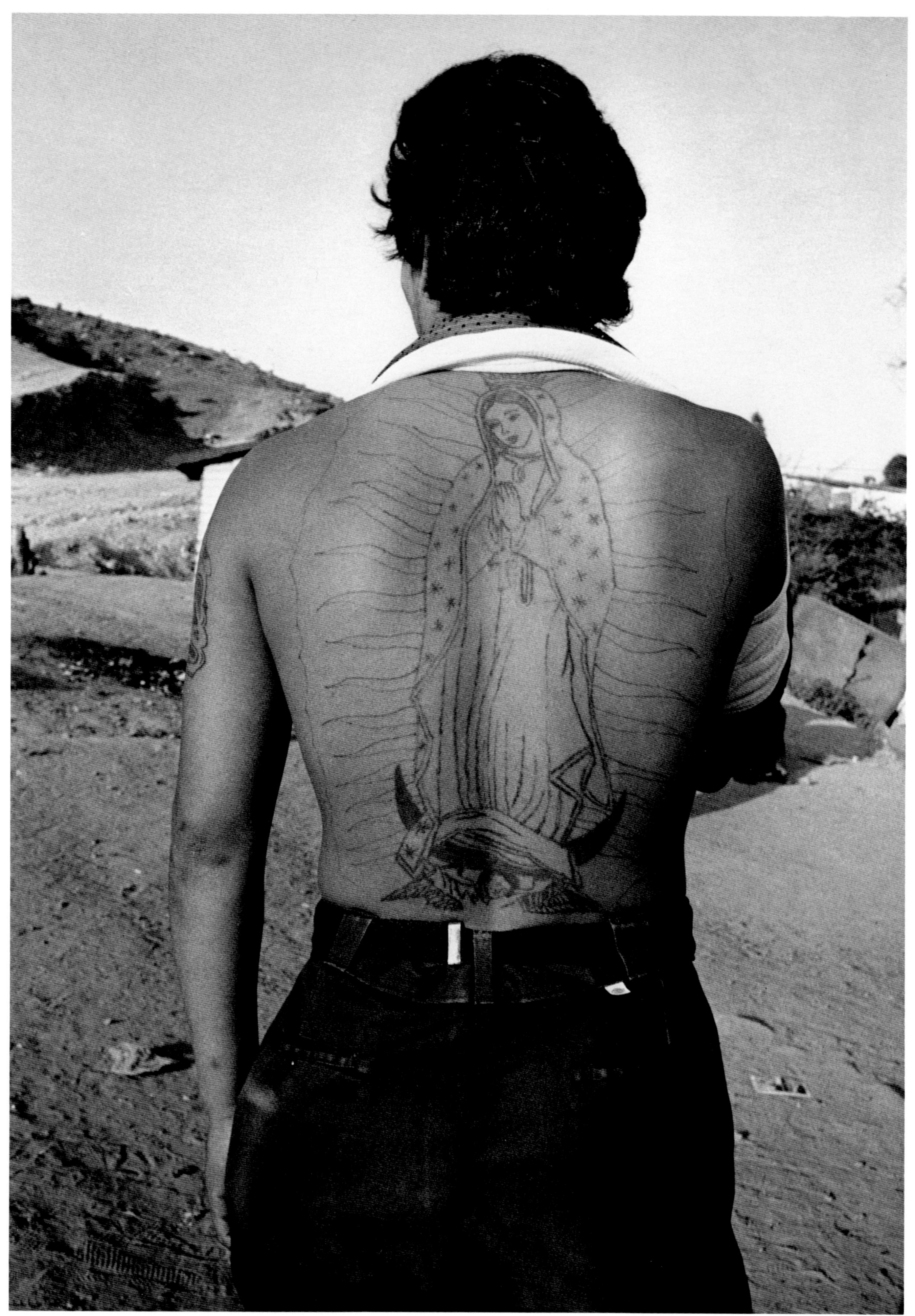

 La frontera (The border), Tijuana, Baja California, 1990

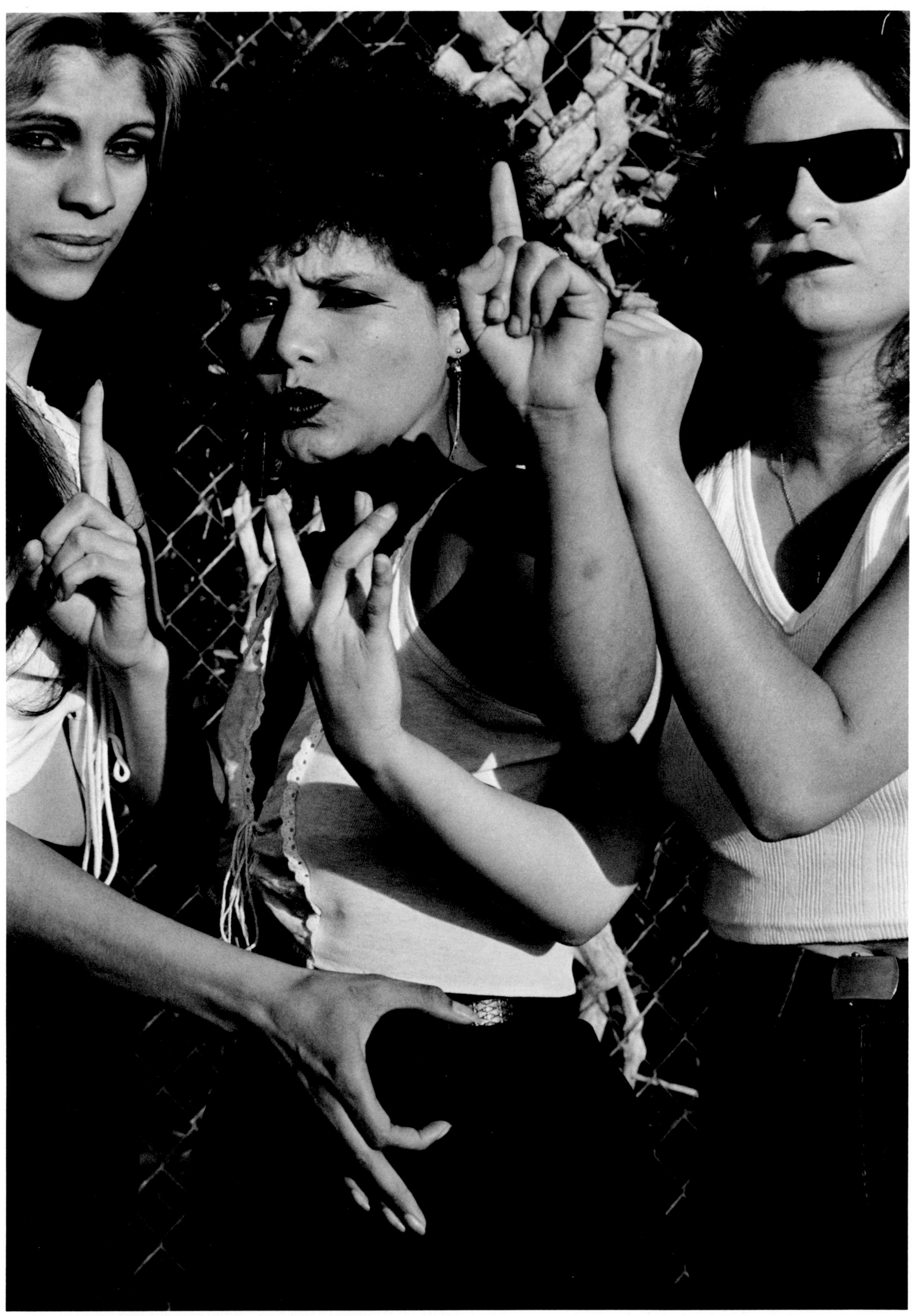

Rosario, Cristina, and Liza, White Fence, East Los Angeles, 1986

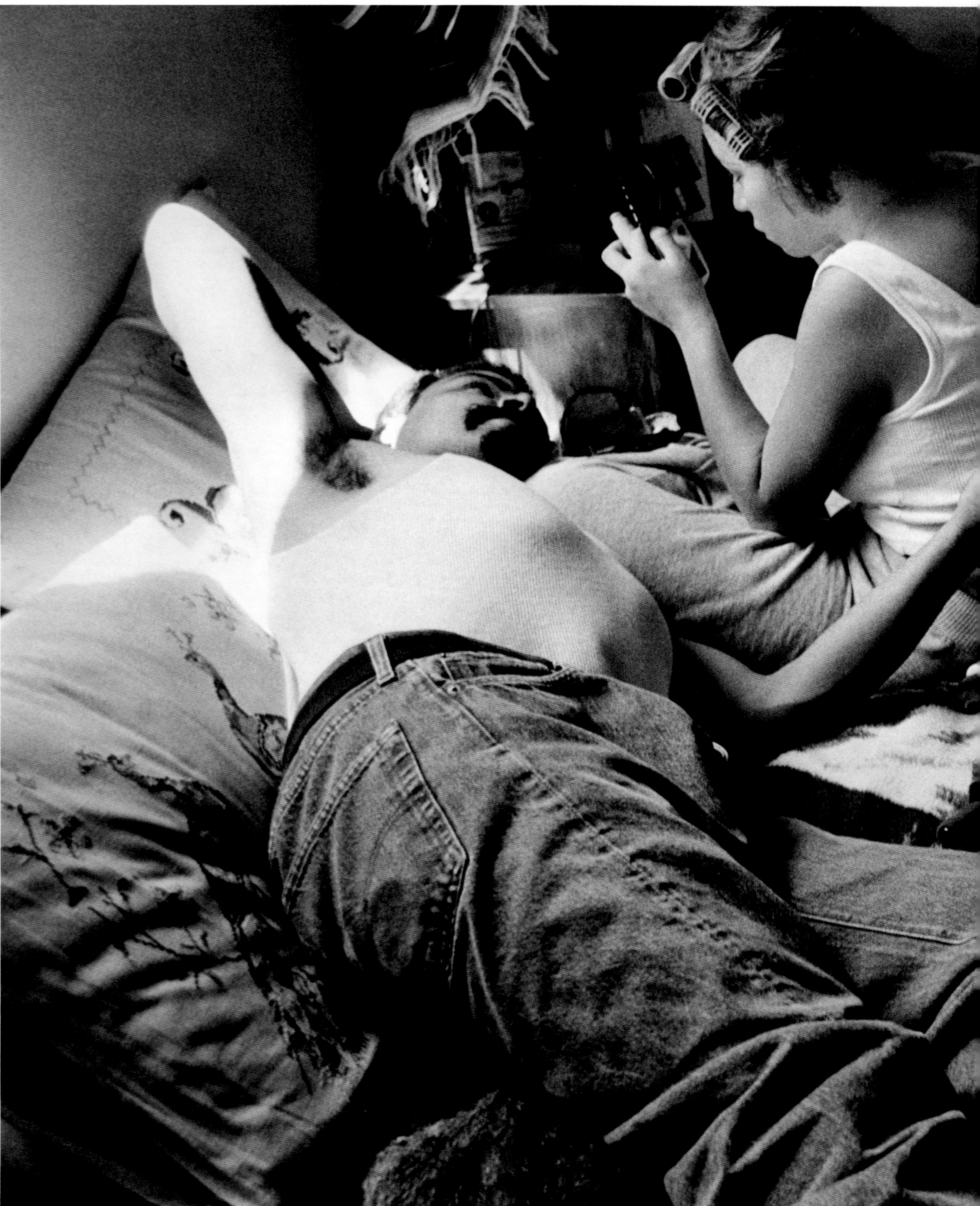

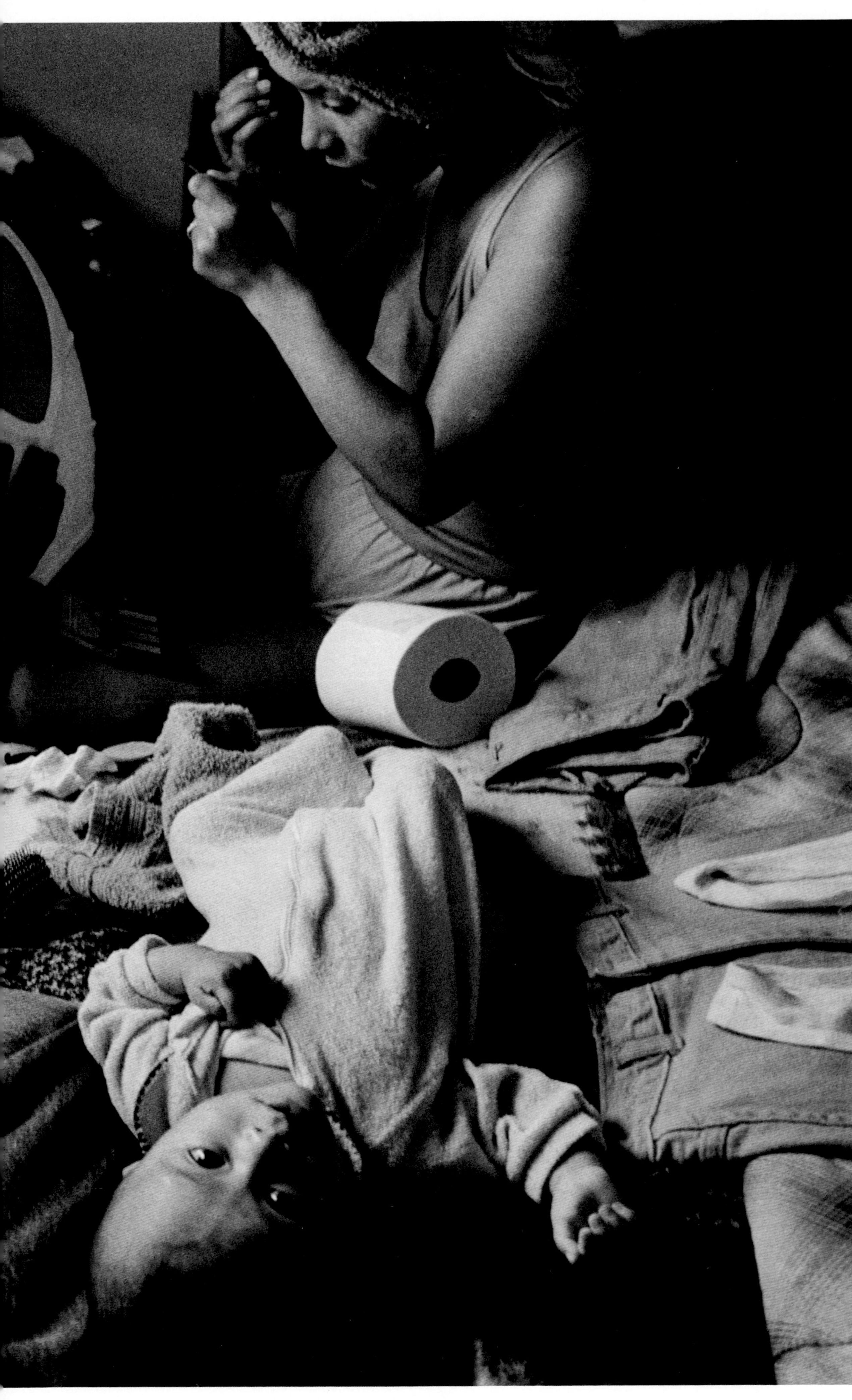

Cholos, White Fence,
East Los Angeles, 1986

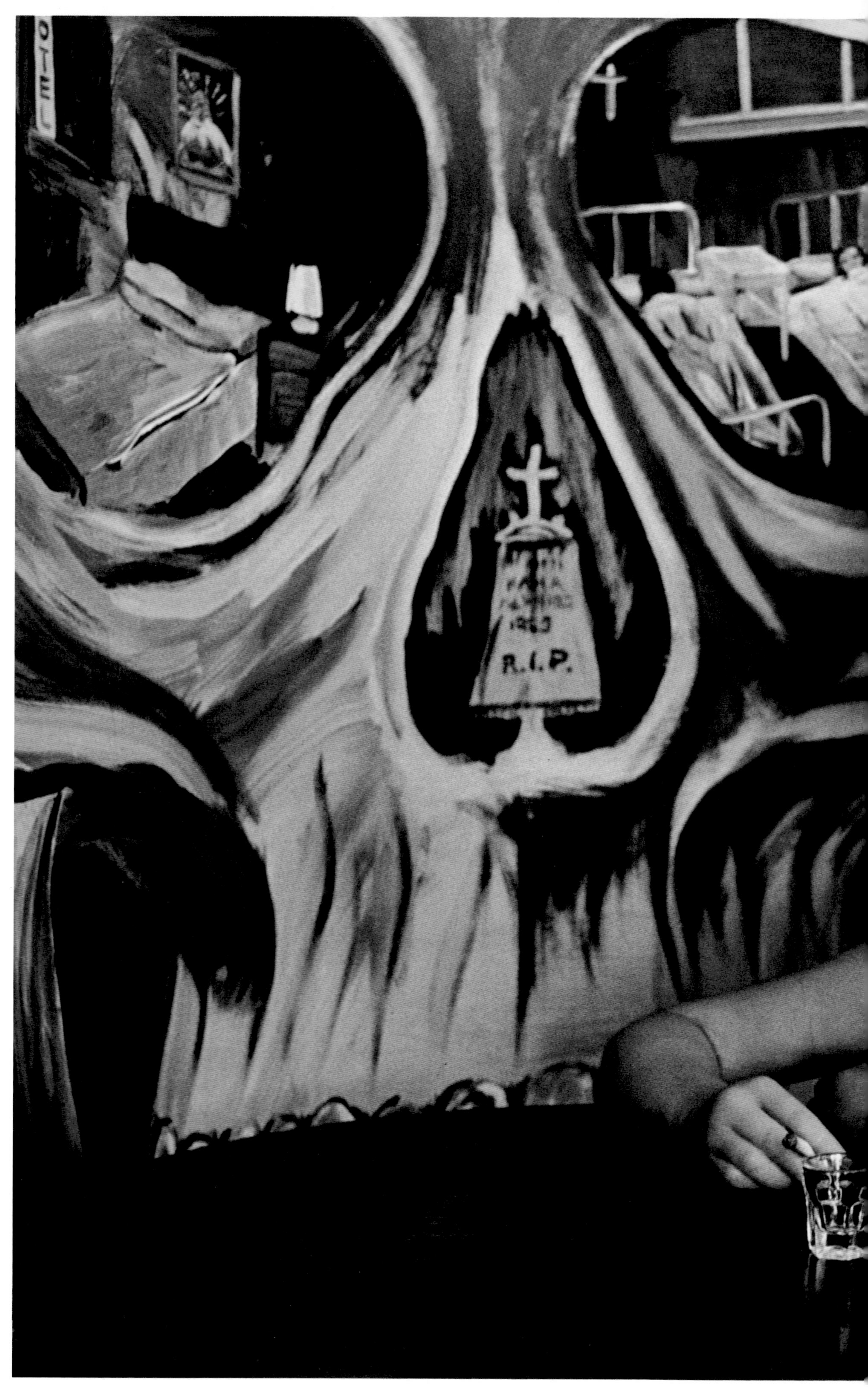

México, D.F. (Mexico City), 1972

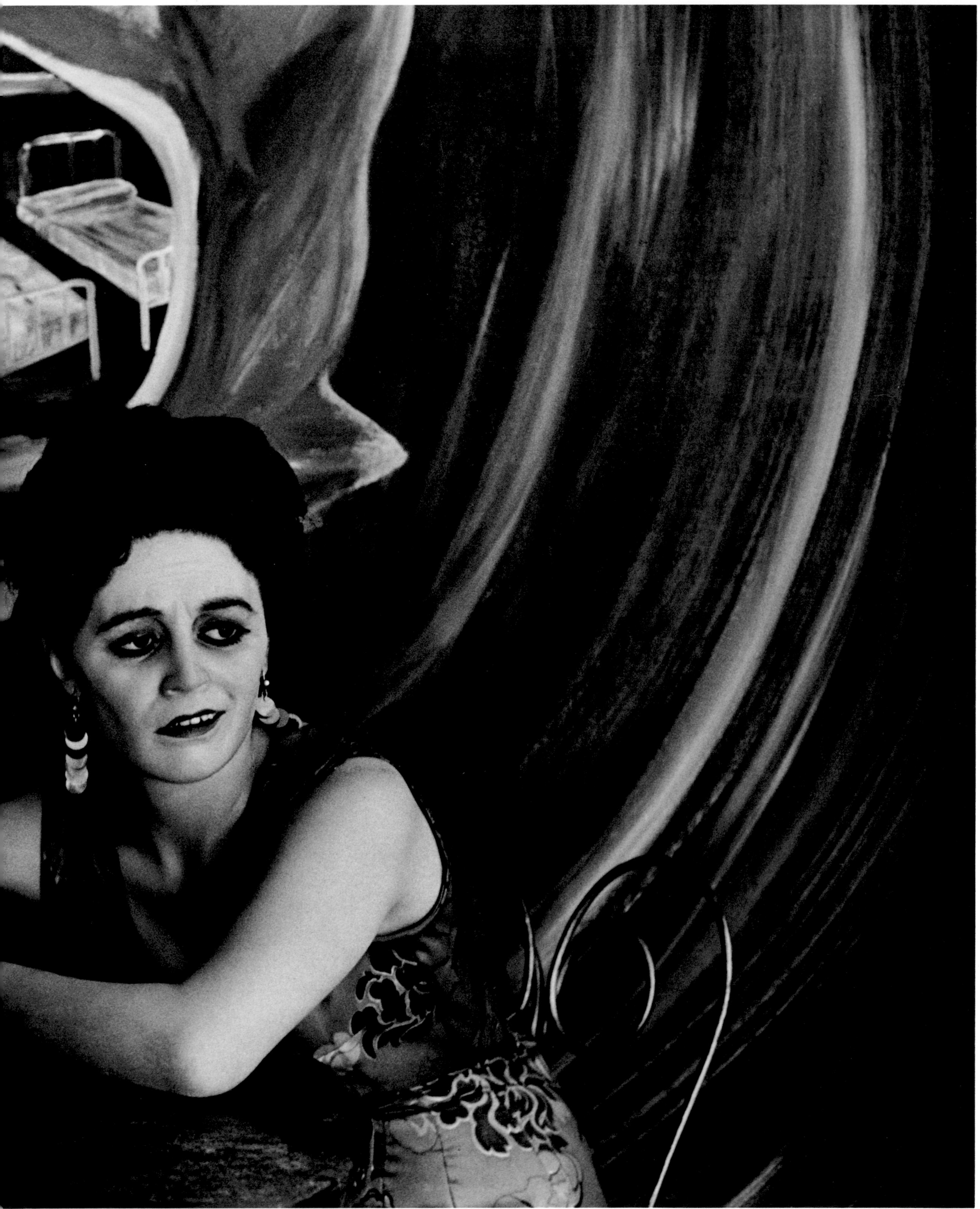

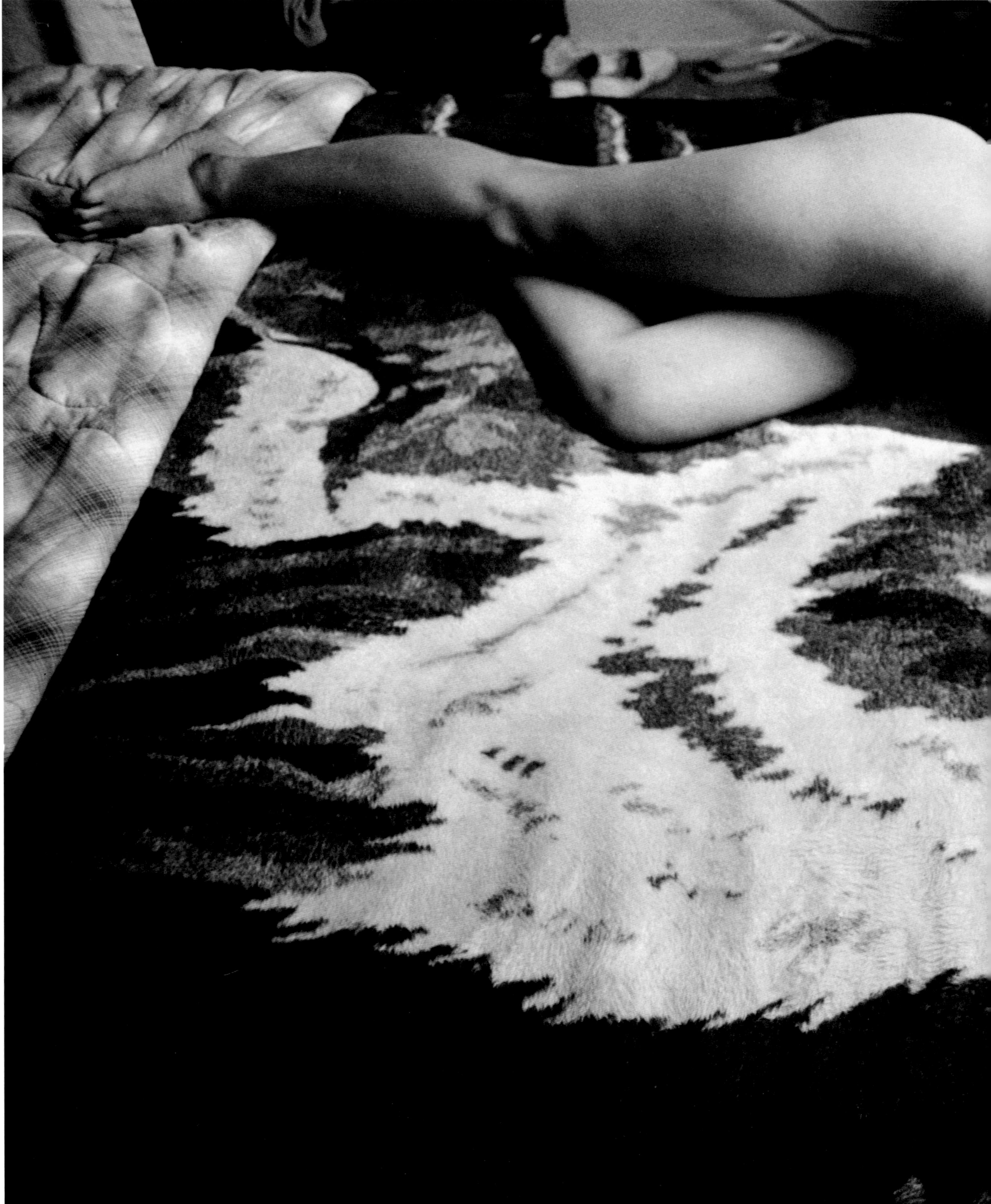

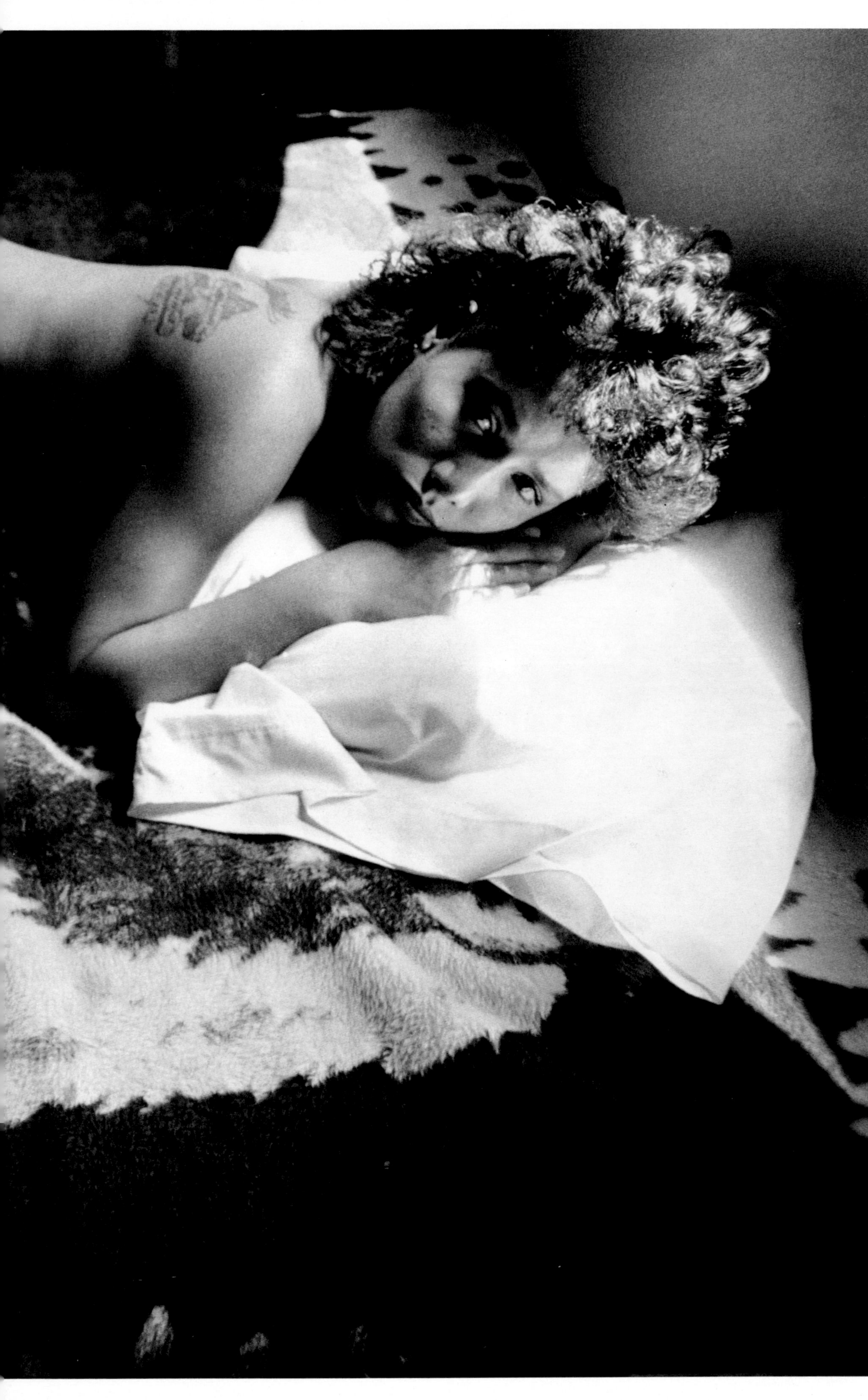

Cristina, White Fence,
East Los Angeles, 1986

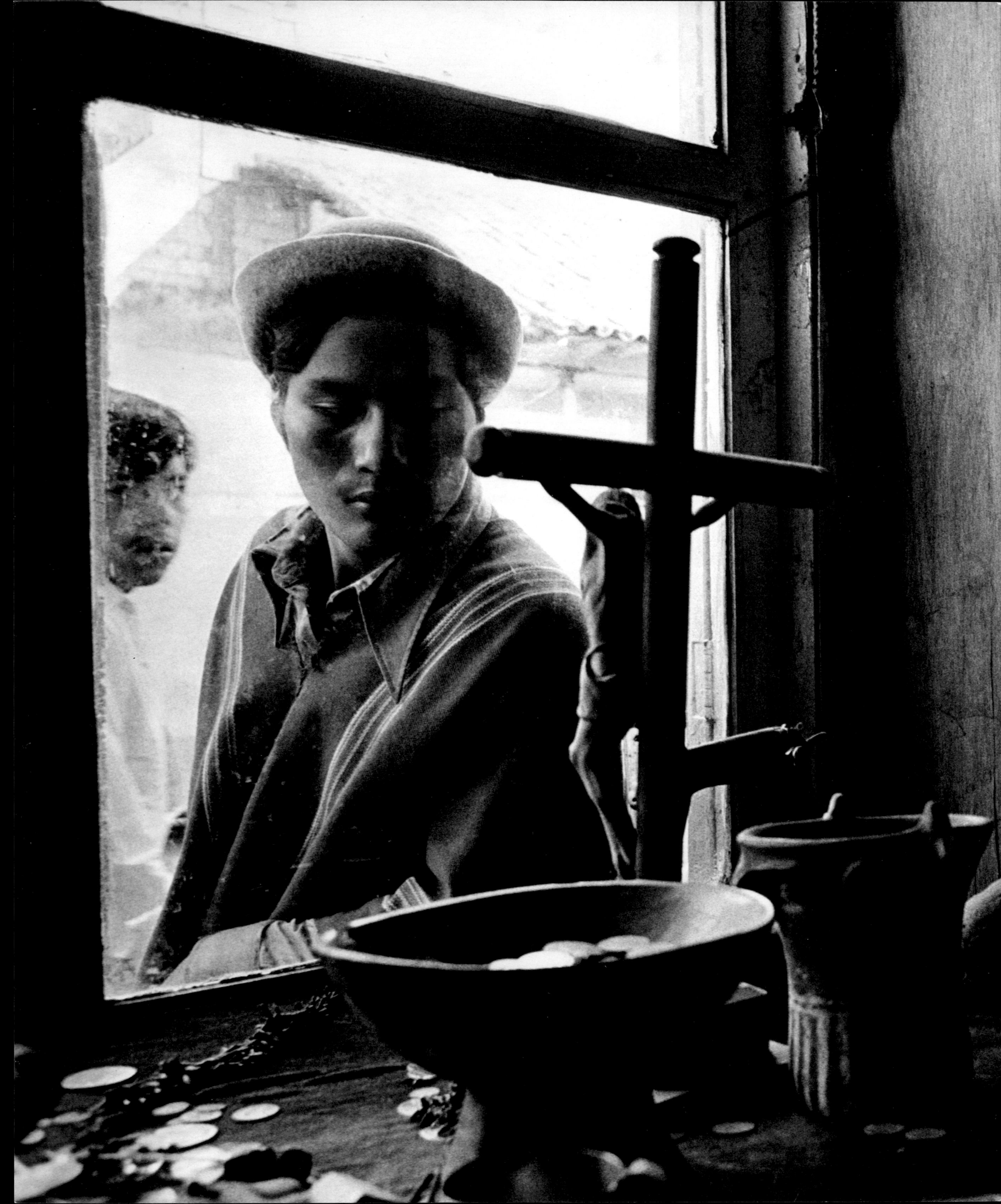

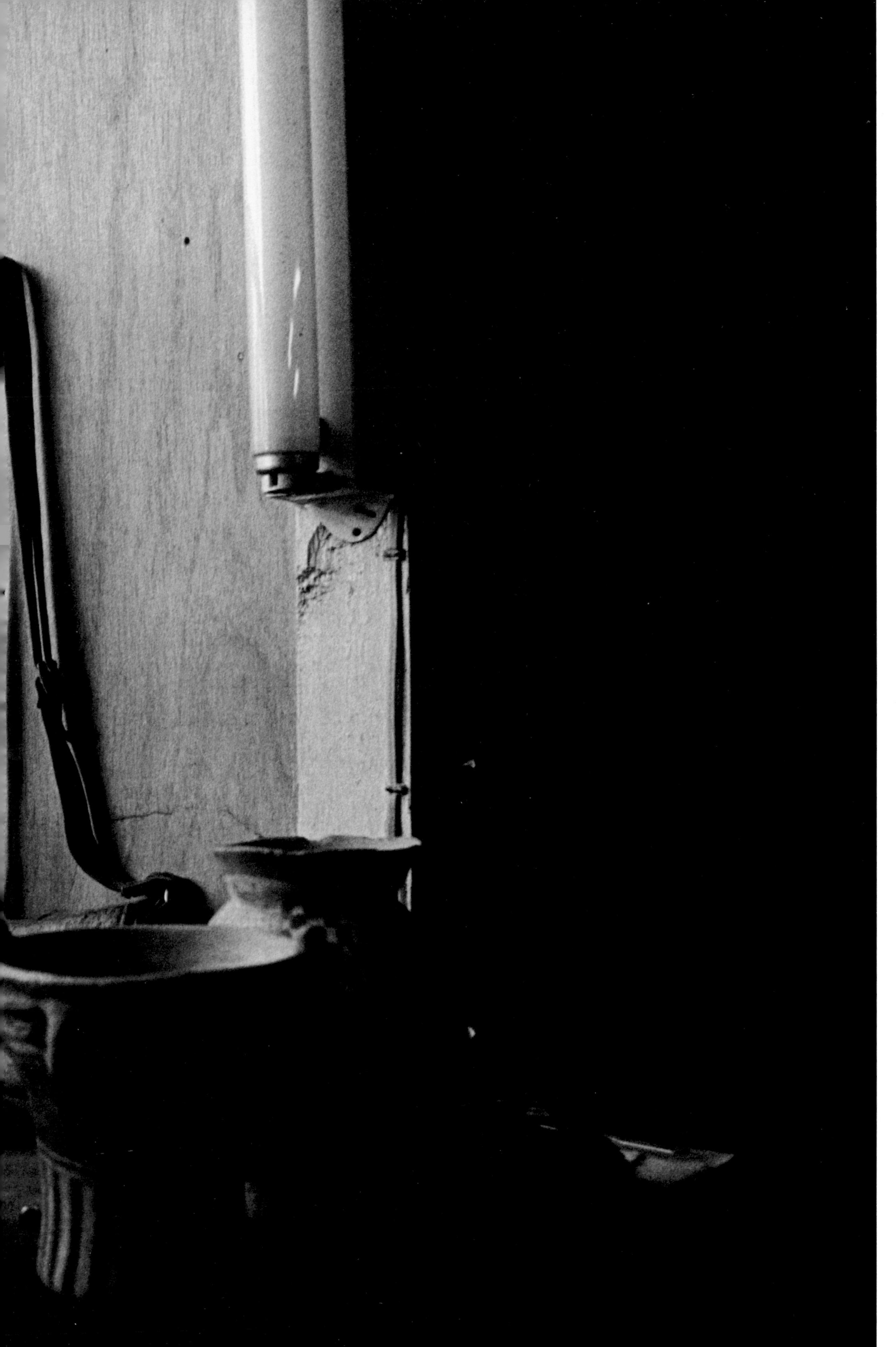

La tienda (Store),
Quito, Ecuador,
1982

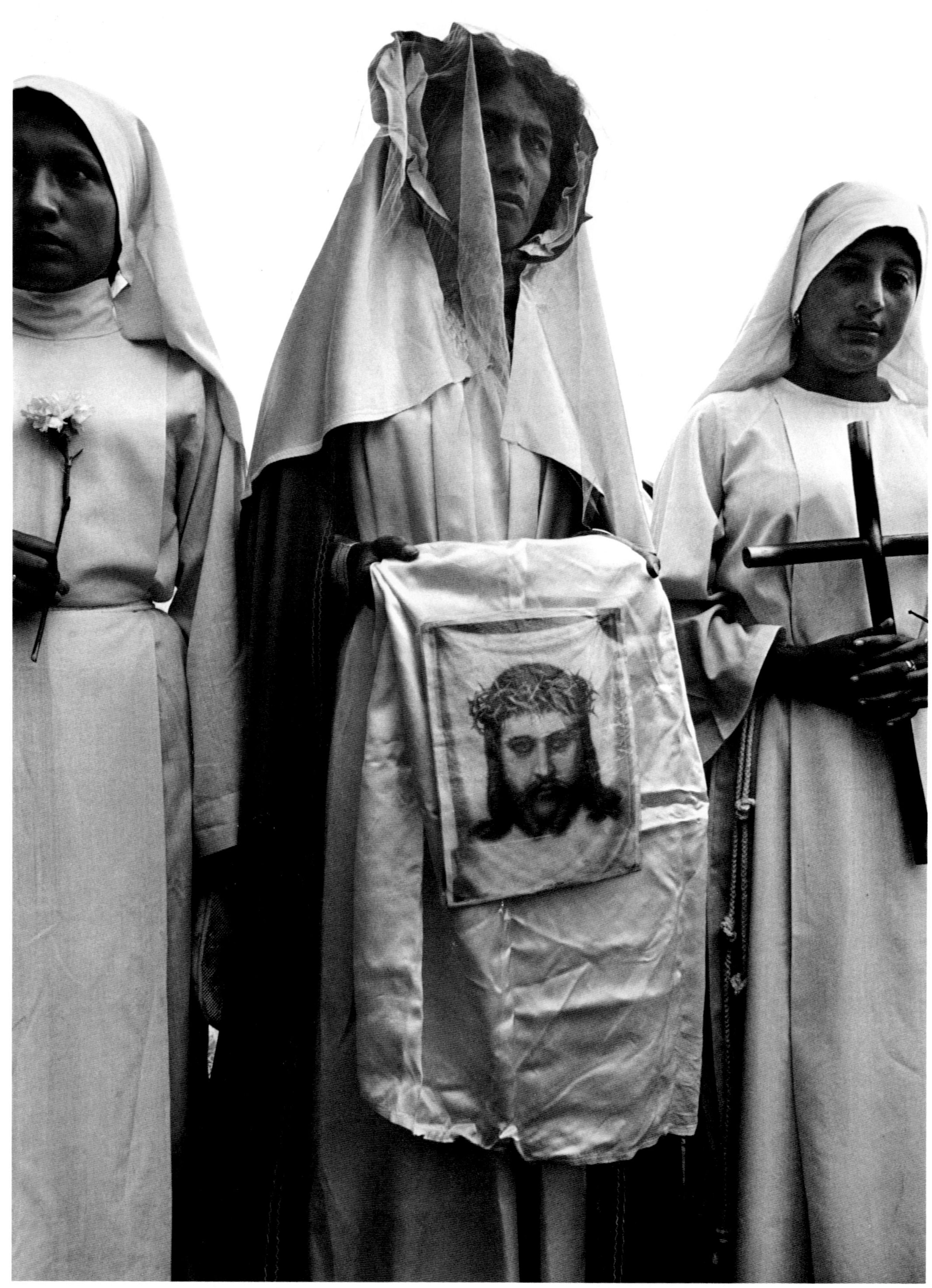

 La Verónica patrona de la fotografía (Veronica, patron saint of photography), Quito, Ecuador, 1982

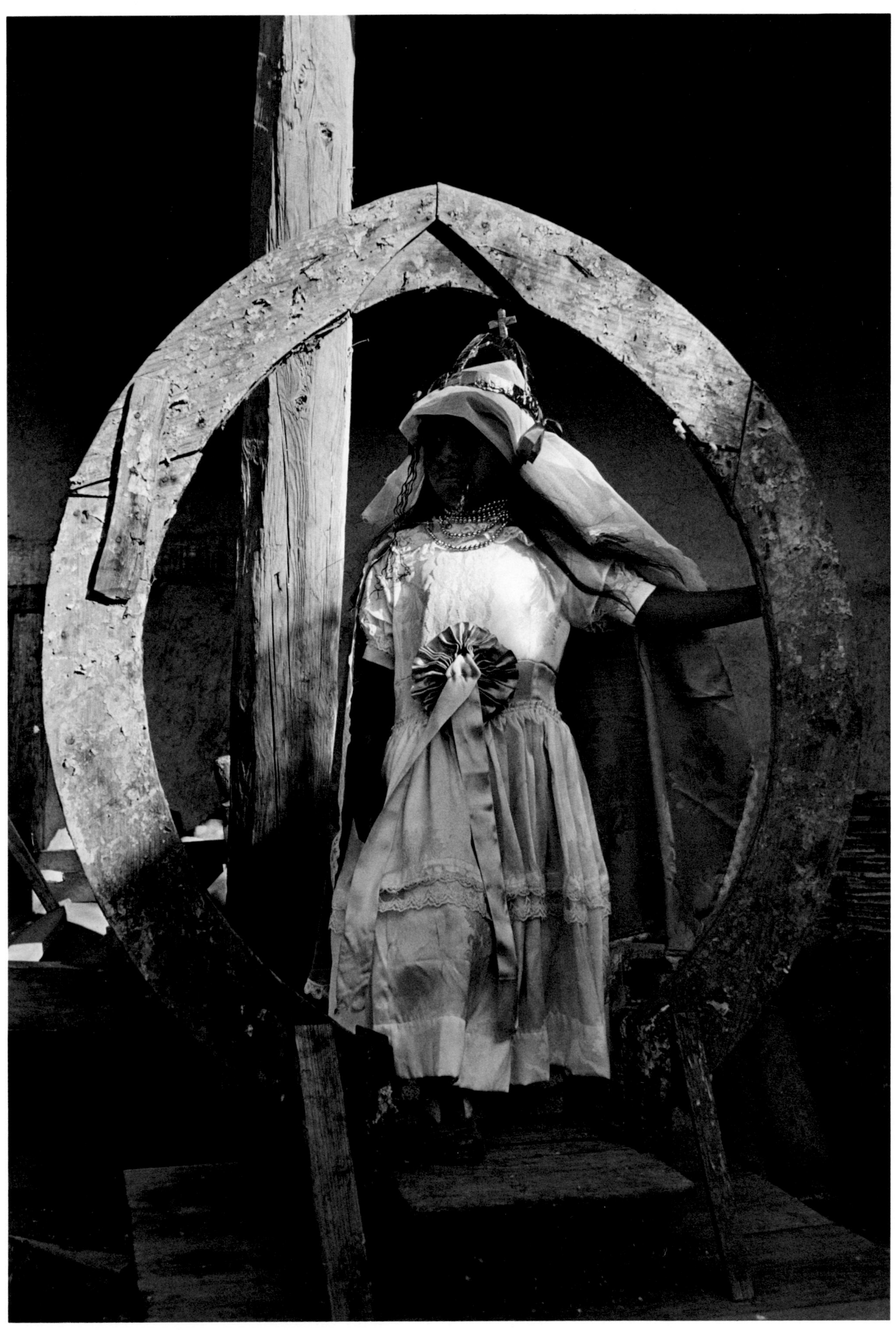

Virgen niña (Virgin child), Ocumichu, Michoacán, 1981

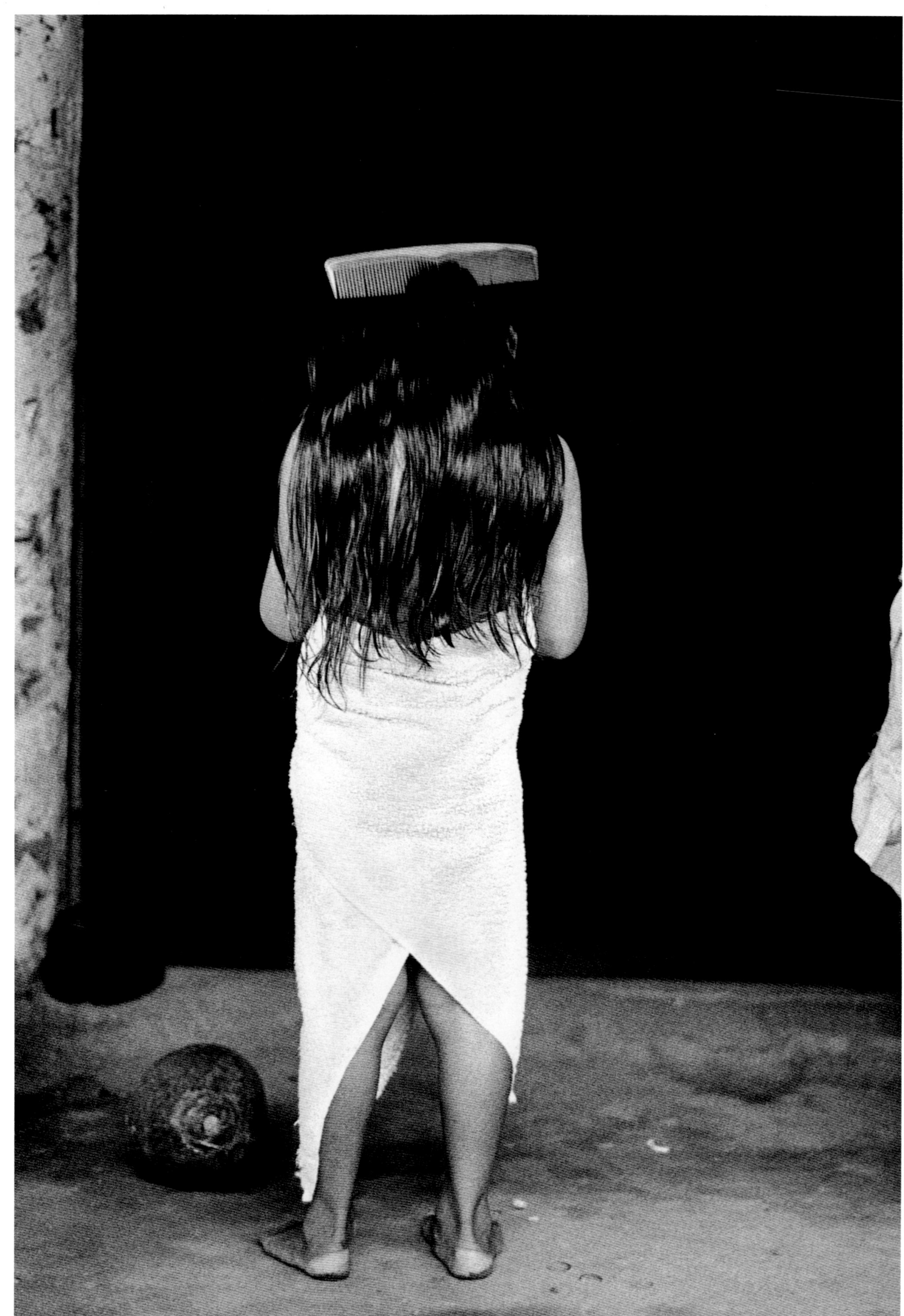

La niña del peine (Girl with hair-comb), Juchitán, Oaxaca, 1979

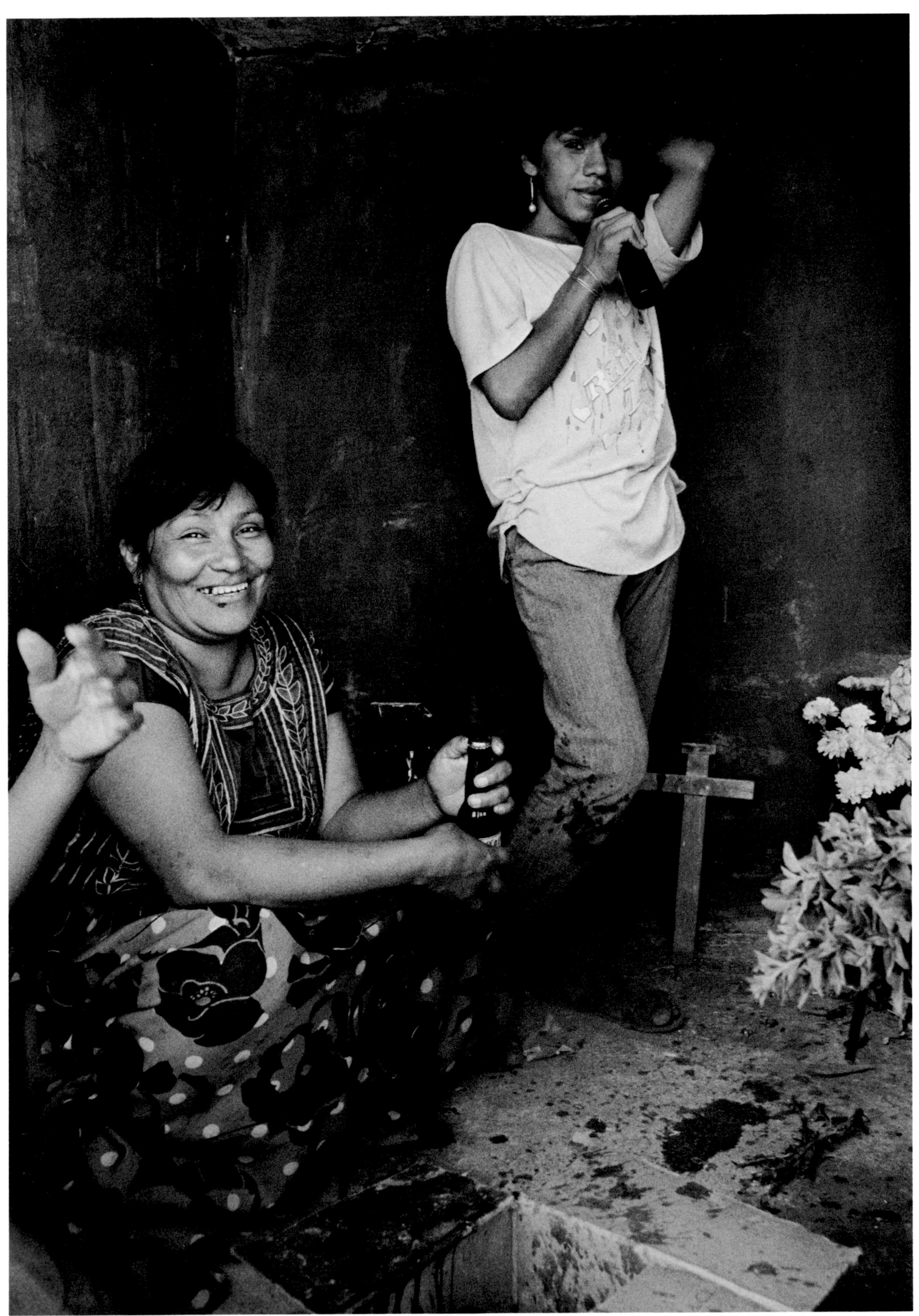

Día de muertos (Day of the Dead), Mexico City, 1975

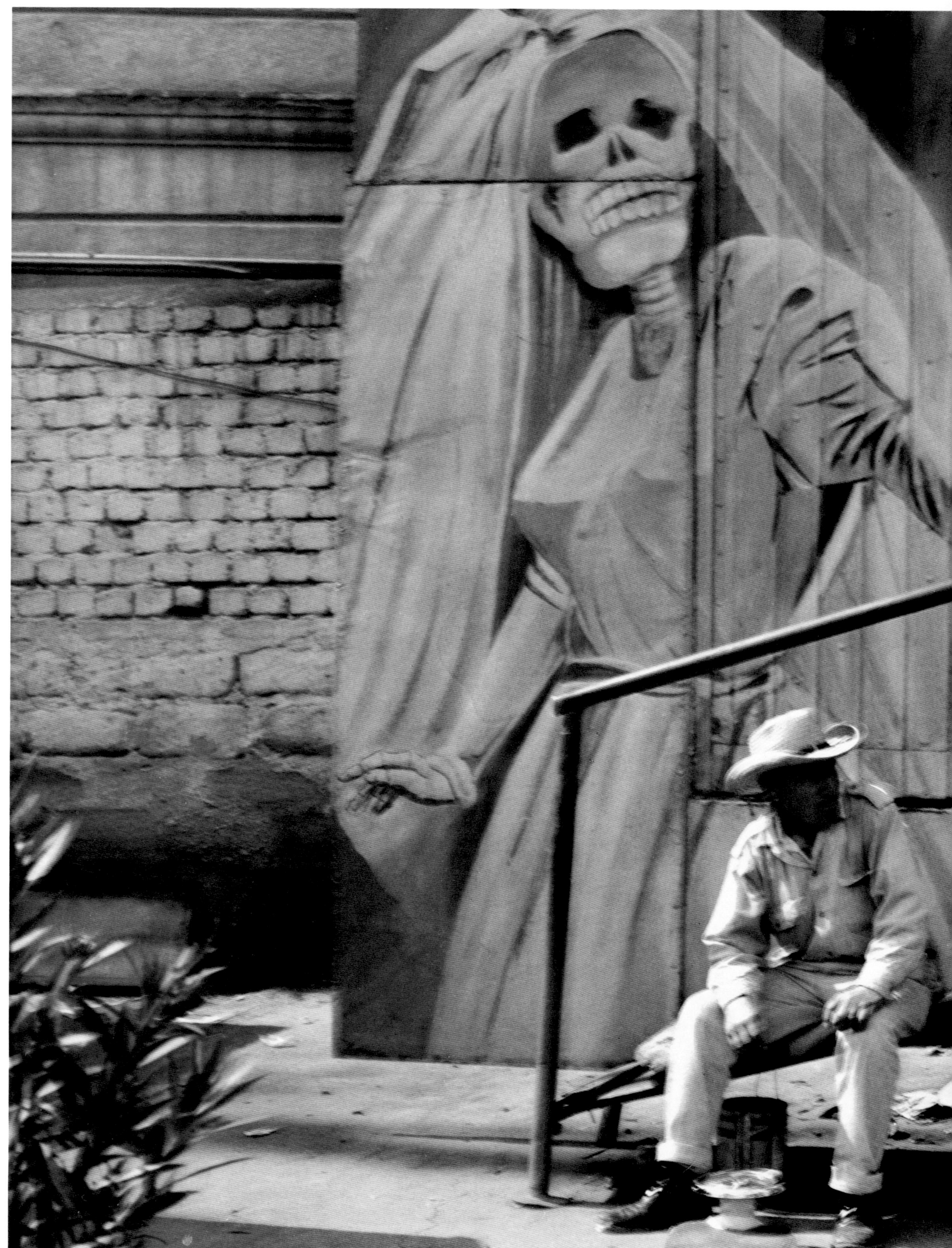

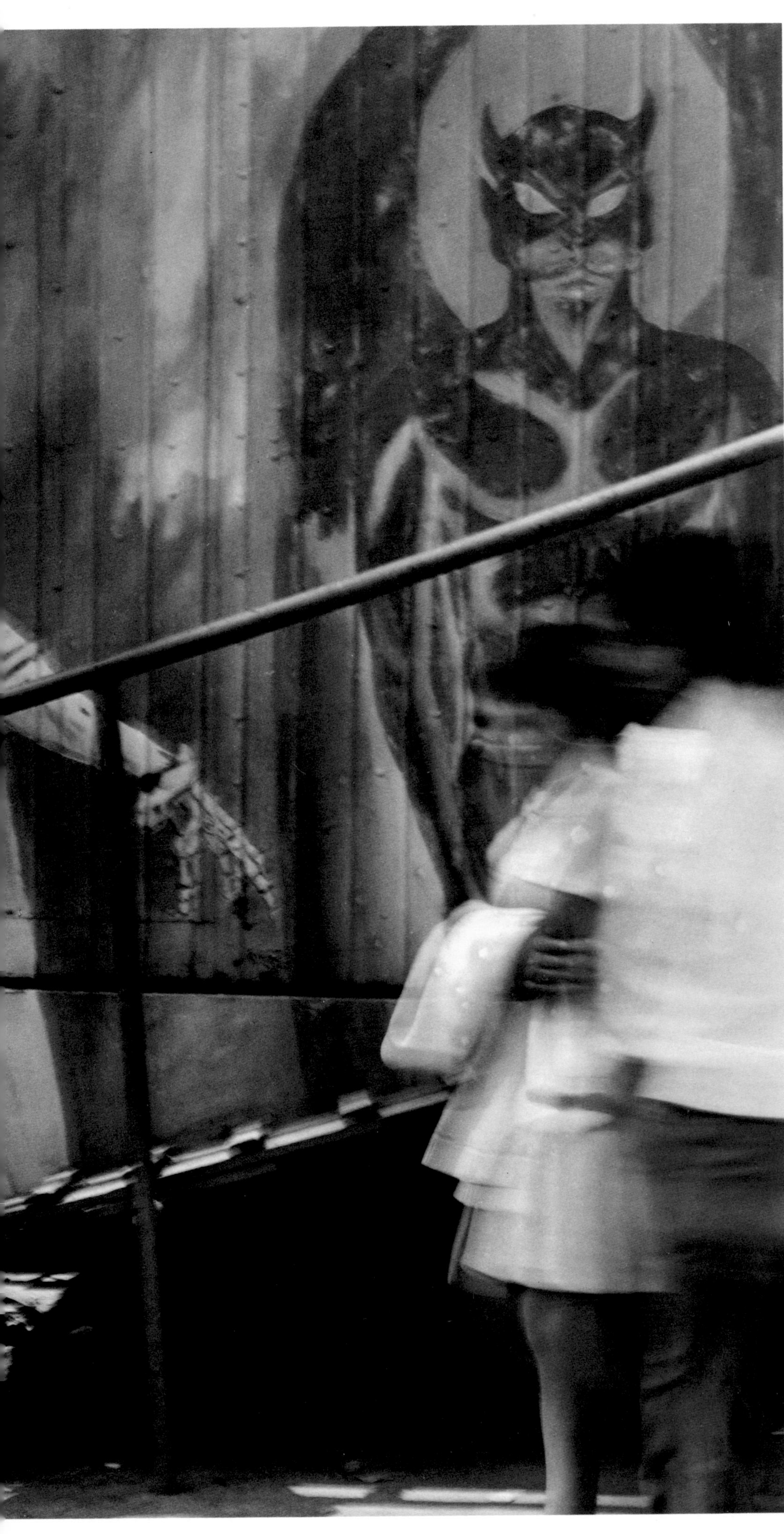

Casa de la muerte (House of Death),
Mexico City, 1975

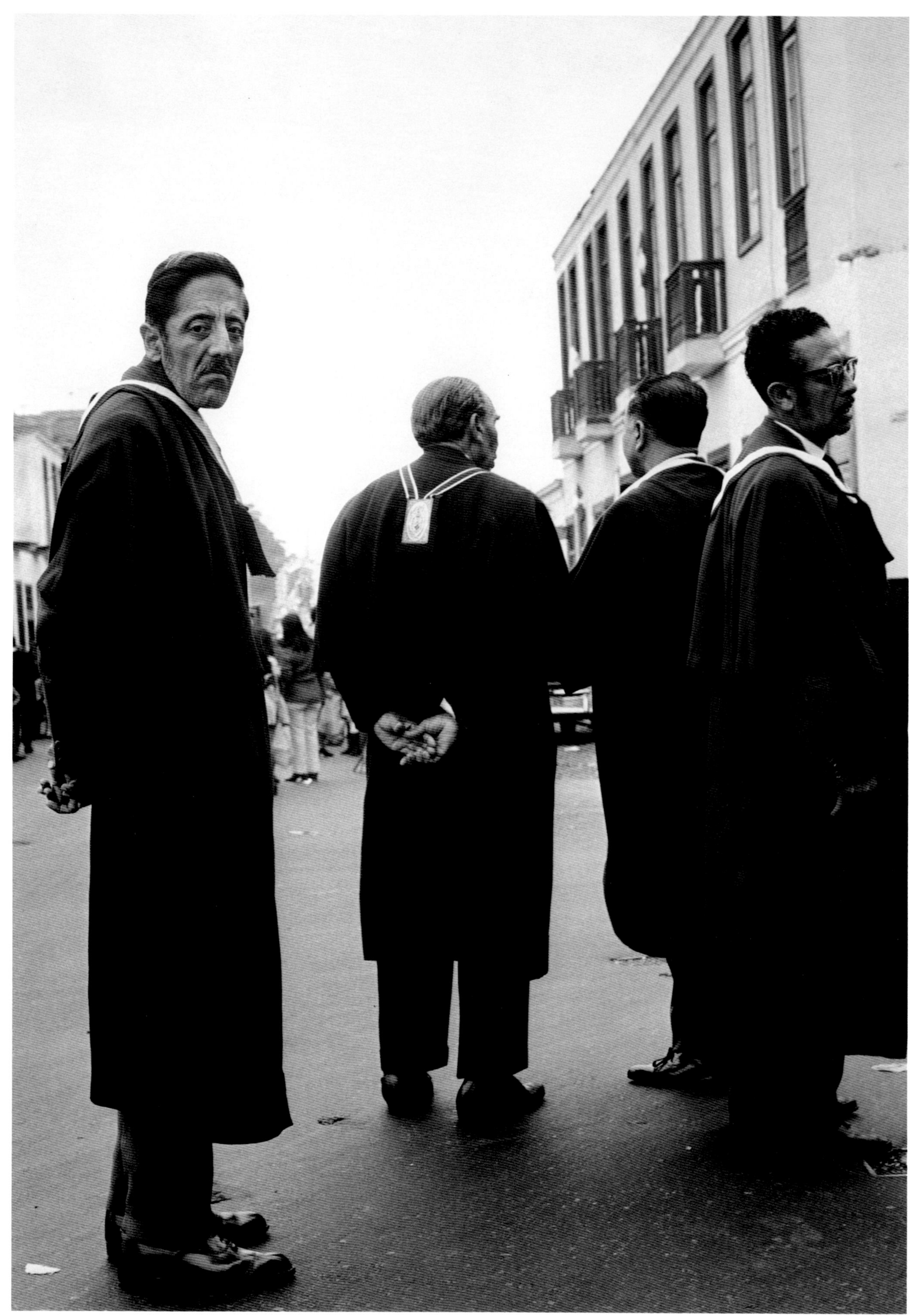

 Caballeros de Colón (Knights of Columbus), Lima, Peru, 1972

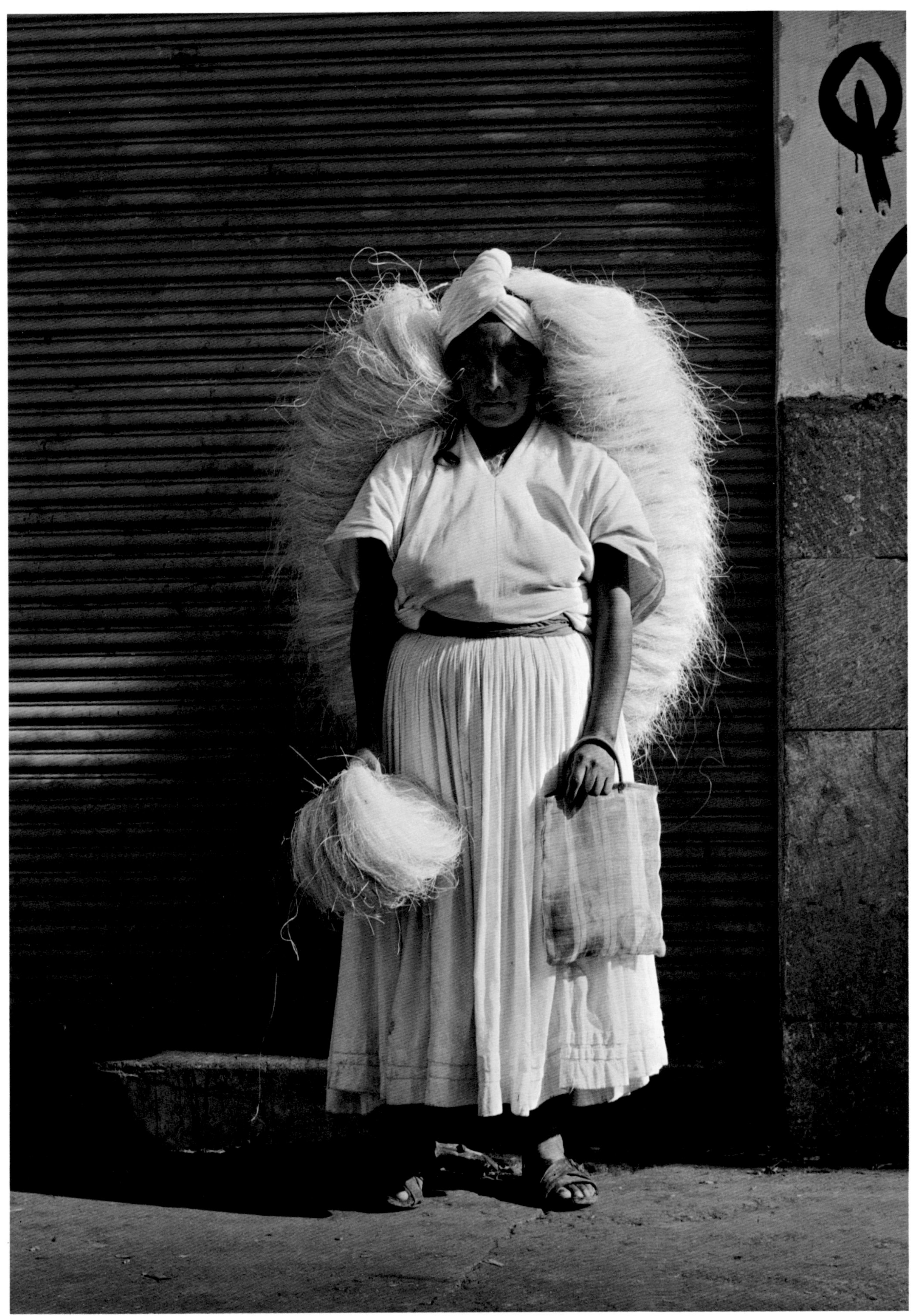

Vendedora de zacate (Sponge vendor), Oaxaca, 1974

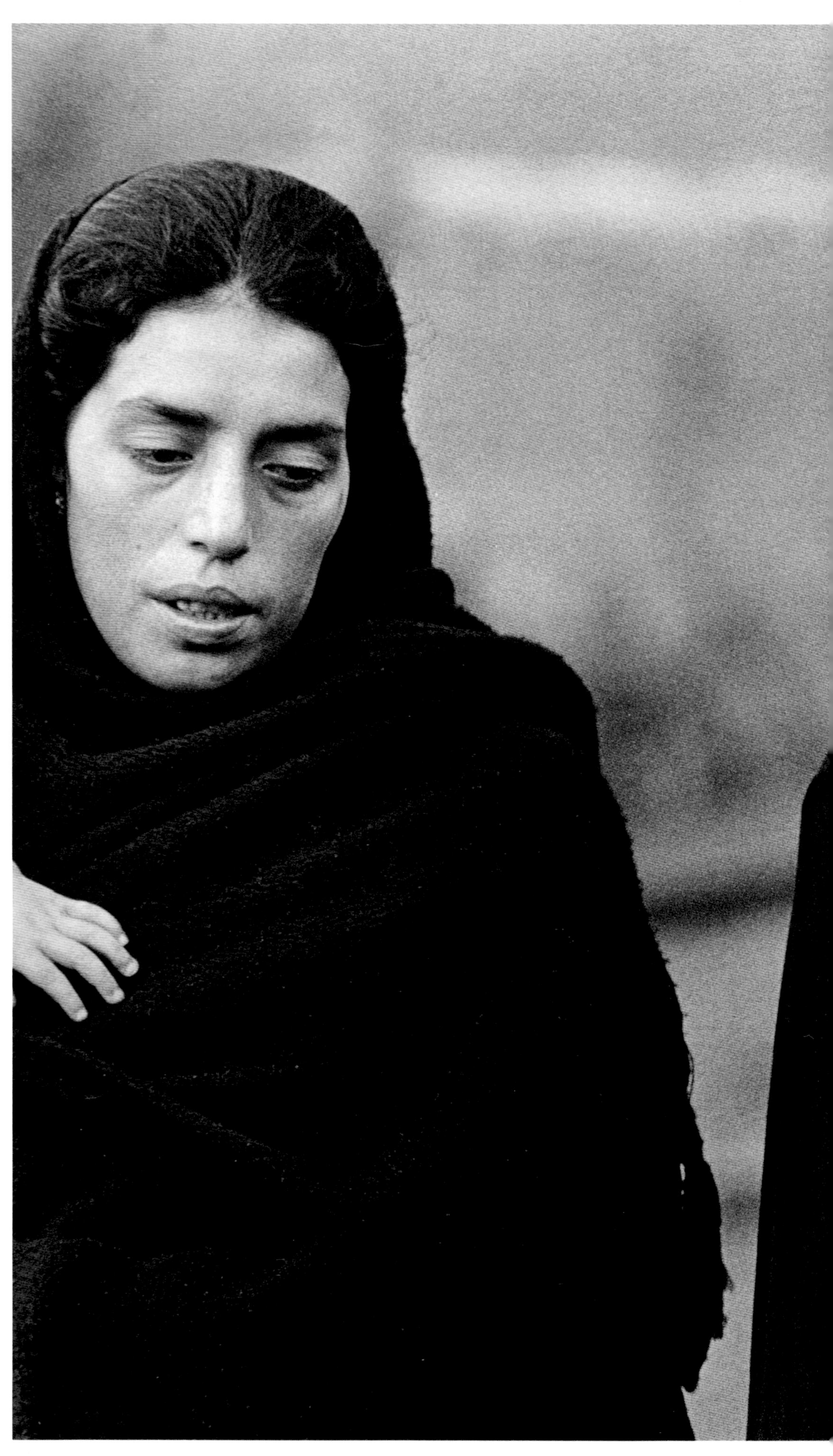

Chiapas, 1975

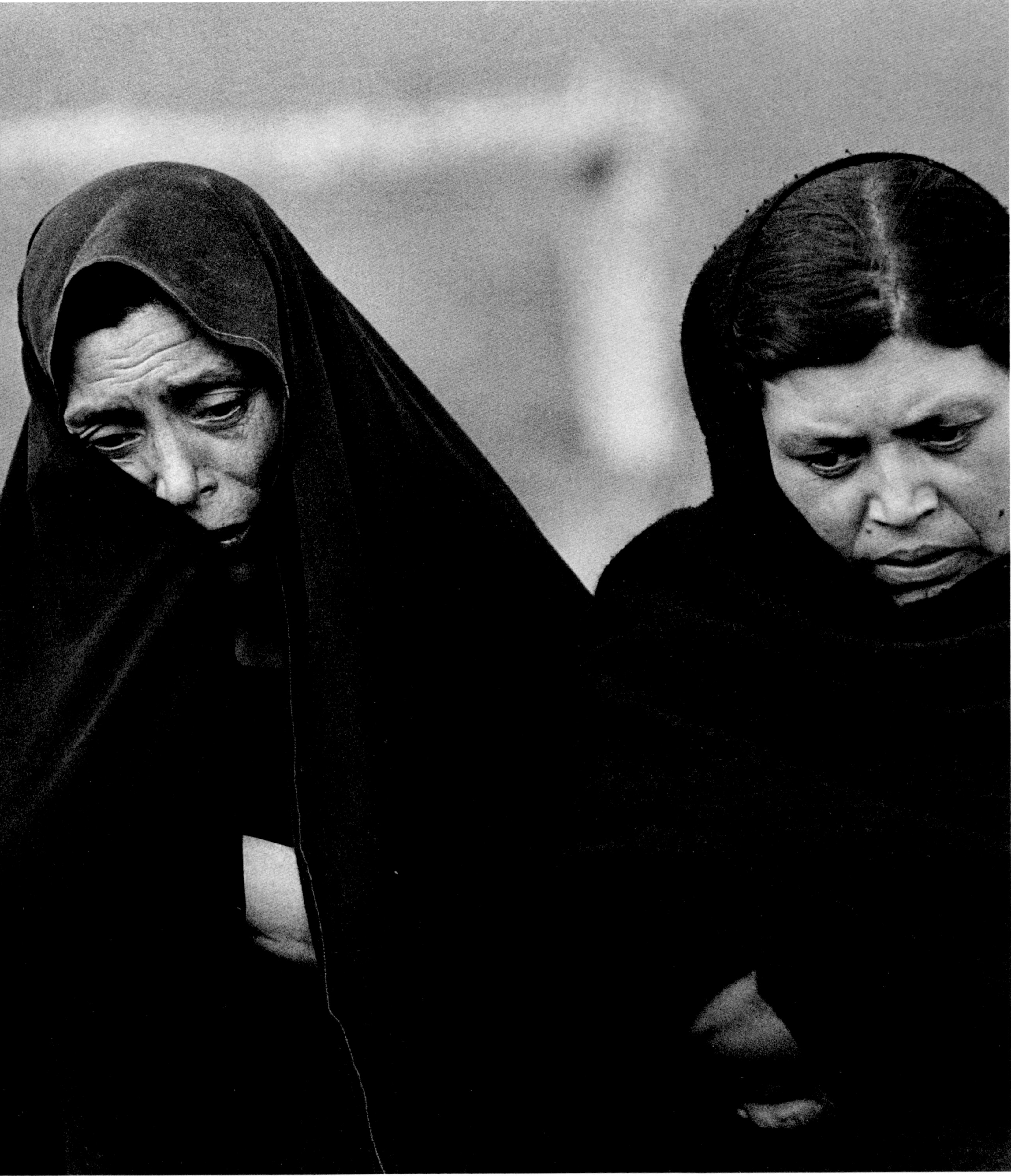

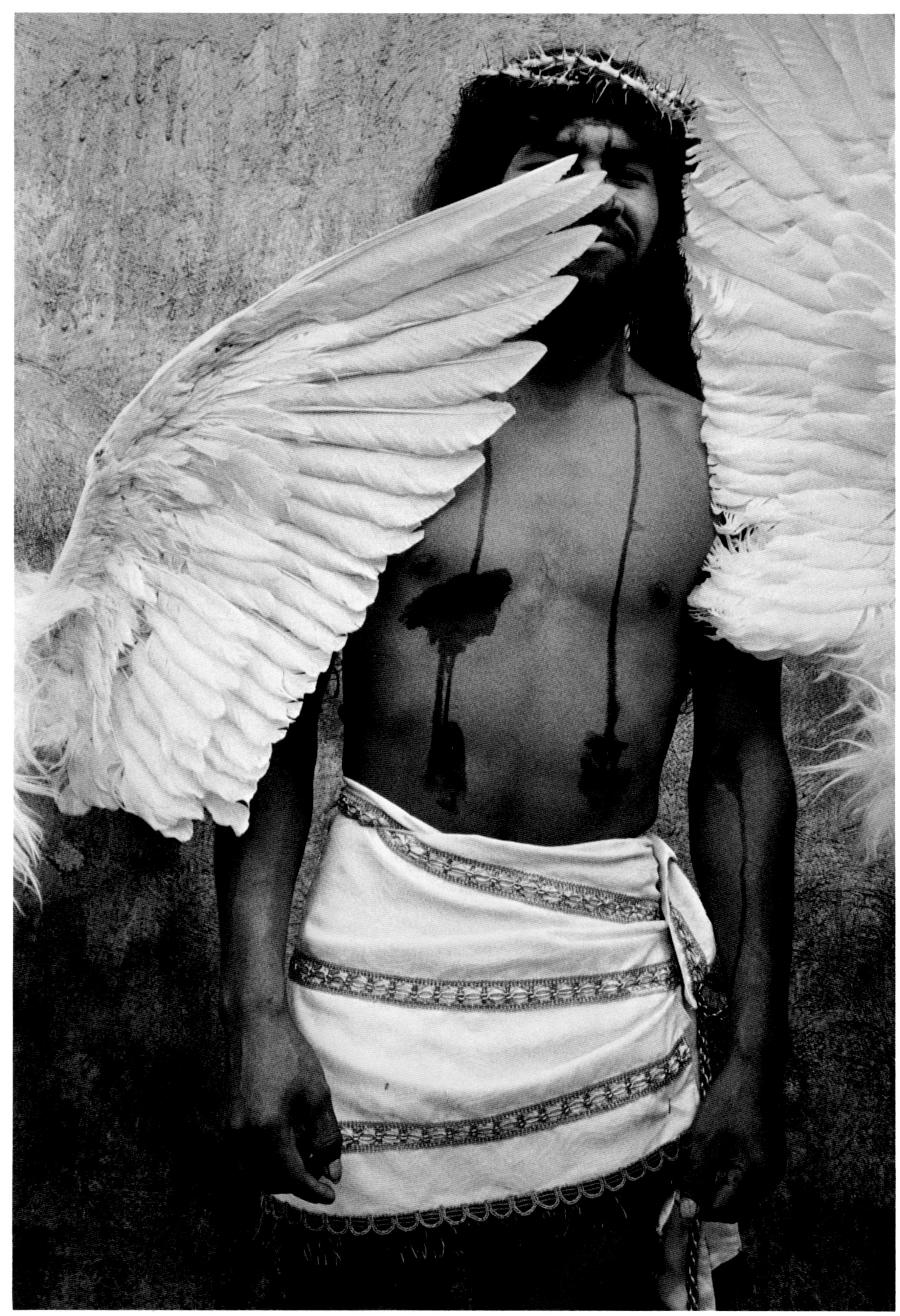

 Above: *Cristo* (Christ), Chalma, State of Mexico, 1990. *Opposite*: *Procesión* (Procession), Chalma, State of Mexico, 1984

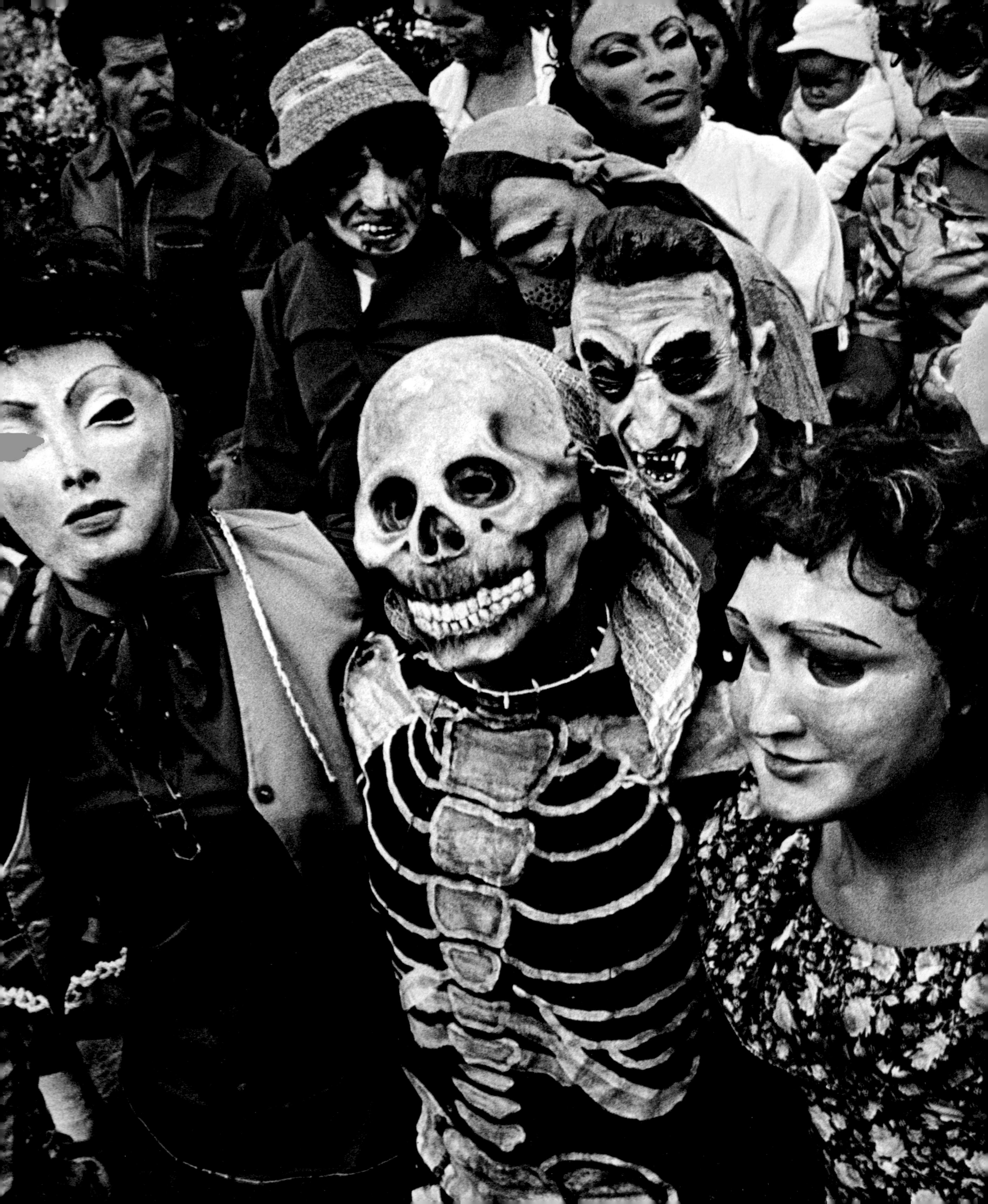

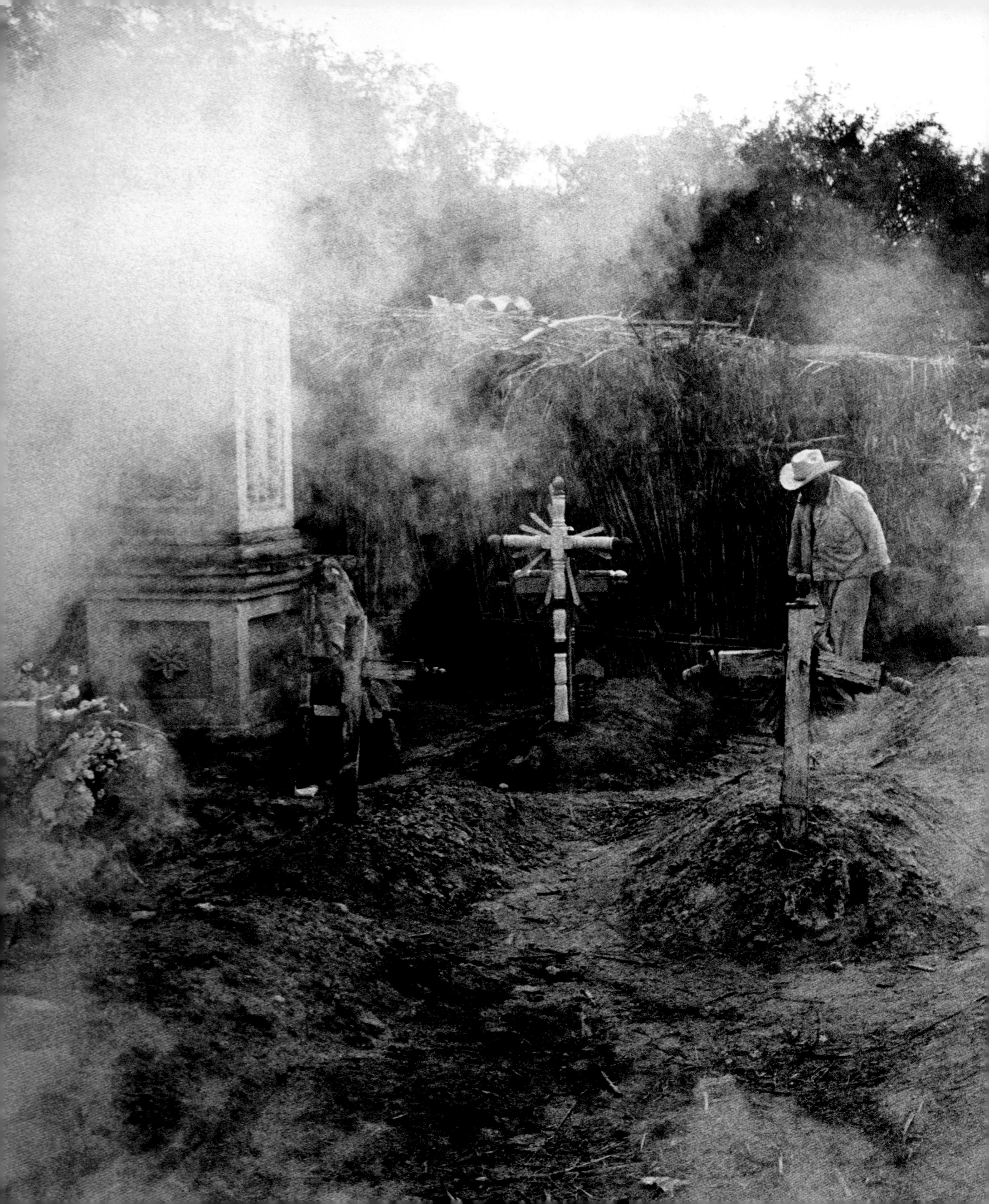

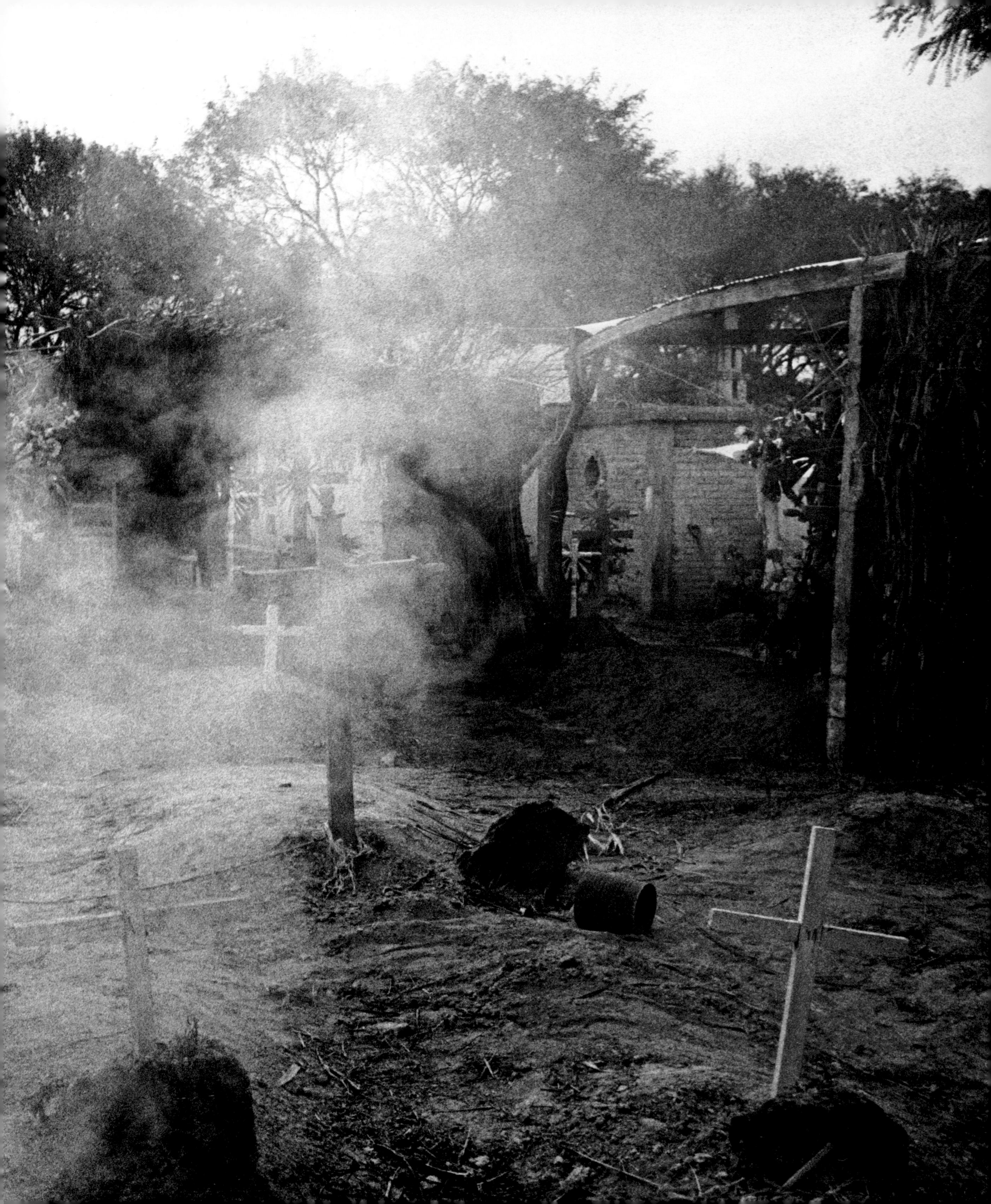

Pages 110–111: *Cementerio* (Cemetery), Chilac, Puebla, 1992
Opposite: *Primera comunión* (First communion), Chalma, State of Mexico, 1984

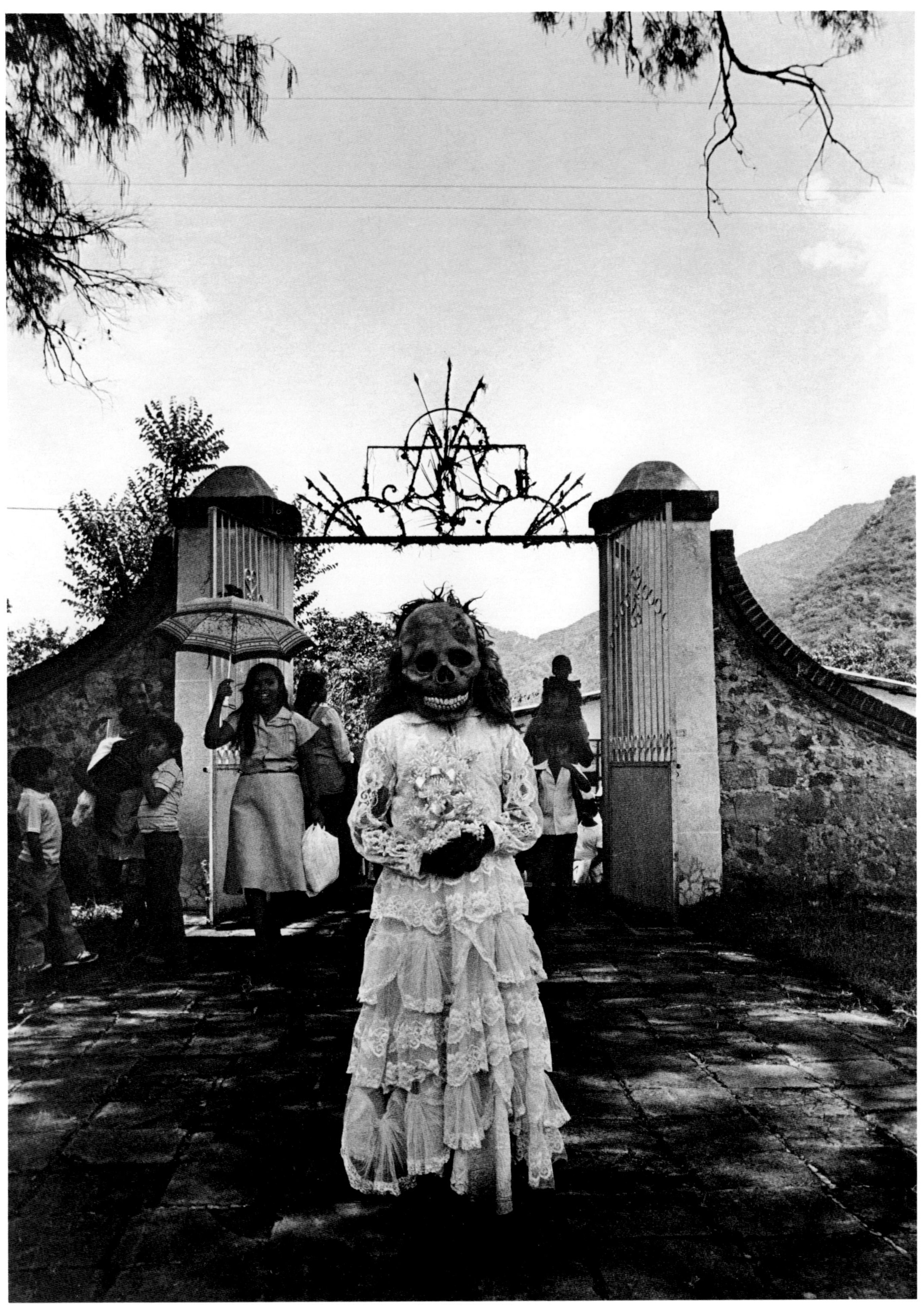

Sahuaro (Saguaro), Sonora Desert, 1979

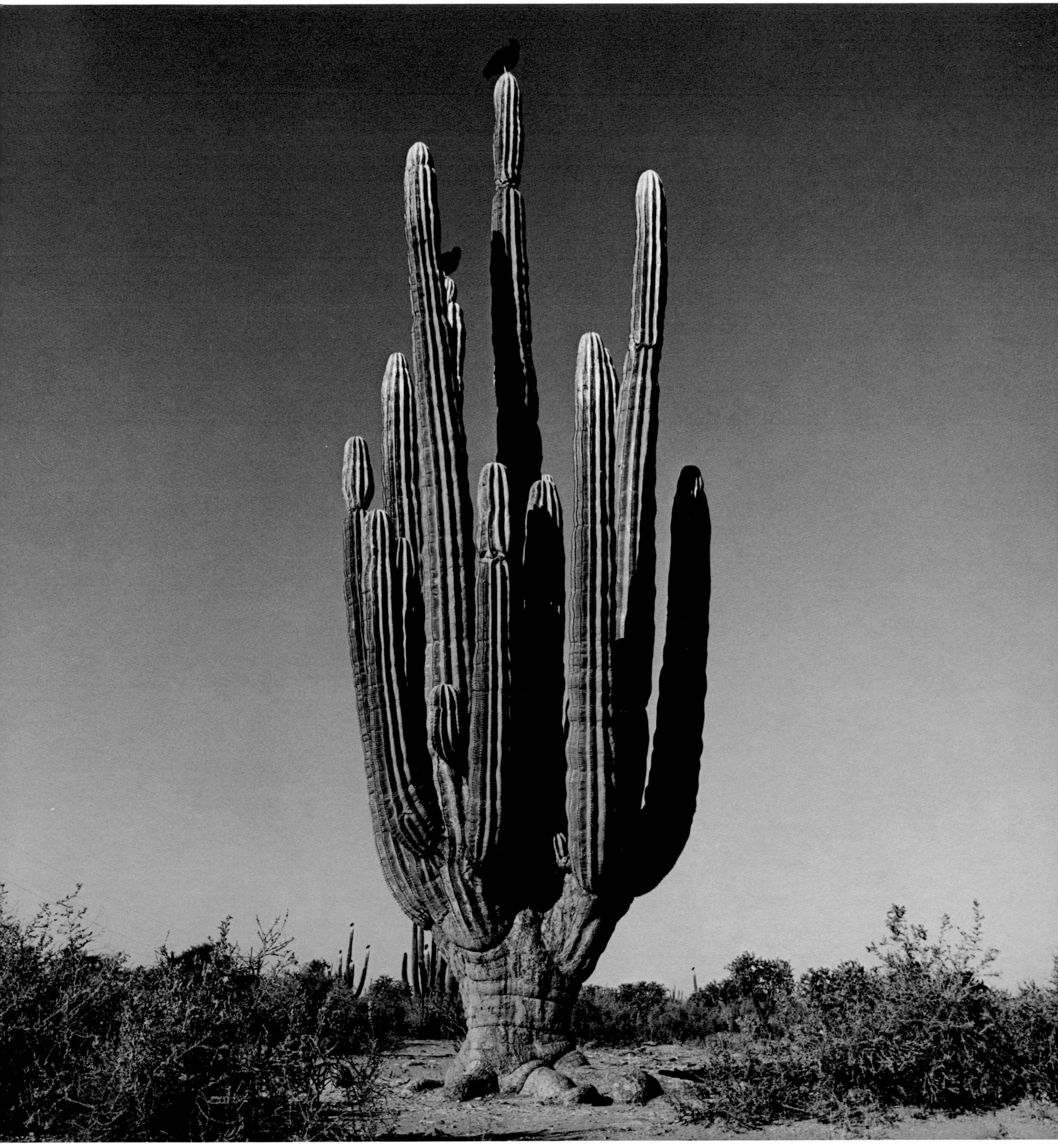

Recurrent Letters

by Alfredo López Austin

CALENDAR

Dear Graciela,

If I were to match my sleepless imagination to the mindful visions of dreaming, I would find you on a promontory set over the world in such a way as to see from one ocean to the other, to approach the vault of heaven, and to surpass the artificial boundaries. Down below, the desert of angel-women painting artificial lines across their faces. Over there, that rift of the boundary separating the world from the vault of heaven. Down below, the seas you can inhale. Above, the vault of heaven composed of wings and scissor-tails, and over there, fish drawing artificial boundaries with their bodies.

You could behold the world, Graciela, at the end of the century, surpassing the artificial boundaries of the self and the other.

The century's coming to an end, despite the artificial convention of a boundary marked by three zeros. Numbers hardly matter. The zeros could well be ones, or threes, or sixes, or one-hundred-and-fours. The century's coming to an end because the time-worn cogwheels no longer lock into gear, and thus stripped, they grind everything down until it is flat and even.

Hopes, too, have been crushed. Possibly the only hope left is that of survival—but it is subject to the laws laid down by the market.

You realize, Graciela, that the only ones left are those who build regions in the sky using tin foil, the feathers of white chickens, hammers and nails. You understand that there are many who still harbor the compulsion to imbibe the meaning of everyday life a sip at a time. You know that there are those who link generations to each other. You've discerned how "here I am" is defended by bodies marked, by virtue of the skin, and offered to the gods, to an ideal, or to the imagination of the artist. In the "here I am," you see a life's meaning. You see the "here I am" defiantly asserted in the face of laws, conventions, persecution, or life itself. You know that "here I am" lays claim to its unique characteristics and obsessions.

But you also realize that the pages of the calendar begin to wane, pages from which you have set yourself to tearing shreds of light.

Let's pretend—while the pages recede—to build regions in the sky with planks and nails. Let's continue—between now and then—to give life meaning by joining it to death. Let's crown ourselves—in the meantime—with a headdress of iguanas, let's bullfight with bicycles, let's wrap ourselves in curtains of grasshoppers, letting slaughtered chickens fly, and witness, devoid of tears or applause, the tragedy of goats.

Let's revel in the light, Graciela, while the pages of the calendar fade away.

XOXOCOTLA

I've thought about you often today. Just a few days ago you spoke of your passion for vultures. We were observing the image of someone exuding "vultureness" as you captured him with your lens. Yours was a singular vultureness—which often happens when an animal's features are corrupted, as is made manifest in human beings. In this vulture, the cadaverine is blended with the smell of rancid sweat, the smell of candles, and accumulated gold. Our conversation drifted from that photograph to more affable topics, and so we discussed the unusual beauty of that black bird which is always wavering between solemnity and fancy.

Today I've been observing different vultures in performance: vulture-children rejoicing around deer-men, jaguar-men, dog-men, hacienda-owners, sharp-shooters, doctors, rascals, and those costumed as the four colors. Together they form a retinue of dancers who have gathered to reenact a hunt. The two hacienda-owners and their respective sharp-shooters pervade the savage world of the rascals to hunt for jaguars and deer. The vultures go in search of their share, with dogs chasing them away from the pieces recovered by the men. In the staged chase, the four colors—two dressed in green and red, the other two dressed in red and green—serve as assistants to the hacienda-owners. The doctors travel with the group in the chance event that something should happen, and the rascals frame the action with their intemperate cries.

I'm impressed by the rascals. Their bristly hair, savage faces and ragged clothes remind me of those frightening assistants to the god of the animals who live in the wildest realms of the forest and whose task it is to guard the springs, caves and streams. They also make certain that the sacred laws of the hunt are followed, and that they lead the herd of wild animals through the tunnels of the hill to spend the night in the house of the god. In the recesses of the earth, they mend the fur of beasts wounded by maladroit hunters. Could these assistants and the rascals be one and the same? At least the rascals act as fierce as the god's assistants.

In Xoxocotla, at the end of the dry season, on a Wednesday in May, rain for the coming season must be requested. This is done inside a cave in the Cerro de la Serpiente, or Serpent Hill, an hour away from the village. Wanting to witness the farmers' gratitude, restlessness and hope, I joined the procession that first began at the home of the village councilman with a prayer recited by the primary participants around the household altar. Large disks of yellow flowers were removed from the altar to be used later as the primary offering in the cave, and then the walk began under the radiant sun.

The retinue started from the councilman's house. We proceeded down the streets of the village amid music and dances. In addition to the actors of the hunt, the Moors and Christians arrived—the fierce Moors with somber masks and beards, wearing large headdresses of colorful half-moons; the Christians dressed in sky blue. Both sides were armed with machetes that have collided for centuries over uncharted lands and seas.

Behind the mask, behind the costume, dark-skinned men fulfill their promise in the ritual of the dance. Each has his story to tell—a sick relative, a lost job, the anguish of love lost, fear of the law. Some are there to render payment with their bodies for the favors they received from the invisible powers. Others have paid in advance. Almost all the parts are played by adult males and young men. But the vultures are a throng of fifteen-year-old adolescents dressed in black whose movements sound tiny bells sewn around the hem of their shortened pants near the back of their knees.

We were joined by the musicians and dancers, each with his fatigue, up to the end of the village. Some of us would travel to the cave. Others would stay behind, playing and dancing throughout the day, involved in the hunt or in combat. As we headed on our way, I saw the faces of the vulture-children. They were restless and eager to howl along with the rascals, to hurl themselves violently at the dying jaguars and deer, to tear out shreds of skin, intestines or eyes with their beaks, and to skirt the snapping jowls of the pursuing dogs. Each one of them, no doubt, has his family story. They serve as delegates fulfilling the promises made by their elders to the invisible powers. But the desire to lift clouds of dust with their feet, to flap their arms, to scream or run, to wound and outwit transcended the limits of the sacred obligation to effect the grandeur of the game.

Identities

Confront someone.
Perceive his otherness.
Respect the other.
Involve myself in the other.
Perceive that his or her otherness, in relation to me, is composed of both sameness and difference.
Understand that to know the other, in relation to me, is to gauge both sameness and difference.
Learn that bridges are built over sameness.
Dialogue.
Respect otherness.
Make myself available to perceiving difference.

Let myself be drawn by difference.
Dialogue, dialogue.
Respect, respect the other.
Gradually ascertain that sameness can have depth.
Gradually prove that difference can be coherent.
Examine differences more closely.
Gradually demonstrate that difference is consistent.
Intensely consider sameness.
Respect, respect, respect the other.
Reconstruct the image of the other in his or her integrity as other, both same and different.
Value the other as other.
Respect the other once again.
Discover myself in the confrontation.
Discover that before the confrontation I had yet to discover myself.
Understand that the self is only formed in the face of the other.
Understand that I am other to another self.
Realize that we are all others.
Realize that all of us are a third person plural.
Understand that every third person plural is composed of "we-are-others."
Value the other as another form of "we."
Understand that the quality of otherness depends on the attendant self.
Understand that the degree of otherness depends on the attendant self.
Understand the self by dint of the other.
Return to myself.
Ponder the fact that when I look in the mirror, it transposes my right side and my left.
Realize that if the mirror-play fails to transpose my left side and my right, then I hardly recognize myself in either figure or movement.
Understand that I haven't been the same each day.
Understand that a person who hasn't been the same each day is self-othered.
Understand that my fullness is formed by memories, recurrences, obsessions and stubbornness.
Understand that even fullness endures the manifestations of time.
Identify myself as an object of study.
Involve myself as an object of study.
Integrate myself as subject/object.
Understand myself as self.
Return to the other, but this time by myself.
Know that communication with an other will never be absolute.
Know that communication will always be viable.
Understand that there are many forms of being other.
Understand that there are many forms of being myself.
Understand that the forms of being other—or of being myself—depend on the nature and point of division.
Conclude that a "we" may vary in zones and intensities of inclusion.
Distinguish alterities.
Value the degrees and qualities of otherness in the other.
Understand that to name all others "brother" is to dissolve otherness.
Understand that to name all others "brother" is to dissolve brotherhood.
Understand that this holds true when calling all others "opponent" or "enemy."
Understand that to deny or to be ignorant of the other blurs vision.
Understand that the blurriness leads to negligence.
Confirm that negligence often ends in brutality.
Respect myself.

Cerro de la Serpiente (Serpent Hill)

Men from three villages should have attended. First came those from Xoxocotla; then those from Atlacholoaya; those from

Alpuyeca failed to show for the second consecutive year. The most devout swept the leaves that had gathered at the entrance of the "charm." The representatives of each group—those who confronted the powers inside the hill—knelt down and prayed at the mouth of the cave. They began removing the stones, one by one, with which they had closed off the entrance to the sacred place during the year. The worshipers crawled in through the narrow opening. There, they were handed the offerings: the disks made of yellow flowers, candles and food, as well as the cane alcohol known as *aguardiente* and burning copal, initiating the ceremony in the name of those of us who remained outside. They say that inside the cave are three wells, and that, given the quantity and quality of the waters, they can tell when the rains will arrive to each one of the three villages in the coming season.

Hours went by. Finally, the representatives looked out from the mouth of the cave and let us know that the secret ceremony had come to an end. After having left their aroma—their substance—in the "charm," the food and alcohol were brought out to serve among those of us hungry mortals who had waited out in the open. I reached for a *tamal* and tasted the dough which had not been seasoned with meat, chili or salt. The ancient codices describe a festivity known as the *atamalcualitztli*, celebrated every eight years in honor of the rain gods. The ritual food was the *atamalli* ("water *tamal*") that would receive no condiment because, on that day, corn should not be affronted with chili or salt.

Have you thought, Graciela, how creeds must be cleared of stones? That belief is no easy matter? You have to reconcile thoughts that emerge from opposite directions. Differences must be assimilated. When they fail to harmonize, scars remain from the inconsistencies. But scars, too, become assimilated.

Here the *angelitos*, or little angels, transport the clouds. They are the children of heaven. They are the small carriers of rain. They open the coffers of rainwater that are buried deep down in the world of the dead, in the cave.

Here death is the dark damp creator of life. Death is the feminine force of the world. It is the universal mother nourishing us, the deep hollow by which we are one day devoured. Who is not indebted? Who has not tasted the nourishment?

Angels and skeletons dance together. Together they collect what they are due.

Don Arcadio had come from Atlacholoaya, accompanied by his grandson who is learning to fulfill his duty. It will not be long before this child will have to substitute for him. Don Arcadio has a swollen knee. Misfortunes from the past that reappear. He uses black military boots and second-hand, navy-blue uniform pants with stripes down the side. Proud of his attire, he explains that one of his sons, a policeman in the city, provides him with clothes. Like everyone else, Don Arcadio has brought his bottle to be filled with the water drawn from the wells. The bottles will be placed at the family altars next to the pictures of saints and virgins, and next to the candles and flowers. When it fails to rain, the devout farmer buries his bottle in the middle of his cornfield. The entire crop will be moistened, at least a little. It will still be thirsty, but it will not wither.

"Some ask for more," Don Arcadio tells me. "They come to the 'charm' and pray for big things. They want to be musicians, or great singers in the choir. Someone I knew was like that. No one dared trying to outdo him on the guitar. He arrived anywhere and started playing. Others would want to play as well, but they were no match for him. The strings would snap and they would stand there stunned, with no guitar and voiceless. The strings would break and, embarrassed, they would have to leave."

A pause just long enough to reaffirm his obsessions.

"Another friend invited me to ride bulls. I was good. I would mount that bull and it wasn't often that the animal managed to throw me off. But he was much better. He would go from village to village, wherever they rode bulls, and there was no animal that he wouldn't fight. No matter how fierce they were, they wouldn't harm him and he was famous throughout the state. One day he asked me, 'Wouldn't you like to bullfight like me? I can teach you how I managed to do it.' But I didn't want to. I've always settled for who I am. Why commit myself? We're all going to hell when we die. It's one thing to spend a brief time there, though, and another to stay there paying for centuries."

Bottles were passed from hand to hand inside the cave and came back filled with fresh water. It was yellowish, somewhat turbid. Everyone recognized his container and some quickly took a couple of sips. Finally, the worshipers emerged into the light. Their eyes seemed distant, lost, and they seemed annoyed by the insistent questions asked by those they represented. They barely spoke a word, but vaguely said, "The weather will be good."

And that, Graciela, was when the people began to leave. In rows along the road, and wading through the river, we reached the village and joined the boisterous frolic among the screeching cries of the rascals, waving the branches we had recently cut.

The village received the good news and everyone brought home a part of his fortune, his indebtedness, his life and his death—stored in a bottle.

I AM

In spite of myself, I am here
seated on the throne I've fashioned with gouges, hammer and nails;
in my kingdom drawn with the artificial lines of my furrows.
In spite of myself, I am here
with the genitals I've fashioned, with which I've known
delight, with which I distribute pleasures.
In spite of myself, I am here
when speaking with the firm cadence of my gestures, of my
hands, of my fingers; with the skin of the blue-colored artifice
I've fashioned.
In spite of myself, I am here
for I am fashioned in spite of myself
and I take chickens for rides on a bicycle
and I transform my dreams into powerful hands of vigil
and I turn into a window in the wall or a wall in the
window
and I brave wearing a face over my mask to fashion
layers of skin like an onion
though timidly, in order to do so, I admit I hide
in the silence of corners.
I am the cross's crossing
and the florid navel of the universe.

BORDERS

Throw a line out in the North and a border is drawn. Everything becomes a matter of direction in the rose of the winds. Or, if you will, it depends on the nature and point of division. Here: the desert. There: the craggy trench. Sand and humus, except for the flooding. Everything a border between north and south, east and west, winter and summer, wealth and misery. The great line hereby drawn to indicate a disjunction with the powerful neighbor, except for the flooding. And there are borders separating loves, traditions, loyalties and moral codes, as well as those measuring time.

The history of the north is like that. It resembles its geography and seasons. In the past, boundaries were marked between nomads and farmers, though these were often erased by trading in turquoise and deer skins, or in raids to steal corn and women. Had the dividing line among the nomads been perpendicular, the Chiricahua would have been separated from the Mescalero. When the white man arrived, inherent divisions were maintained. In the ceaseless rustling of the winds you can hear stray voices on the barren plateau: Spaniards—old Christians—dragging the luckless figure of a black slave. Afterwards came the enterprise of the Conquest and colonization, but history and myth, as well as reality and fantasy, confronted each other with a deep-seated sense of boundary, even on the solid ground of business concerns. Stories upon stories emerge from such encounters. At one end, the practical sanity of the noble fortune-hunter. At the other, and at the same time, the friar driven to madness in his futile search for the legendary Seven Cities of Cíbola.

And the demarcations accumulate over time. During the time of the Revolution, many men and entire families fled north—some seeking, others unwilling to find. Any corner of the country could have been their point of origin. Today, they are followed by those run aground in their failed attempt to cross the border. A melting pot of identities has been forged. There are marks of "here I am" on either side of these demarcations: here, the old northerner facing the recent arrivals who claim to be *norteños* because they soon learn to face themselves. There, on the other side, the *pocho* faces the Chicano in divisions that create hierarchies among a lineage founded on deracination.

That's why you have to speak loudly in El Norte. Everyone must stake out his presence, create a contrast, mark their territory. Identity should be determined by the group, and at the expense of life. The group, the clan, the gang. "I'm here. I am. We are. We're here. We're the best." The frame—the markings—will impose the code. Yesterday it was the pachuco. Today it's the *cholo*.

Identity becomes a question of pride, a challenge, the skin. *Cholas* will exclaim (even with the cry of deaf-mutes): "Here we are. We are women, *cholas*, number one. Me, a *chola*. and my passions, my conquests, and my son, my offspring, my son a *cholo* as well, the son of a *chola*, who will bear the fruit of *cholos*, my son, the first among the foremost."

Throw out a line in the North and it will be blurred with thousands of others. The deleting line will forge identity. In the North, we're the "we-are-others."

We're the ones with lines painted across us.

ANGELS

Mexico, Graciela, is a land of *angelitos*, little angels. Dark-skinned angels, with wings made of white chicken feathers, haloes and stars made of tin foil, and sometimes beaming with the eyes of a little devil. Everyone knows that's the way they are. What everyone *doesn't* know is their relationship to death and devils. Because Mexico is also a land of death and devils.

Here, *angelitos* transport the clouds. They are members, as such, of a teeming and complex army led by the rain gods. Long, long ago, they used jade disks to frame their eyes, large lip-plates onto which bits of sharp teeth were introduced, and they used to soar through the skies with a vessel full of water in one hand and a club in the other. When the traveling child shattered the vessel with his club, the farmer would hear thunder and could expect heavy rain to fall over his *milpa*, or cornfield.

Other components of that same army had different duties. There were those who watched over fountains, springs, streams, caves, ravines, and forests; those who purged the underground river streams; those who herded fish and wild animals; those who drove the wind; those who filled each blade of grass, each plant, each bush, and each tree with green sap and burgeoning forces; those who caused the chill of sickness in men and women, or those who whitened the fields with hail. It was the army of the mother goddesses, of the rain gods, and of death.

Insignificant? No. In ancient times they believed that all life was derived from death and that, likewise, all death was derived from life. It was a cycle, a succession of triumphs between the cold dank lords from below, and the warm glowing gods from above. For each side to fulfill its duties, by turns, was the only worldly form of preserving life and death.

The promise of life remained linked to the darkness of the underworld. In the region of the dead—in the depths of the earth, in the hollow womb of the mountains—potential riches were hidden in coffers. These were filled with rain and wind, with plant, animal and human soul-seeds, with forces of regeneration, with jade; but also with hail and cold-spells and illnesses. Those who kept watch over the earth, death, and rain could well be generous, measured, and seasonable in the opening of those coffers, but also greedy, cruel, and untimely whenever they pleased.

When the Christians arrived, their angels were readily accepted and were compared to those heavenly children who carried vessels and clubs. (Perhaps that is why the piñata, originally from Europe, was also accepted here with equal enthusiasm.) Beside them, death continued to promise fruitfulness and the birth of wealth, and the dead continued to fulfill their function as generative agents—which is to say that angels joined the chilly army.

And devils? Well, not everything was easily accommodated. The Christians referred to the Devil as the lord of evil, God's enemy, inhabitant of the underworld, the gatherer of souls, the executioner of a blazing hell, the lord of corruption, and so forth. Indigenous peoples doubted that a god could be considered either absolutely good or absolutely evil—which is why they were gods, in order to act as they pleased. That particular lord would have to be a dispenser of good and evil, and to be confronted as such. Indeed, an enemy of God, if Christ is identified with the sun. Inevitably, they would be opponents, each one the leader of respective armies, to produce the seasonal cycle. Inhabitant of the underworld? That was precisely where to find the key in identifying the Devil. Gatherer of souls? Clearly, for he was the lord of the dead, the debt-collector, and the lord of corruption, for new life blossomed from corruption. But what about the flames? This was truly disconcerting, for the indigenous underworld was freezing cold. And so, whether hell was cold or hot remained a topic of debate, or became an inextricable mystery of faith.

Have you thought, Graciela, how creeds must be cleared of stones? That it is extremely difficult to assimilate something when it lies at a distance? That assimilation and accumulation are not one and the same? Faith is not simply about storing items, but about accepting inconsistencies. It's difficult, but one is at home there. The waves of history pound and shape traditions with their beating. It is difficult to believe. You have to adjust each day, for centuries, for millennia.

Scars are left in the resolve. Everything has to be assimilated, although the True Face is never the true face, one's own face.

Do all angels fly, Graciela? I don't think so. There are those with feet planted firmly on the ground.

Paradigms

I keep insisting. Those who affirm universals claim to have conquered the value of the individual. To what individuals are they referring? To those capable of struggling for personal happiness? To genius? To someone who is saved or eternally condemned for strictly inherent reasons? To those who dress with no constraint but with that of the frame around a mirror? To someone shouting "me" from the top of a hill? To someone who decides he can buy one of three thousand trinkets? To someone who allows himself the temporary luxury of ignoring history? To those who compete for profit even if it means having to annihilate their opponent? To those devoid of brothers? To someone effacing his individuality? To someone who endlessly entertains the idea of "me," crying "me," dancing "me"? To those so singular as to fulfill their function as mute producers and unstoppable consumers?

I know other individuals. They, too, struggle courageously for their personal happiness. They know how to struggle between vulgarity and genius. They also climb the top to cry "me," to cry "we." They enjoy and suffer intimately as well. They, too, buy and sell, choosing whom to love or hate—and doing so, by and large, in company. Endlessly, these men and women claim "me," "me," "me" till the day they yield their breath. Except that their "me" is considerably complex. They believe that they transcend their flesh like the roots of trees growing from the walls of ruins. They establish systems, loves, alliances, pacts, loyalties and hates, in keeping with the way their "me" travels along the sinuous wandering of roots. The self moving here and there and over there, joining the pasts and the futures, dreaming and wakefulness, the regions in the sky and those of death, binding death to life to death to life to death.

I keep insisting. There is more than one paradigm of the individual over the vast face of the earth.

Tradition

We are living years of reaffirmation. Difficult years.

In less stormy times, men and women showed greater awareness, and the play of identities simply produced the necessary tension to maintain the healthy condition of difference, without succumbing—ingenuously—to the idea of a universal brotherhood that destroys the nature of fraternity, nor—disingenuously—to the notion concealing the aims of assimilation. I'm me, you're you, us and all of you in planes of respect and reciprocity. Let's mark our differences in order to work and live together side by side. There are those who say ideal cities have never really existed—like that of Toledo, where Muslims, Christians and Jews once lived in coexistence. They're right. But let's set aside the search for ideals in order to build potential, more desirable worlds.

We live years of painful reaffirmations. It is the reaction—often times extreme, desperate, furious, suicidal—of those who demand the respect toward the particular meaning of their existence, the recognition of their past, and the validation of their inherent life project. A reaction against universal man, that is, against those who impose their values by means of force.

History is forgotten.

What lies in the immediate future? What lies in the future? The gearless wheels of our era are turning too fast.

Villages cling to traditions by which they have shed thorough meaning onto their life. With the patience of millennia, they amass intellectual values that are created, shared, and transmitted among individuals, modified daily through experience, history, and collective hopes. Each village understands the world with that accumulated wisdom, and acts accordingly. They thereby order thought and work, and their conceptions and patterns of behavior maintain a global sense, coherent and integrated into their existence. Traditions are not the dead weight of petrified customs that keep one from adapting to new historic conditions. On the contrary, they offer cultural responses to change, albeit a change that preserves the sequence between the founding past, the fullness of the present, and a future that must be projected with responsibility.

Imposing values by force of power, universal man deals in absolute truths, universal values, categorical imperatives, irrefutable knowledge, the only true and accurate points of view, optimum wealth—distribution will be negotiated later, exclusive methods for eternal salvation, refined taste, international legalities, open tracks, immediate communication, globalized markets, world police, progress, and—why not?—an ideal brotherhood. The conditions of sale are reasonable. Only a few things are expected in return. The list includes land, gold, sweat, awareness, autonomy, and the soul; distinguishing features, true fraternity, collective responsibilities, and the abandonment of traditions, as well as the past and the future. The only thing expected in return is the disintegration of the individual.

There are those who nevertheless persist in asserting "I am."

Where are you headed with your camera, Graciela? I watch you in your quest for reaffirmations, as if in search of others, ourselves, the "we-are-others."

Alfredo

Chronology

1942
Born May 16, in Mexico City, the oldest of thirteen children.

1962
Marries; this marriage produces three children: Manuel, Claudia, and Mauricio.

1969–1972
Enrolls in the Centro Universitario de Estudios Cinematográficos at the Universidad Nacional Autónoma de México.

1970–1971
Works as assistant to Manuel Álvarez Bravo.

1974
Travels to Panama, where she produces a photo-essay on the country, its people and its leader, General Omar Torrijos.

1975
First exhibition, "Tres fotógrafas mexicanas," first shown at the Galería José Clemente Orozco in Mexico City, and the following year at the Midtown Y Gallery, New York City.

1979
First trip to Juchitán, Oaxaca, Isthmus of Tehuantepec, with the support of Francisco Toledo.

1980
First solo exhibition, "Graciela Iturbide," at the Casa del Lago in Mexico City, and later at the Casa de Cultura in Juchitán, Oaxaca. Awarded Acquisition Prize at the I Bienal de Fotografía, in Mexico City.

1982
Exhibition at the Centre Georges Pompidou, Paris, France.

1983
Production grant from the Consejo Mexicano de Fotografía.

1986
Awarded prize from the UN-International Labor Organization for her portfolio *El empleo o su carencia* in Chile.

1987–1988
Receives the W. Eugene Smith Award from the W. Eugene Smith Memorial Foundation, for her work in Juchitán. Subsequent exhibition of that series, "Juchitán pueblo de nube," travels to England, Argentina and Japan.

1988
Receives a Guggenheim Fellowship for her project *Fiesta y muerte*. Receives Grand Prize, Mois de la Photo in Paris.

1989
Receives Hugo Erfurth Award in Leverküsen, Germany.

1990
Awarded International Grand Prize in Hokkaido, Japan. Major exhibition, "External Encounters, Internal Imaginings: The Photographs of Graciela Iturbide," at the Museum of Modern Art in San Francisco, California. Invited by Médecins sans frontières to photograph in Madagascar.

1991
Receives award at Rencontres Photographiques in Arles, France.

1993
First exhibition of "En el nombre del padre" at Galería Juan Martín, Mexico City; Galería Foto Optica, São Paulo, Brazil; Museum of Modern Art, Rio de Janeiro, Brazil.

1996
Major retrospective, "Graciela Iturbide: La forma y la memoria," at the Museo de Arte Contemporáneo de Monterrey, MARCO.

1998
Major retrospective, "Graciela Iturbide: Images of the Spirit," at the Philadelphia Museum of Art.

Selected Bibliography

BOOKS

Avándaro. Text by Luis Carrión. Mexico City: Editorial Diógenes, 1971. Photo-essay on the events surrounding the week-long music festival that came to be known as the Mexican "Woodstock."

Los que viven en la arena. Text by Luis Barjau. Mexico City: INI-Fonapas, 1981. Photo-essay on the Seri Indians of the Sonora desert.

Sueños de papel. Text by Verónica Volkow. Mexico City: Fondo de Cultura Económica, Colección Río de Luz, 1985. Selected images. One of several titles in a prominent series of books produced during the 1980s, primarily featuring photographers from Mexico and Latin America.

Juchitán de las mujeres. Text by Elena Poniatowska. Mexico City: Ediciones Toledo, 1989. Photo-essay on the visible presence of women in the public life of Juchitán, on the Isthmus of Tehuantepec.

En el nombre del padre. Text by Osvaldo Sánchez. Mexico City: Ediciones Toledo, 1993. Photo-essay on "la matanza," or the yearly traditional slaughter of goats in Huajuapan de León, Oaxaca, Mexico.

Fiesta und Ritual. Texts by Erika Billeter and Verónica Volkow. Switzerland: Benteli-Werd Verlags A.G., 1994. Selected images.

Graciela Iturbide: La forma y la memoria. Text by Carlos Monsiváis. Monterrey, Mexico: Museo de Arte Contemporáneo de Monterrey, MARCO, 1996. Catalog to a museum retrospective tracing the photographer's work from 1972 to the present.

ADDITIONAL TEXTS AND PERIODICALS

Christian Caujolle. "La cámara como pretexto." Catalog essay, Fundació "La Caixa," Girona, Spain, 1992; Palacio de Bellas Artes, Mexico City, 1993.

Deborah Caplow. "Graciela Itubide. In the Tradition of Mexican Photography." Catalog essay, Museum of Modern Art, Seattle, Washington, 1991.

Diana Du Pont. "External Encounters, Internal Imaginings." Catalog essay, Museum of Modern Art, San Francisco, 1990.

Elizabeth Ferrer, "Manos Poderosas: The Photography of Graciela Iturbide." *Review: Latin American Literature and Arts*, no. 47 (New York, Fall, 1993), pp. 69–78.

Frederick Kaufman. "Graciela Iturbide." *Aperture*, no. 138 (New York, Winter, 1995), pp. 36–47.

Alfredo López Austin. "Exposición de placas." *El alcaraván*, vol. 4, no. 14 (Oaxaca, October–December, 1993), pp. 85–86.

Elena Poniatowska. "Abracadabra patas de cabra," *La jornada* (Mexico City, September 11, 1993), p. 29.

Osvaldo Sánchez. "La mirada del paria." *Reforma* (Mexico City, May 15, 1996), p. 16c.

Roberto Tejada. "La Matanza." *Thèmes*, no. 4 (Belgium, March–April, 1995), pp. 18–29; "Graciela Iturbide and La Matanza." *Sulfur*, no. 36 (Ypsilanti, Michigan, Spring, 1995) pp. 128–130.

Raquel Tibol. "La lírica visual de Graciela Iturbide." *Proceso*, no. 291 (Mexico City, May 31, 1982), pp. 51–52.

SOLO EXHIBITIONS

"Graciela Iturbide," Casa del Lago, Mexico City; Casa de la Cultura, Juchitán, Mexico, 1980.

"Graciela Iturbide," Museum of Modern Art, Georges Pompidou Center, Paris, 1982.

"Juchitán," Casa de la Cultura de Juchitán, Mexico, 1985; Cantonal Museum of Fine Arts, Lausanne, 1987.

"Graciela Iturbide," Centro di Ricerca per l'Immagine Fotografica, Milan, 1987.

"Juchitán pueblo de nube," Side Gallery, Newcastle, England, 1989; Centro Cultural de México, Paris; Cameraworks, London, 1989; Museum of Photography, Hokkaido, Japan, 1990; Museo de la Recoleta, Buenos Aires, 1989.

"Juchitán de las mujeres," Galería Juan Martín, Mexico City, 1989; subsequently traveled to various sites in Mexico, 1990.

"External Encounters, Internal Imaginings: Photographs by Graciela Iturbide," Museum of Modern Art, San Francisco, California, 1990.

"Graciela Iturbide," Ernesto Mayans Gallery, Santa Fe, New Mexico, 1990.

"Neighbors," Museum of Photographic Arts, San Diego, California, 1990.

"Visiones: Graciela Iturbide." Le Mois de la Photo à Montreal, Maison de la Petite Patrie, Montreal, 1991.

"Recontres internationales de la Photographie" (retrospective), Chapelle du Méjan, Arles, 1991.

"Graciela Iturbide," Museum of Photography, Seattle, Washington, 1991.

"Graciela Iturbide," Galería Visor, Valencia, 1992.

"Graciela Iturbide," Fundació "La Caixa," Girona, 1992.

"En el nombre del padre", Galería Juan Martín, Mexico City; Galeria Foto Optica, São Paulo; Museo de Arte Moderno, Río de Janeiro, 1993.

"Graciela Iturbide, " Musée de la Photographie, Centre d'Art Contemporaine de la Communauté Française de Belgique, 1993.

"Graciela Iturbide," Sala de Exposición de Telefónica, Madrid, 1993.

"Graciela Iturbide," Chicago Cultural Center, Chicago, Illinois, 1993.

"Graciela Iturbide," Universidad de Salamanca, Salamanca, 1994.

"Graciela Iturbide," Adair Margo Gallery, El Paso, Texas, 1995.

"Graciela Iturbide," Gallery of Contemporary Photography, Los Angeles, California, 1995.

"Graciela Iturbide," I Kwangju Bienniale, Kwangju, Korea, 1995.

"Graciela Iturbide: La forma y la memoria," Museo de Arte Contemporáneo de Monterrey, MARCO, Monterrey, 1996.

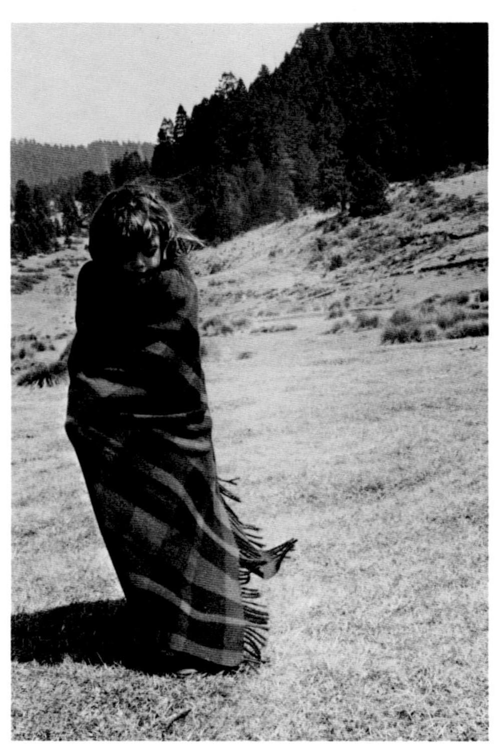

To Claudia,
who will always keep me company.

I would like to extend my gratitude to Francisco Toledo, for his continued support in the fulfillment of my photography,
to Pablo Ortiz Monasterio, for his clarity over the years in our collaborative efforts of selecting and editing the work,
to Christian Caujolle, for his professional enthusiasm and encouragement,
to Mexico's Consejo Nacional para la Cultura y las Artes (National Council for Culture and the Arts),
to Alicia Ahumada, for her dedication and accomplishment in producing the prints for this book,
to Michael Hoffman and Melissa Harris, for their faith and commitment as publisher and editor of this book.

—Graciela Iturbide

The exhibition, *Images of the Spirit: Photographs by Graciela Iturbide,* has been organized by the Alfred Stieglitz Center of the Philadelphia Museum of Art.

The exhibition and publication have been supported by the U.S.- Mexico Fund for Culture, sponsored by Mexico's National Fund for Culture and the Arts (FONCA), The Bancomer Cultural Foundation, and The Rockefeller Foundation. Additional support for the exhibition was provided by The Pew Charitable Trusts.

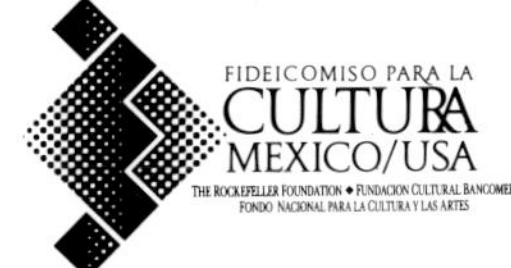

Aperture gratefully acknowledges the support of this publication by the following companies representing their commitment to the life and culture of Mexico and to Mexican artists of distinction.

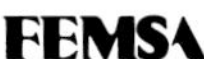

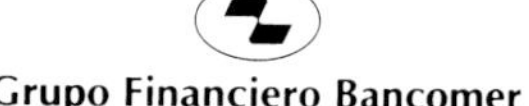

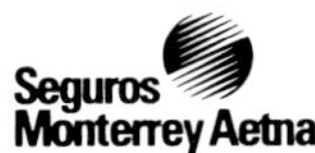

The Photographers for Photographers Fund, established by Aperture in 1993 by the generosity of many of the most significant photographers of our time, has provided additional support to ensure publication of *Images of the Spirit.*

The tour of the exhibition, *Images of the Spirit: Photographs by Graciela Iturbide,* includes the following venues:

North America

June 14, 1998 – August 9, 1998
Philadelphia Museum of Art
Philadelphia, Pennsylvania

October 23, 1998 – December 24, 1998
The William Benton Museum of Art
University of Connecticut, Storrs, Connecticut

February 27, 1999 – May 2, 1999
San Jose Museum of Art
San Jose, California

May 21, 1999 – August 29, 1999
Mexican Fine Arts Center Museum
Chicago, Illinois

June 1, 2000 – September 24, 2000
The National Museum of Women in the Arts
Washington, D.C.

February 9, 2001 – April 22, 2001
Museum of Fine Arts
Santa Fe, New Mexico

International

April 1, 1998 – June 15, 1998
Musée d'Art American
Giverny, France

Spring 1999
Biblioteca Panizzi
Reggio Emilia, Italy

Unless otherwise noted, all photographs in *Images of the Spirit* were taken in Mexico.

Library of Congress Catalog Card Number: 96-83971
Hardcover ISBN: 0-89381-681-7
Paperback ISBN: 0-89381-828-3
Catalog edition ISBN: 0-89381-832-1

Book and jacket design by WENDY SETZER
Printed and bound by MARIOGROS INDUSTRIE GRAFICHE SPA, Turin, Italy
Duotone separations by THOMAS PALMER

Aperture Foundation publishes a periodical, books, and portfolios of fine photography to communicate with serious photographers and creative people everywhere.
A complete catalog is available upon request.
Address: 20 East 23rd Street, New York, New York 10010. Toll-free (800) 929-2323.
Phone: (212) 598-4205. Fax: (212) 598-4015.

Visit Aperture's website: http://www.aperture.org

Aperture Foundation books are distributed internationally through: CANADA: General Publishing, 30 Lesmill Road, Don Mills, Ontario, M3B 2T6. Fax: (416) 445-5991. UNITED KINGDOM, SCANDANAVIA, AND CONTINENTAL EUROPE: Robert Hale, Ltd., Clerkenwell House, 45–47 Clerkenwell Green, London EC1R OHT. Fax: 171-490-4958. NETHERLANDS: Nilsson & Lamm, BV, Pampuslaan 212–214, P.O. Box 195, 1382 JS Weesp. Fax: 31-294-415054.

For international magazine subscription orders for the periodical *Aperture*, contact Aperture International Subscription Service, P.O. Box 14, Harold Hill, Romford, RM3 8EQ, England. Fax 1-708-372-046. One year: $50.00. Price subject to change.

To subscribe to the periodical *Aperture* in the U.S.A. write to Aperture, P.O. Box 3000, Denville, NJ 07834.
One year: $40.00. Two years: $66.00. Toll-free (800)-783-4903.

First edition

10 9 8 7 6 5 4 3 2